UNBELIEVABLE
LIVING IN THE SON

GRAHAM BEE

Unbelievable: Living in the Son
Published by Graham Bee
Email: unbelievable.grahambee@gmail.com

Copyright © 2014 by Graham Bee

This book is copyright. No part of this publication may be reproduced, stored in a retrieval system, or transmitted in any form or by any means—electronic, mechanical, photocopy, recording, or any other—except for brief quotations for printed reviews, without prior permission of the author.

ISBN 978-0-9924515-1-6
First printing March 2014
This edition January 2015

Bible quotations in this book are taken from the following translations:

The Amplified Bible (AMP), Copyright © 1954, 1958, 1962, 1964, 1965, 1987 by The Lockman Foundation. Used by permission.

The Contemporary English Version (CEV). Copyright © 1991, 1995 by the American Bible Society. All rights reserved.

The Modern Language Bible: the New Berkley Version in Modern English (MLB). Copyright © 1945, 1959, 1969, 1987, Hendrickson Publishers Marketing, LLC. All rights reserved.

The Holy Bible, New International Version ® (NIV). Copyright © 1973, 1978, 1984 by Biblica Inc.® Used by permission. All rights reserved.

The New King James Version (NKJV). Copyright © 1982 by Thomas Nelson, Inc. Used by permission. All rights reserved.

The Holy Bible, New Living Translation (NLT). Copyright © 1996. Used by permission of Tyndale House Publishers, Inc., Carol Stream, Illinois 60188. All rights reserved.

The Holy Bible, Revised Standard Version (RSV). Copyright © 1946, 1952, 1971 by the Division of Christian Education of the National Council of Churches of Christ in the United States of America. Used by permission. All rights reserved.

Editor: Owen Salter
Cover photo: Paul (Buzz) Bee
Cover design and book layout: Jenny Godfrey, Concept Designs & Marketing (www.concept-designs.com.au)
Printed by: Lightening Source International

Precisely twenty years ago the entire trajectory of my life was transformed when I crossed paths with Graham Bee. Because of his influence, I have been engaged in the thrills and spills of cross-cultural mission activity ever since. Graham's candid confidence in God's capacity and willingness to do much more than anyone could ask or think is the bedrock of his faith, the fragrance of his life and the premise of Unbelievable. With understatement and humility the hallmarks of every chapter, Graham points us to the glory of his all-powerful God. This book will captivate you – Graham knows the talk and walks the walk.

Simon Longden, CEO/Director, Pioneers of Australia

Unbelievable is not only the title, but an accurate description of this book's 'ride' with Graham Bee through his life. It is a ride complete with bumps, and turns, and unexpected hardships and joys. But it is a ride where we see at every corner evidences of an incredible, almost unbelievable God. Graham tells his story with the humility of an Australian farm hand dreaming to become a top stud breeder. And he tells it with the passion of a man whose dreams are made even bigger when he catches hold of the heart of God for the nations. It is the kind of genuine life story we need to read, to inspire us and give us courage in our own "tiny part" in God's bigger story.

Dr Louis Sutton,
International Director, WEC International

Some people live ordinary lives and others live extraordinary lives. Graham Bee is someone who has lived an extraordinary life. Growing up in rural South Australia, training for missionary service in Tasmania, serving with WEC in Ghana and senior leadership roles with WEC have given Graham a rich story to tell. Through it all you see God's faithfulness to his servant and experience a life given over to the Lord. "Many plans are in a man's mind, but it is the Lord who directs his steps" (Proverbs 16.9).

(Rev.) Tim Costello,
CEO World Vision Australia

Unbelievable will challenge you as it challenged me to believe in a powerful and life changing God. A God who takes ordinary people, with their fears and inadequacies, and does extraordinary things. I was moved by Graham's humility and genuine desire to discern God's will and to submit to it. He enjoyed almost two decades of fruitful ministry in Ghana, and later, along with his wife Marj became Australian Directors of WEC. As the pastor of the Narwee Baptist Church I witnessed the pain and suffering of the whole family as Marj went to be with her Lord after a brave battle with cancer. But I watched Graham trust God for the future, and he continued to see that nothing is impossible with God. I commend this God-centred book to all who want to be inspired in their walk with God.

(Rev.) Angelo Gratsounas,
Senior Pastor Narwee Baptist Church, Sydney.

…inspiring, motivating. You will be blessed.

Grant Lock,
Author of Shoot Me First.

We absolutely loved your wonderful book. In every way it was special. It is so well written and so easy to read. Your sense of humour and positive attitude are great and the special little stories that kept coming up were so interesting. We couldn't wait to get to the next chapter. Each was just like a flower opening up bright and beautiful with a challenge in every one. Your honesty and openness was such a blessing to us. We are sure it is going to be a great blessing to others.

Jenny and Evan Davies
Former International Directors of WEC.

Jan and I got to know a young nurse named Marj Winchcomb 50 years ago when she made a serious commitment to Christ whilst at Narwee Baptist Church, Sydney. I remember the missionary convention in which she received God's call to study with WEC. Then over the years we have followed with prayerful interest Graham and Marj's missionary journeyings. This book is a 'page-turner'. I warmly commend it.

(Rev. Dr.) Rowland Croucher,
Founder John Mark Ministries

CONTENTS

Foreword i
Acknowledgments iii
Introduction v

Prologue vii

1 Impossible? Not with God 1

Australia (1945–1972)
2 Born at Calvary—twice! 11
3 Learning to appreciate differences 17
4 Teenager on the move 21
5 Murder at night 25
6 Working Bee 29
7 A fork in the road 33
8 Carrots and a ukulele 39
9 Caught rather than taught 47
10 God still speaks today! 53
11 Learning to live by faith 57
12 The green light 61
13 Finding a life partner 67
14 Opposites attract—or attack 73

Ghana: The Kpandai Years (1972–1983)
15 Good price, just for you! 79
16 That first handshake 85
17 Tractors, tyres and tithes 91
18 Wonderful people, terrible roads 99
19 A bowl of rainbow soup 103
20 Double trouble and twice the pleasure 109
21 Paul's brush with death 113
22 No house. No money. 117
23 The accident 125
24 For such a time as this 133
25 Coups and counter coups 137

26	Sssspitting cobras	143
27	Jesus cares for our children too	149
28	Twenty-two days	153
29	Protection and provision	159
30	Hospital, hernia and hen's eggs	165
31	ECG on the move	169

Ghana: The Tamale Years (1984–1989)
| 32 | New move, new ministry | 177 |
| 33 | Finishing well | 183 |

South Australia (1990–1995)
34	New property	191
35	The Bees are back!	195
36	Middle East bomb shelter	201
37	Kalashnikovs, Kurds and land mines	207

Sydney (1995–2002)
38	Bigger challenges ahead	217
39	Here to make a difference	221
40	Amazing Korea	227
41	The winner is Sydney!	233
42	The dreaded C word	237
43	On my own again	243
44	A second treasure	247
45	How much more, Lord?	253

The Gold Coast Years (2003–Present)
46	A home on the Gold Coast	261
47	The recent years	265
48	East Timor miracles	269
49	Green fingers: nurturing plants as well as people	279
50	Reflections	287

Notes — 291

FOREWORD

What a good read! I was taken on a roller coaster ride of emotions as I read through the life story of Graham and Marj and then Becky. How encouraging to see the work of God in taking ordinary people and, by His grace, making them extraordinary and fruitful even in faraway lands – often in the midst of adversity and hardship.

I first met Graham and Marj at a WEC International Leaders Conference in 1984, and the following year visited them as Field Leaders of the WEC Team in Ghana when that nation was at its lowest ebb in a terrible economic crisis in 1985. Yet Graham gives indication of how that nation has since seen much church growth and Gospel breakthroughs – all contributing to the subsequent uplift for the country at every level. Then as Graham and Marj moved into more international ministry involvements, we had many more times of fellowship in that close-knit band of WEC leaders – we identified with each other in the joys and sorrows of our ministries and families.

I am amazed as I read what Graham has written to see how many parallels in ministry there are. We both gave about the same number of years to Africa – our 17 to their 18, but he in largely rural ministry and me in urban slums, we fought the same diseases – malaria, hepatitis, skin cancer. We both suffered the loss of our dear first life-partners through a sudden appearance of secondary cancer at 54 years of age, and both of our dying wives laid plans for future life partners to take their place!

My heart is full of praise to our wonderful Lord Jesus Who has been the Focus of their lives and the Source of their fruitfulness. So may He receive all the glory, and, you, Reader, the blessing as you read this book!

Patrick Johnstone
WEC International
Author Emeritus, Operation World
Wisbech, England

i

ACKNOWLEDGEMENTS

Thank you to my prayer team, who have prayed this book into the visible—Brian Allbutt, Evan and Jenny Davies, David Godfrey, Joy Ham, Trevor and Jen Kallmier, Grant and Janna Lock and Annette Rattray. I am aware that many of our regular prayer partners have prayed too, and I thank you for your faithfulness.

My friend, Grant Lock, author of *Shoot Me First*, has been my mentor since the inception of this book, and has greatly encouraged me and enriched the outcome. Thank you to each of my editorial readers—Sue McGuire, Marilyn Rowsome, Jo Smith, Robert Troedson and John Yearn—for your input and dedication to this task.

Becky's editing skills, as well as those of Owen Salter, have greatly enhanced this book and made it much more interesting and readable. Jenny Godfrey's professional and creative layout and design make the book much more attractive. I have greatly appreciated their cooperation and expertise.

Patrick, your leadership in WEC and friendship over many years have encouraged and blessed me. I thank you for writing the foreword.

During our years of ministry, our family has been blessed by the prayer and financial support of many individuals, as well as Narwee Baptist Church Sydney, Edwardstown Baptist Church Adelaide, Fairfield Christian Family Brisbane, and Mosaic: a Baptist Church Gold Coast. Thank you for your commitment to spreading the gospel to the ends of the earth.

My WEC colleagues all around the world have inspired me, encouraged me and blessed me over these 45 years. Friends and colleagues in Ghana, Australia and East Timor—you have a special part in this story, and whether you are named or not, know that you have been a treasured part of my journey.

Marj and Becky, who have journeyed with me, loved and cared for me, encouraged me constantly and nurtured my soul—there would be no story without you.

My children and their partners, Julie (Jules) and Wes Morgan, Paul (Buzz) and Belinda Bee, and Merilyn (Mez) and James Nelson, have shared both the pain and the joys along the way. Much of my story is also their story. It is my prayer that my grandchildren, Shenaya, Isabella, Tyrel, Joel, Charlie, Joshua, Samson and Eli (Elijah), along with Wes's boys, Jeshua and Jamieson, will be encouraged to take God at His word, and step out in faith to find and follow God's pathway for their lives too.

INTRODUCTION

Amazing, incredible, awesome—I could have used any of these words to describe God's interventions throughout my life. However, each time George Mansour, my Egyptian friend in Sydney, hears one of my stories, his immediate response is a heartfelt 'Unbelievable!' George's enthusiastic response was one of many voices that encouraged me to write my life story, so I have chosen the title *Unbelievable*, which the dictionary defines as extraordinary, astonishing, remarkable—so remarkable at times it can be difficult to believe. These words describe my life with God and the events that are recorded in this book.

In sharing these stories from my life journey, my desire is to point to Jesus and His power that has been at work in me and the circumstances of my life all the way through. He took my ordinariness and transformed me as I committed to 'Living in the Son' and drawing from Him daily all I needed.

In this book I refer a lot to God, and I mean God in all His fullness: Father, Son and Holy Spirit. I also include here a number of Scriptures that have underpinned my life. They explain the beautiful exchange—what Jesus has done and continues to do for me and how I live in reponse.

Jesus said:

Live in Me and I will live in you. (John 15:4 AMP)

Whoever lives in Me and I in him bears much (abundant) fruit (John 15:5 AMP)

If you live in Me—abide vitally united to Me—and My words ... live in your hearts, ask whatever you will and it shall be done for you. (John 15:7 AMP)

Paul said:

You are complete through your union with Christ. (Colossians 2:10 NLT)

God's secret plan ... is Christ himself. (Colossians 2:2 NLT)

In [Christ] lie hidden all the treasures of wisdom and knowledge. (Colossians 2:3 NLT)

This is the secret: Christ lives in you, and this is the assurance that you will share his glory. (Colossians 1:27 NLT)

I have been crucified with Christ—[in Him] I have shared His crucifixion. (Galatians 2:20a AMP)

Christ lives in Me. The life you see me living is not 'mine', but it is lived by faith in the Son of God ... (Galatians 2:20b MSG)

His peace will guard your hearts and minds as you live in Christ Jesus. (Philippians 4:7 NLT)

It's in Christ that we find out who we are and what we are living for. Long before we first heard of Christ and got our hopes up, he had his eye on us, had designs on us for glorious living, part of the overall purpose he is working out in everything and everyone. (Ephesians 1:11–12 MSG)

My readers, may this book encourage you to look to our unbelievably awesome God. He longs to be an intregal part of your story, and for you to be part of His great and glorious story.

Graham Bee
Gold Coast,
Australia
January 2015

PROLOGUE

Marj is dying. She knows it. I know it.

Chemotherapy has not helped, and now the specialist has confirmed it. There is nothing else he can do.

We are alone together. My heart is breaking. With the shock that follows the prognosis comes a chilling numbness.

Questions flood my mind: What do I do? What can I say? How can I help? What about our children?

God, where are you?

In the fog of bewilderment, there are no easy answers. In the silence, tears roll down my cheeks. Reflecting on the deep love that we share and the experiences we have been through together, I cannot comprehend what life will be like without Marj.

Like a low-beam headlight shining through the mist on a foggy night, a totally unexpected ray of hope shines. It reveals a glimpse of the way ahead.

Marj says, 'Graham, darling, I am concerned for you and your future. What will you do?'

'My future? There's no need for you to worry about me. My future is in God's hands. I'm here to love and care for you.'

What a woman she is! Marj is lying on her death bed and her thoughts and concern are for me!

Marj squeezes my hand. Strengthened by the oxygen tubed in through her nose, she says, 'Graham, you're still young. You'll need another good wife. I've been talking with God about it.'

Drawing another deep breath, she looks directly into my eyes. They are brimming with tears. She continues, 'I think a lovely lady who will make a good wife for you is …'

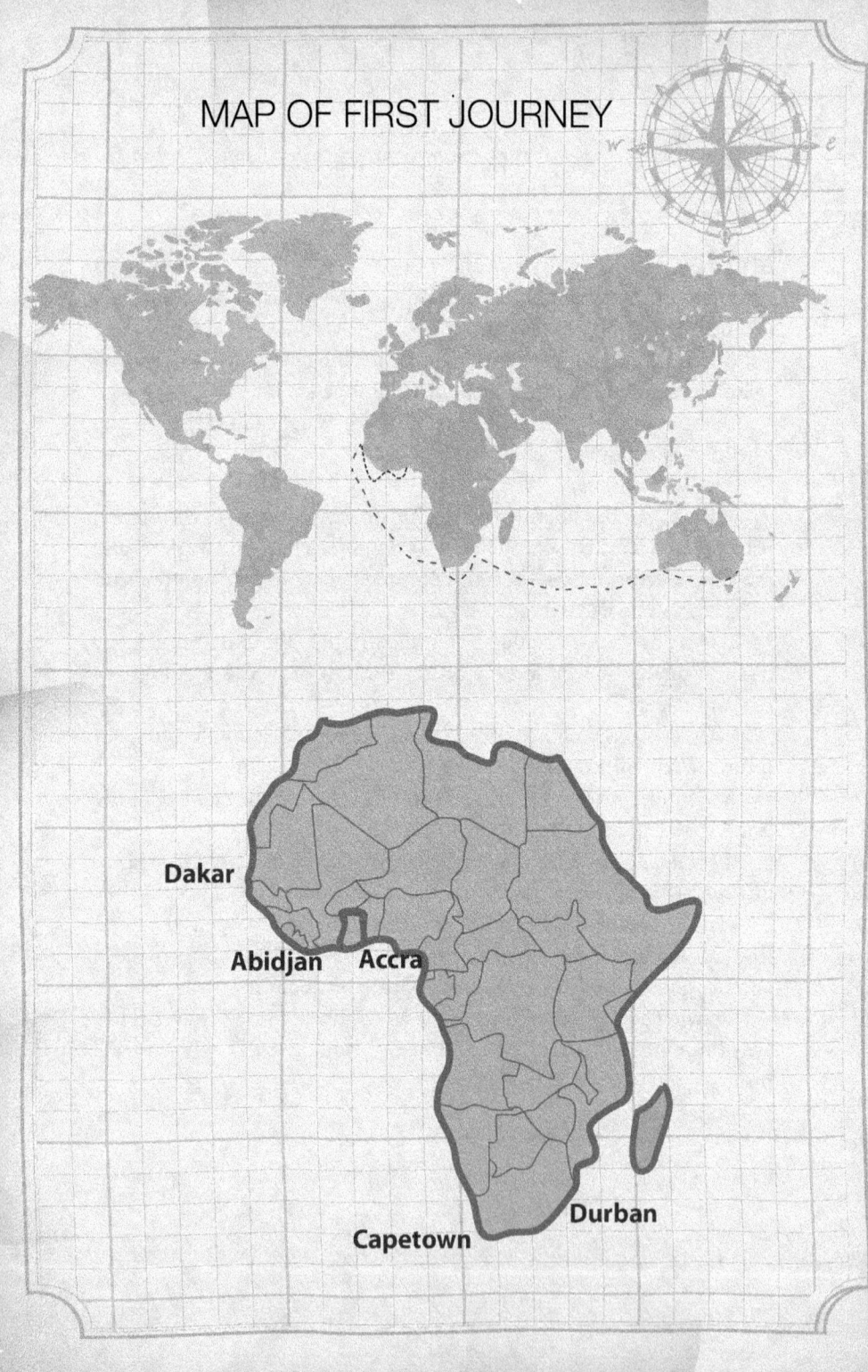

Chapter 1
Impossible? Not with God[1]

A sudden change in weather conditions whip up wild seas which toss the ship about like a piece of driftwood. Cups and saucers fly across the cabin and crash onto the floor. Hurriedly we try to secure anything that is loose. The staff frantically do what they can to assist passengers. They are run off their feet passing out sick bags and assisting people back to their cabins. They warn us that the storm could last for days.

Having an internal cabin near the engines makes it worse for us. The strong winds and heavy rain make it impossible to get up on deck for fresh air to ease the nausea and escape the smell of diesel and vomit. Many passengers, like us, end up on their bunks, groaning in agony. Lying down only gives slight relief.

This is not at all what I had anticipated when the voyage began just one week ago. We were filled with hope and excitement of a new adventure. In my mind I try to relive those days, hoping to take my thoughts off the unrelenting pain and misery.

***

June 3, 1972 is an unremarkable day in world history, but a momentous day for me. A new chapter in my life is beginning. I have a clear sense of purpose and adventure and my expectations are high. I am on a mission.

Just beyond the shadow of the Harbour Bridge, we board the ship. My wife Marj and daughter Julie are with me. Each step up the gangplank is also a step forward in my faith journey. The future stretches before me like a distant horizon. I cannot even try to imagine what lies ahead. What I am sure of is that, like the daily presence and magnificence of the sun, the Son has promised, 'I will be with you. I will never leave you nor forsake you.'

Our imminent departure is announced and reinforced with a loud blast of the ship's horn. We throw rolls of streamers down to those on the dock who have come to farewell us. Holding on to our end gives us one last, tenuous connection with family and friends. As the ship pulls away, the streamers break. Tears roll down our faces as Marj and I excitedly wave goodbye.

Slowly we steam out from the magnificent Sydney Harbour, leaving behind the iconic bridge, our Sydney friends and life as we have known it. There is a real buzz and anticipation among the 1500 passengers. In no time we sail through The Heads and into the open seas beyond. Marj and I stand by the side railing, contemplating life from an ocean perspective. A thousand thoughts course through my mind. The luxurious meals, the lounges, the swimming pool, the various games rooms and the deck chairs to relax on await us. There will be plenty of time to enjoy them. But the start of a new adventure with God is a moment to savour.

It has taken months of preparation but now we are on our way. Our ship is the P&O Line *SS Orcades*. It was commissioned two years after the end of World War Two and set a new standard in style and accommodation. Now it is as old as I am—26 years. We leave Sydney together. The *Orcades* is on its last voyage to England before being scrapped; I'm on my first journey outside of Australia, praying and hoping that my journey will have a more positive ending than that of the ship.

***

Not everyone understands what we are doing. At the meal table an elderly passenger engages us in conversation.

'What! There's no electricity there? And … and no running water?'

'That's right. And no flush toilets or phones either,' I reply.

The well-to-do passenger furrows his brow and almost stutters over his reply as he tries to comprehend. 'But … but … you're leaving Australia? You're going to live in a Third World country? You're crazy! Have you been checked out recently?'

'Well, not specifically,' I chuckle. 'But I do realise that just as we're leaving Australia, many refugees are lining up to get here.'

'Yes, of course. They're seeking a safer, more prosperous future, where life is easier. And ... and here you are—giving it all up!'

'This is a carefully thought through decision,' I answer softly, trying to allay the elderly man's fears. 'There are more important things in life than comfort and ease.'

Out on the deck of the ship I hold tightly to Julie, our beautiful, wriggly eight-month-old daughter. My lovely wife of eighteen months, Marj, is beside me, basking in the sunshine. The refreshing sea breeze and the glistening water add to the sparkle and magic of the moment. I wonder if life can get any better than this. I expected my journey in missions to involve sacrifice, frugality, isolation, loneliness and sickness. But wow, we sure seem to be living it up right now! Maybe, just maybe, things will be different for us.

We sail south and then west around the Australian coast. The ship calls in at Melbourne, Adelaide and Fremantle to take on additional passengers. We are able to disembark briefly at each port to farewell precious family and friends. The wrench of separation from loved ones hits us hard; it is made even more intense for me by the thought that I might not see my mother again. *Lord, I entrust them all into your care.*

Fremantle is our last glimpse of Australia. It is full steam ahead as we sail towards the huge continent of Africa.

***

The farewells at each port encouraged us, and now we want to make the most of our voyage. We advertise a daily morning Bible Study and around sixteen passengers attend. What a mixed bunch! Leading the study we try to involve everyone, yet avoid getting caught up with doctrinal differences. It is an opportunity to present a positive message of freedom in Christ.

After just one week, following each study we flop, seasick and exhausted, on our beds to recuperate. The *Orcades* does not have stabilisers, and passengers rename the ship 'The Rockades'. At times even the thought of food is too much for my stomach. I feel disappointed that having paid for our all-inclusive fares, I can't enjoy all the delicious food. Who knows when we will see such an extravagant smorgasbord again?

I also develop pleurisy, and our crawling baby, Julie, hates the confinement of the cabin. We struggle to be up with her in the lounge or on deck when we would much rather stay horizontal on the bed. Julie's body clock is slow to adjust to the time changes as the ship heads west. Most nights, just as all the revellers are heading for bed, I find myself crawling around the lounge floor with her, trying as hard as my weak body will allow to keep her happy and occupied.

We see nothing but ocean for nearly two weeks. One day blurs into another. Then, one morning, as our eyes eagerly scan the horizon for a sign of land, South Africa comes into view. We are ecstatic to be able to step onto land.

The ship spends one day in Durban and another in Cape Town. We are disturbed by what we see of South Africa's apartheid policy. Signs direct whites to particular shops, transport facilities and businesses they can use, while other signs indicate where blacks and 'coloureds' can and cannot go. Residential areas and even public toilet facilities are racially segregated. In some areas we visit, the racial tension is palpable.

Marj whispers to me, 'I'm so glad we're going to West Africa and not staying here. Some people are treated as though they're less than human. It's appalling.'

'You're right,' I agree. 'At least in Ghana the Africans themselves govern, and people are free to get on with their lives, regardless of race or colour.'

***

A month after leaving the shores of Australia, we dock in Dakar, the capital of Senegal. The ship is continuing to England, but this is where we disembark. We watch on as all our luggage is taken out of the hold. Other passengers, standing on deck in small groups, chatter among themselves: 'What? Is someone getting off here? Surely not! This is the end of the world!' We chuckle, not letting on that we are those people. We are grateful to be leaving the *Orcades* but struggle to find our land legs.

For the next 12 days we are in transit while we wait for another boat to take us around the coast to Ghana. Our accommodation is the WEC guesthouse, run by the mission organisation we are part of—an unusual concrete, igloo-shaped building. The workers kindly provide meals and help us with formalities, even though we are an interruption to their normal busy routine.

Our first insights into life in West Africa do not encourage us. We expected heat and humidity, but two things leave negative impressions. It is mango season, and the concrete footpaths of Dakar are strewn with discarded mango seeds covered in flies and maggots. We have to tread carefully. Even worse is the putrid smell of the shanty towns on the edge of the city. The slums have wide drains which are open sewers. We are appalled to see children playing right by those drains, and we are very glad we are not staying here.

Senegal is a Muslim country and Christian churches are not prominent. On Sunday morning, we attend a small Bible study and are thrilled to discover that the Ambassador of Ghana, a fine Christian man, is also there. When we left Australia, we only had the approval number for our Ghanaian Residence Permit. We still need a visa to gain entry and have officials stamp the permit in our passports.

'Come to the Embassy on Monday morning,' the Ambassador offers, 'and I will personally ensure you get the visa you need.' He is as good as his word. On Monday I breathe a sigh of relief as the smiling Ghanaian clerk hands over our stamped passports. We thank God for such a timely encouragement.

***

Due to the uncertain timing of our arrival here, we were not able to pre-book tickets for the ongoing boat trip. Each day we head off to the port to check on the availability of ships going to Ghana. Eventually we find a Polish cargo boat willing to take us plus our 15 drums and boxes. We are informed that the journey should take one week.

This vessel is very basic, but thankfully the weather is kind. We reach Abidjan, the port for Cote d'Ivoire (Ivory Coast), a few days later. Unexpectedly, the captain informs us in broken English, 'I am sorry,

Mr Bee. Crew decide they need a break. So we spend weekend here.'

It is heartbreaking for us to be so close to our destination and then have this further delay. We are still struggling with nausea and are desperate to get off the boat.

'Julie hates being confined to a cabin and this is no tourist boat,' Marj says. 'Look up the WEC Directory, Graham. I think there may be workers here.'

Flipping through the pages, I relay the good news to Marj. 'The Kennedys live here, but it doesn't give a residential address. I have no idea how to find them in such a large city.'

Marj encourages me. 'Let's pray about it. Remember what we wrote on our prayer cards before we left, that nothing is impossible for God.'

Alastair and Dr Helen Kennedy, from the UK, are the first WEC workers to reside in Abidjan—a city of around one million people. The only clue that might help us find them is a post office box number and a postcode. We have no residential address, no phone number, no visa and no local currency, and we speak no French!

As we pray together about what to do, I sense Jesus saying to me, 'Just start walking, Graham. I will guide you.'

'Lord, I want to trust you in this, but I don't have a residential address and I've never been to Cote d'Ivoire before.'

Jesus' reply is swift. 'Graham, if you really trust me, there is nothing to worry about!'

'Lord, you do realise we haven't even got a phone number or any local currency, and I can't speak the language. Oh ... of course you do!'

Somewhat reluctantly I turn to Marj. 'Darling, I feel the Lord is saying to me that I should leave you and Julie on board, start walking and trust Him to guide me.'

Marj squeezes my hand in agreement. 'I believe He is able to do this. I'll be praying for you, but you need to take those first steps of faith.'

I walk away from the port and come across a post office, eventually finding someone who speaks English. 'This is not the post office you are looking for,' he says. 'You need to get a taxi and follow the directions I give you.' He tells me the way, but I have no chance of remembering even half of it.

I am disappointed, but with no money for a taxi, I have no option but to set off walking again. I make a mental note of some landmarks in case I need to find my way back to the ship. My praying intensifies, and I affirm out loud, 'All things are possible with God.'

Right then, a blue Volkswagen Beetle pulls up at the kerb in front of me. On the back window, in English, are the words ALL THINGS ARE POSSIBLE WITH GOD. I stop, mouth open in amazement.

The young African driver gets out and, seeing me staring at the words, asks, 'Do you believe it?'

'I sure do!' I reply excitedly. 'I've just prayed those exact words.'

After I explain my need, he says, 'If you wait while I finish my business, I'll take you to some people I've seen carrying big black bags and selling Christian books.' I wonder if they might be Mormons or Jehovah's Witnesses, but I sense God is leading me in the right direction.

The driver, I find out, is a Catholic priest who tells me, 'I have recently returned from training in Ghana—that's why I speak English and have an English text on my car.' He is quite likely the only person in the whole of Abidjan like that, and incredibly God has brought us together on this particular street at this precise moment. Had he been one minute later, or had I taken a few minutes longer to decide what to do, I would have missed him. Not only is God's leading and direction spot on; His timing is impeccable too.

We set off together, but after quite a long drive I realise, nervously, that I have no idea how to get back to the ship. Thankfully we arrive at the Christian Literature Crusade bookshop and I know I am in good hands. I thank the young priest profusely for his timely assistance. I would not be surprised if he were an angel in disguise, such is the miraculous help he has given me.

Christian Literature Crusade grew out of WEC and the workers of the two groups in Abidjan know each other well. Once I explain who I am looking for, Doris and Lotti call a taxi, ask the driver how much the fare will be and put the money in my hand. They carefully explain to me, 'When the taxi stops, give the driver the money, walk across the road and knock on the door.'

Bang, bang, bang! I hammer on the heavy wooden door and wait.

Thankfully the Kennedys are home. They are utterly amazed that an Aussie WECer has somehow turned up on their doorstep. After a welcome cold drink and a brief conversation, we hop into their little car, drive back to the port and pick up a smiling Marj and little Julie. We enjoy a wonderful weekend together on terra firma, rejoicing in God's goodness. It is such a physical relief, and it means we feel stronger to cope with all the challenges ahead.

But even more than that, this unbelievable demonstration that God is journeying with us fills us with anticipation and excitement as we set sail for Ghana.

AUSTRALIA
(1945–1972)

Mum and Dad and 10 siblings[1]

Graham – 10 years old

Chapter 2
Born at Calvary—twice!

Adelaide, South Australia
1945–1957

Conceived in wartime and born just after the end of World War Two, I am never quite sure if I am a 'Booster' or a 'Boomer'.[1] But I do know I was born at Calvary—in fact, twice!

***

'Australia is at war!' Every radio station in the country carried Prime Minister Robert Menzies' announcement on 3 September 1939. Almost a million Australians, men and women, served in World War Two alongside those from other nations, mostly helping to defend other countries. Australia itself was attacked in 1942 when Japanese aircraft bombed towns in north-west Australia and three Japanese midget submarines entered Sydney Harbour. Finally, after six long years, the last enemy forces surrendered and the war ended in August 1945.[2]

My father, Alfred Bee, did not fight in the war. As an iron moulder he was considered an essential worker and was not required to register for service. He worked in various foundries in the Adelaide suburbs. Dad's father, Alfred Snr, had migrated to Australia from the UK in 1888 when he was 21 years old. He later married an Australian woman, Mabel Waters, and found employment for a time as a chef at the Royal Adelaide Hospital. I did not get to meet Mabel as she died two years before I was born.

My mother, Marion Bee, trained as a seamstress, but during the war worked in the Islington factory making parts for Beaufort bombers. Her parents, George and Marion Sim, lived in Welland, South Australia. They were good, upright, salt-of-the-earth people, and regularly attended the Hindmarsh Congregational Church. With limited transport, we did not see them often, but Sim family get-togethers were always warm, enjoyable and something to look forward to.

I was born in Adelaide's Calvary Hospital a few months after the end of World War Two. Six years later, while a student at Eden Hills Primary School, I was also 'born again' at Calvary, receiving salvation through Jesus' death on the cross. Retired British naval officer Commander Harvey, a children's evangelist, conducted meetings at my school during lunch hour and after school. He showed us his sword and the gold watch given to him by the Kaiser long before the first world war. It was a reward for rescuing German sailors in distress, and we kids held him in awe. His bright, wide-eyed personality commanded our attention and obedience, and we all respected his authority. He led us in singing rousing choruses accompanied by his piano accordion. My favourite was his unique way of singing 'Brrrrighten the corner where you are'. Talk about making an impression!

Challenged with the need to make a personal commitment to Christ, I responded. I kept a follow-up letter of encouragement for years. It helped remind me of the decision I had made to follow Jesus all my life.

***

So what was life like for me as a firstborn post-war child? What situations and relationships impacted me and formed me?

Times were tough with rationing in place, and people had to make do with very little. The economic cost of the war and its impact on the whole of society was felt for many years. Our first home, in North Adelaide, consisted of several rented rooms in a house we shared with another couple. I remember only a few stories Mum told me of those days:

'Our bread and milk were delivered each day by horse and cart. The milkman would come very early in the morning, before we got up, and deliver bottled milk. You were always up later in the morning, Graham, ready when the baker came to feed the horse a piece of bread. One day when you were sick, the horse refused to continue on his rounds until someone else gave him a piece of bread.'

'We had smelly bucket toilets in small buildings out the back. They were emptied regularly by workmen who accessed them through a laneway at the rear of the property.'

I wish now that I had pressed her to tell me more of those early experiences.

Life was uncomplicated, but work was hard. There were very few machines and gadgets to ease the load. In the years before refrigerators became common, we used ice boxes to keep a few essential food items cool. Large blocks of ice were delivered twice a week and placed in the top of the ice box. The evaporation of the melting ice cooled the food and helped it last longer.

A wood-fired copper was used to boil and wash our clothes. To heat the water meant struggling to get a fire going under the copper. It was especially difficult when it had been raining and the wood was wet. Mum often coughed because of the smoke, so I tried my best to help. I was fascinated as Mum scrubbed the steaming clothes on a corrugated glass washboard—no wonder her hands were always rough. From the concrete rinsing tubs, she put the clothes through a hand-operated wringer. Usually she hung them up to dry on the Hills Hoist clothesline outside, but on wet days she hung them on lines under cover. It was strenuous and tiring, but after a quick cup of tea, she got on with the rest of the day's work.

Change was difficult, but slowly we made progress. Dad bought a block of land in Eden Hills, in the outer suburbs of Adelaide, as we didn't have enough money to buy a house or have one built. At every opportunity, he mixed concrete by hand and moulded building blocks. When there was no more room in the backyard at North Adelaide, he transported the blocks up to Eden Hills. Later, when he began to build, we moved to a relative's house over the side fence from our block. Eventually we moved into the uncompleted house. Dad travelled down to the city to work each day and continued to labour on the house in his spare time. He was an extremely hard worker.

I was envious of other families who went on holidays and returned eager to share their experiences. We never went away together as a family, not even once. Even a day out as a family was a rarity as Dad took every opportunity to work. Twice Mum took us to stay at the beach for a few days with relatives, and occasionally I stayed with a cousin; but otherwise, holidays for our family did not happen. After their marriage, Mum and Dad had a short honeymoon on Kangaroo Island, but the next holiday they had together was not until an interstate visit 50 years later!

I was their only child at this point and Mum and Dad sometimes took me to dances in the city. From the time I could walk, I enjoyed beating the drums whenever I got a chance. When I was three and four, two sisters were born, so Dad went to the dances alone. He often arrived home in the early hours of the morning drunk. Poor Mum had to clean up the mess after he vomited. Thankfully, he didn't continue this behaviour for long, but an indelible memory remained with me. I determined alcohol was not for me, and to this day I don't drink it or even like the taste.

Grandpa never remarried, and when he could no longer cope on his own, he came to live with us. Dad and Grandpa often had heated disagreements. Each insisted on doing things his own way. Their relationship was tense and could erupt at any time. On top of everything else Mum had to contend with, and despite the tension Grandpa brought to our household, she graciously fed and cared for him until his death.

Mum conscientiously took us to church and Sunday school at the bottom of Willunga Road. We thought nothing of walking the mile down the hill and back. She was befriended by some members who encouraged her to attend a special evangelistic tent mission. This was held on vacant land down near the Eden Hills Railway Station. I was with her when she responded to the invitation given by a fiery visiting Irish evangelist to give her life to Christ.

Mum then had a personal relationship with Jesus, and she was a faithful follower. She had a godly influence on all the family. She was quiet, committed, compassionate, prayerful, gracious, warm and friendly. I felt so blessed to be her son and to have her godly example and support in whatever I did.

What about Dad? Initially he resisted encouragements to follow Mum. For a brief time he got involved in the Masonic Lodge. However, one day, when coming home from work on his motorbike, he was knocked over by a car running a red light. He tried to stand but couldn't and looked down to see a bone sticking out through the skin. His leg was put in traction, and eventually in plaster. The bones did not set well and consequently were slow to heal and left him with one leg slightly shorter than the other. He was unable to go to work for many months.

One day, bored and tired from resisting frequent invitations, he agreed to accompany a friend who travelled around different country venues each week speaking at open-air gospel meetings. He made a decision to follow Jesus and gave up drinking. But Dad's commitment fluctuated—sometimes he was keen but at other times his fervour waned. The main hindrance was his love of beer and his inability to stop drinking before he became intoxicated. Thankfully, he was never violent and remained committed to supporting the family.

***

Thirty years later, alcohol again got the better of Dad and he lost his licence following an accident. The car was written off, so he had no means of getting to the pub easily. I was overseas at the time and wrote him a letter, sharing my concern that if he didn't stop drinking something worse could happen. Later, no longer able to drive, crossing the road on his way to work, he was almost killed when sent flying through the air by a speeding car. For many years I had been under the impression that he had overcome this temptation, but my younger siblings told me stories of still having to go out and find him on the street and help him home.

I later learned what finally caused him to give up drinking. One day his only sister, Ivy, came to visit. She boldly challenged him about his drunkenness and he promised her he would stop. Two days later, while crossing Prospect Road in Adelaide with two of her friends, the three ladies were knocked down by a car and killed. This shook Dad up badly. It took this tragedy to get through to him, but he finally gave up drinking.

Dad never played football or cricket but he was a keen follower of both. In the days before TV, we listened to the crackly shortwave radio broadcasts of Australia playing England in Test Matches. He attended Aussie Rules football games with his friends and took me along. When he stopped going, I often walked the mile to the railway station, caught the steam train or the new diesel train into the city centre, and then took the bus to wherever my team, Glenelg, was playing. Although I was only nine, my parents had no qualms about me going on my own. I appreciated the confidence they had in me, and this helped me develop a sense of responsibility.

God used many things in developing my character, including our humble living conditions and the specific location of my home.

Chapter 3
Learning to appreciate differences

Eden Hills
1948–1957

'Graham, come quickly!' yelled my friends.

'What's happening?'

'Another bus has just pulled up! We might get some more money!'

My little friends and I rushed down to the side of the road. Curious tourists jammed their faces against the bus windows and watched as a swarm of brown-skinned children appeared on the footpath below them. We were like bees around a honey pot. Those watching seemed oblivious to the fact that there was a white child among them.

Lining up on the side of the road with the younger children from Colebrook Home is one of my earliest memories. This was the only home for Aboriginal children in the city of Adelaide and the children were a novelty to the tourists who came in buses. They threw threepences and sixpences out of the bus windows to us waiting children. I scrambled to get one or two coins for myself. Sometimes the tourists threw lollies, but it was the money we liked most!

***

The house Dad built was in Barunga Street, Eden Hills. It was directly opposite Colebrook Home, where 50 children, mostly part-Aboriginal, were housed and cared for.

Colebrook Home was operated by the interdenominational United Aborigines Mission (later UAM Ministries). Various churches supported the ministry, and after their traditional Harvest Thanksgiving services donated the produce to Colebrook. The Home was supervised by two widely-acclaimed, caring and respected Christian ladies, Matron Hyde and Sister Rutter, and their helpers. My mother appreciated these ladies and developed a close friendship with another very committed Christian helper, Sister Lovibond. We often attended Christian meetings held at Colebrook, and whenever I had the opportunity, I would go and play with the children or invite a particular friend to my place.

On weekends, we were sometimes given permission to walk through the bush to Sturt Creek. There were lots of interesting things to do there and I really enjoyed swimming in one of the cool waterholes. On other occasions, we watched the trains go by from the back of the 10-acre property or climbed trees and looked for birds' nests. Discipline of the children was firm, but my parents were too. If I disobeyed, the most common method of correction was for the consequences to be administered to the 'seat of learning'!

The Home was held in high regard. A 1951 Aborigines Protection Board report said:

> A float entered by UAM in the Jubilee Celebrations provided convincing evidence of the great advance in Aboriginal welfare work in this state. Many young aborigines from Colebrook Home, and older persons, who were trained in this institution, illustrated the various trades and professions in which they were engaged. The nursing profession was represented by several nurses and, in addition, music, weaving, and other industrial and scholastic phases of the training provided were displayed.[1]

Sadly, during this era, there was still much prejudice towards Indigenous people. The children were not able to attend schools with white children. They were educated in their own school until the way finally opened for them to attend local schools. I interacted frequently with them and grew to respect, love and appreciate them.

All this happened at a time when the Australian Government's restrictive White Australia immigration policy was still practised. Adelaide's suburban Eden Hills was a very unlikely place for a young boy to develop sensitivity to, and love for, people of other cultures. But that is exactly what I experienced.

I still had no understanding of the circumstances from which these children were removed. I realised they were different and that some had real behavioural problems. The majority, though, I found to be warm and friendly. Although they were well cared for, they were separated from their families. It made me feel so thankful for my own home and family.

For those children, real treats were few and far between. To get maximum pleasure out of an ice cream, for instance, they would come right up close to my face and, while I watched on enviously, give a long slow lick accompanied by sounds of 'Mmmhhh! This is so nice.'

One of those who lived at Colebrook later became a celebrated member of society. Lowitja (Lois) O'Donoghue received numerous awards and in 1984 was named Australian of the Year.[2] She also had a number of responsible positions as a nurse and public servant, and in 1992 became the first Aboriginal Australian to address the United Nations. Another notable person, Doris Kartinyeri, reflecting on her years at Colebrook stated, 'The atmosphere these Sisters created is a pleasurable memory.'[3]

Later, I learnt about the circumstances that surrounded the removal of these children from their families. Indigenous children were taken from their parents and placed in care for their education and physical welfare. Sometimes it was with their parent's permission, but on many occasions children were removed against their parents' will. I am sure it was done with good intentions, often by government departments, but it was frequently traumatic for both children and parents. Both those removed with parental consent and those without are now regarded as part of what many Australians refer to as 'The Stolen Generations'.

In many instances, this practice resulted in abuse and ill treatment. After the full extent of the damage to the lives of many of those treated in this way became known, in 2008 the Australian Prime Minister made a national apology and said 'Sorry' on behalf of all Australians: 'We apologise for the laws and policies of successive governments that have inflicted profound grief, suffering and loss on these our fellow Australians.'[4]

Just recently, I realised that these early experiences are where my affinity with people of other cultures began. God knew that much of my life and work would be spent in a multicultural environment, and without my knowing it He was growing certain values and attitudes within me.

I was content and happy. But change often comes when we least expect it.

Chapter 4
Teenager on the move

Meadows, South Australia
1957–1965

'We're moving! You children will have a whole 10 acres to run around in and we can grow our own vegies and fruit trees.' Dad's smile was huge and his enthusiasm catching. 'There's a double garage and a big workbench with lots of room for tools on the wall behind the bench. We'll have a proper workshop and can make things together.'

Mum and Dad believed their calling in life was to have a large family and to bring us up according to biblical principles. They created a loving, stable family environment and did all they could to provide and care for us. So in my seventh year at school, they sold the house in Eden Hills and moved us all to a small 10-acre farm at Meadows in the Adelaide Hills. They saw this as the next step in their vision of raising a large family in a healthy rural setting.

We were all sad leaving our friends, but the sadness was tinged with anticipation. Mum, Dad and we six children squashed into the old FJ Holden car—a gift from Dad's sister, Aunty Ivy. With windows wound down, we breathed in the fresh country air and eagerly peered out, keen to get a first look at our new home. Our shared impressions fuelled the excitement we felt.

'Look! The heads of the oats growing in our paddocks are trying to peer over the fences.'

'I had no idea 10 acres is this big!'

'Doesn't the countryside look so lush and green?'

'Spring is such a great time of the year—I wonder what the farm will look like in other seasons?'

We had cows, and chickens. We planted vegies and baled our own hay. I developed a love for all things country. My plan had been to attend Unley High School in the city and then to train as a teacher. But this move changed the direction of my life significantly.

I was attracted to farming as a career, so I decided to attend Urrbrae Agricultural High School, five kilometres from the Adelaide CBD. This meant getting up at 6 am each morning to get to the main road to catch the 7 am bus. Usually I walked, but if the weather was not good, I got a ride to the bus stop with Dad. It was a 90-minute bus trip to Adelaide and then a 20-minute walk to Urrbrae. After school, the reverse happened. I arrived home around 6 pm.

Mum's days were full, looking after our large family without the help of many modern conveniences. She made clothes for the children and did the washing, ironing, cleaning, mending and darning of socks. She still made time to sit with me and have a daily Bible reading and prayer while I ate breakfast. Her priorities were clear. She was a wonderful example to me.

I was quite shy and found it difficult to make new friendships. Our move to Meadows didn't help. I only attended Meadows Primary School for three months before I started high school back in the city. I had limited opportunities to meet local people, and I didn't have many close friends my age. I was, however, appointed captain of the local under-16 cricket team in my last year at high school.

We attended the local Methodist Church. The minister taught a social gospel without the need for a personal relationship with Jesus. On some Wednesday evenings he had to be called from the manse as he had forgotten it was prayer meeting night—no wonder few others attended. Disillusioned, Mum and Dad decided to go elsewhere.

Each Sunday we travelled to the more evangelical Strathalbyn Church of Christ. What a contrast! Their enthusiasm was evident. Before the Sunday evening Gospel Service, people gathered to pray in a galvanised iron garage at the back of the church. The inside walls were lined with people as we earnestly prayed for others to be saved. We were blessed by the warm and inclusive fellowship and the pastor's sound biblical teaching. It was not surprising that nine of us from this small church later went into missionary service within Australia and overseas. It was here I was baptised and encouraged in my walk with Christ.

Due to distance, we usually only travelled to church on Sunday mornings and occasionally on Sunday evenings. So each week we had a number of meetings in our home, led by Harold Filmer, a local Christian farmer. Some people thought he was a bit fanatical as he was bold in using every opportunity to share his faith. He was a man of integrity, well respected in the community, and had a great influence on my life.

A Bible study on Wednesday evenings, a prayer meeting on Friday nights and a Christian Endeavour meeting on Sunday afternoons supplemented our church attendance. I was one of nine children by this time, so we only needed a couple of other local kids to join us and we had a crowd! I gained some experience in leading and speaking at these meetings. We often had missionaries from various mission societies speak at the prayer meetings. But the first Friday of each month became a regular 'Prayer Force' meeting for WEC International, an interdenominational and international mission agency. Ralph and Berte Moan led these meetings and often brought a WEC missionary to share about their work. Gradually my interest in missions grew. I began to pray daily for specific missionaries, and soon decided to financially support two of them.

In 1959 Billy Graham conducted crusades in Adelaide. Our small home fellowship sought to impact local people and hired a bus on several days to take people to the meetings. A growing concern for people to come to know Jesus Christ personally became a part of my life.

Towards the end of Year 10, I had an opportunity for work experience. Mr Filmer kindly agreed for me to work with him on his dairy farm. I thoroughly enjoyed this and decided to investigate the kind of farming jobs that might be available to me in the future. Mum and Dad got the shock of their lives when I came home one evening and told them I had agreed, subject to a preliminary visit, to work on a stud dairy farm in Meningie. It was approximately 160 kilometres away. I would have to leave home and live there, but I appeased them with the fact that I would return home once a month for a four-day long weekend.

My quick decision to find work was due in part to knowing that in the next two years, two of my sisters would start high school. Family finances were very tight and Mum and Dad would struggle to support us all. I felt that by doing this I could relieve some of the pressure on them. Dad continued taking on extra jobs at weekends and public holidays to supplement his regular wage. Mum's joy and gratitude was heart-warming when I presented her with our first vacuum cleaner and pop-up toaster, bought with my wages.

The lifestyle and workload in Meningie challenged me, but I really enjoyed showing our cows in some of the local shows. My greatest thrill, though, was taking some to the annual Royal Adelaide Agricultural Show. I excitedly reported back to my friends, 'Winning championships with the cattle is amazing. My dream now is to one day become a stud breeder of "Illawarra", Australia's own specially developed dairy breed.'

In Meningie I attended church with my boss's family most Sunday mornings, but there was not much in the teaching to encourage my spiritual growth. At 15 years of age, and without a driver's licence, it was difficult to get to youth group. I was quite shy and didn't make the effort to find a lift.

Despite that, I enjoyed both the work on the farm and returning home for my long-weekend break each month. Leaving my family to go back to the farm at the end of each visit was never easy for me—or for them. During my years at Meningie, my youngest brother, Peter, was born. Our family then numbered 10. Dad, especially, seemed pleased that they had managed to have five boys and five girls.

***

One evening, just as I came in from work, the phone rang.

'Mrs Williams, is Graham home yet?'

'Yes, he's just walked in, Mrs Bee. I'll get him for you.'

Mum's voice was trembling as she told me, 'I've been trying to ring you all afternoon. I was told you were out. I have some bad news for you. Something terrible has happened. Your sister Marilyn was involved.'

Chapter 5
Murder at night

1962

'What is it, Mum? What's happened to Marilyn?' I asked, my heart pounding.

'Your sister was tied up.' Mum took a breath, trying to break the news slowly.

In the time it took her to brace herself and get the words out, the evening television news had started. 'We begin tonight's bulletin with a shocking story.' A picture of a farmhouse at Bull Creek flashed on the screen. I knew that house! It belonged to our friends, Geoff and Fay.

With one ear tuned to the report being aired, I tried to listen to what Mum was saying. Through tears, she continued with her heartbreaking news.

'I wanted to tell you personally before you saw it on the news. The media cameras have been everywhere! I'm so sorry to have to tell you, but Fay has been tragically murdered. Marilyn was staying with her for a few days while Geoff was away. She's OK, but it's been a horrendous ordeal for her.'

While I listened to Mum, pictures of the farm surroundings flashed on the screen. There was no doubting the truth of what she was telling me. The reporter continued, 'An 11-year-old girl staying in the house displayed great bravery by escaping. She carried the crying son across the paddocks in the cold and dark of the night to get help from neighbours.'

Abruptly, the news presenter moved on to the next story.

While I struggled to comprehend what I had just seen and heard, Mum filled me in a bit more. 'I'm currently caring for their little boy. The young man who did this stole their car and was arrested 270 kilometres away. He was caught trying to cash a forged cheque to pay for petrol.'

Living so far from home, I was shielded from much of the trauma of this event, but I was still shocked. How could such a thing happen in our quiet country community? It was not until my next visit home that I felt the full impact. A young life snuffed out prematurely. A family's dreams—not broken, but shattered. A young boy having to live out his future without knowing his mother's love and care. It left a shadow over many of our lives.

***

Geoff and Fay had moved into our area in 1959 to take over a dairy farm. Geoff was training to be a pilot with Missionary Aviation Fellowship. They hoped the farm would help fund their preparation for missionary service. They quickly became very close family friends and key members of our small home fellowship.

Their compassion and care for others was evident, so it came as no surprise to us that a call from the Welfare Department to our church resulted in Geoff and Fay giving a young man a chance to sort out his life.

Fifteen-year-old Harry came from a dysfunctional family. He'd had a rough start to life—an illegitimate child at a time when society still frowned on this. He grew into a troubled teen and authorities were worried about his future prospects.

Harry seemed to get off to a promising start with Geoff and Fay. For three months he helped on their dairy farm and fitted in with their family. He attended church with them and appeared to progress well. He even made a profession of faith, so there was no indication that something like this would happen.

Life was busy for Geoff, trying to juggle the family, the farm and ongoing pilot training. Concerned about the pressure he was under; Fay suggested he go away for a few days' break. She checked to see that 11-year-old Marilyn was available, both to keep her company and to help look after her young son while she milked the cows.

Geoff and Fay's loving and thoughtful act cost Fay her life.

Mum, despite having her hands full with our own family, lovingly cared for Geoff's son. Two dear Christian friends stayed with Geoff to help him through the difficult first week. Then other caring friends graciously surrounded him with love and practical support for the next three months until the farm was sold. He needed time to grieve and to adjust to the new situation. The first nine months were traumatic as he wrestled with his grief and uncertain future. The pain and loss he felt were deep.

He was just 23.

***

I am amazed at the resilience of people like Geoff and Marilyn who, with Jesus' help, are able to move on from being victims of circumstances beyond their control to being people whose lives continue to bless others. Years later I asked Geoff, 'How was it possible, after such a tragic event, for you to get up and move on?' I have never forgotten his answer.

'The key, Graham, is forgiveness. I came to faith in God when I was 13. Jesus' teaching on how we should react to those who harm us has truly become part of how I live my life. As difficult as it was, I realised that, in obedience to God's Word and for my own sake, I needed to forgive Harry. By not allowing bitterness and thoughts of revenge to control me, it allowed me to focus on what lay ahead. The public sharing of this act of grace was misunderstood by some in the local community. Forgiving didn't make things any easier, but it did help me to move on.'

And Marilyn? She discovered that a supportive family, and a personal trust in Jesus, made all the difference. It was still a journey, however. Daily learning to draw on divine strength and enabling, she was able to confidently face the future. Rather than dwelling on her past, she chose to follow God, and eventually married Geoff Ellery, a minister with whom she has had a lovely ministry in both Australia and New Zealand.

***

In the will of God, no experience is wasted. God used even dark and difficult times like these to strengthen my trust in Him. Just as Joseph, Daniel and his three friends trusted God during adverse situations, I began to understand how holding on to God and His promises makes a huge difference to the outcome. In spite of their situation, and because of their faith, the light of these men shines down through the ages to bless us today. This lesson would ultimately serve to keep me steady when my own journey took me through 'the valley of the shadow of death'.

Chapter 6
Working Bee

My body ached after working all day putting in new fence posts. A hot bath relieved the soreness only slightly. After dinner, I sank down onto the sofa to relax, but I had to jump up when my boss's wife called me to the phone.

'Graham, you'd better be quick. It's your father and he sounds like he's in a hurry.'

'Are you sure it's Dad? He hates talking on the telephone. Something must have happened.'

To my relief it was not bad news—quite the contrary.

'Graham, Mum and I are really keen for you to return home. I've been asking around and I've found a good job for you here in the Meadows area. It's a large farm; you'd have more responsibility, and higher pay.'

'Wow! Thanks, Dad! It sure sounds inviting.'

He informed me that I would have to buy a car. With early morning starts, I would need to drive myself to and from work each day. Any hesitation on my part disappeared with the mention of a car. After learning to drive on the farm, I loved driving and already had my licence.

I'd had two and a half wonderful years working in Meningie and would have been happy to stay, but I heard the wistfulness in my father's voice.

'Dad, you know it's just lack of finance that has held me back from buying a car already. This is all very sudden, but it feels right to be coming home closer to family again. The Williams family has been good to me, but maybe it is time to move on. I'll have a chat with them tonight about resigning, and then tomorrow I'll give the other folk a ring to confirm I'll take the job.'

It was with mixed emotions that I left the Illawarra stud behind, but

I still carried my dream of being a top stud breeder secure in my heart.

***

I purchased my first car—a second-hand Ford Cortina—with a loan. It provided me with a new level of independence, and enabled me to travel further afield and meet other Christian young people.

Hawthorn Farm Bible teaching weekends, at nearby Mt Barker, attracted many keen young people from all over Adelaide. This is where I first heard about the biblical principles of dying to self—of living the crucified life in absolute surrender and dependence on God. Alan Catchpoole, a renowned speaker, did not mince words: 'It means being prepared to give up your selfish ambition: to put aside your personal goals and plans and embrace God's will for your life.'

I needed time to think about this and its implications. It was a step further on than I was prepared to take at the time.

After the years in Meningie without a lot of fellowship and teaching, I was keen to keep learning and growing. But one thing I struggled to understand in the Bible was the Israelites' behaviour. They had seen so many wonderful acts of God on their behalf. God had devastated the nation of Egypt through 10 terrible plagues, and the Israelites had experienced a miraculous deliverance from the Egyptian army when the Red Sea opened up. Yet they frequently doubted God and disobeyed His clear instructions. I wrestled with this, not comprehending how they could respond to God's goodness and faithfulness by doubting and complaining.

Gradually the Lord began to open my eyes to see that I was just like them. As His child I was blessed with so much, yet often I also doubted, disobeyed and chose to follow my own desires.

In my naivety, I had expected that Father God would protect me, His child, from any danger. But after the tragedy of Fay's murder, I found myself still trying to come to grips with how to trust God in the ups and downs of everyday life. I longed to experience the 'highs', the miraculous and the blessings I read about in Scripture. Others had shared their stories; I wanted God to be real in every circumstance of *my* life as well.

In time, I learned that before the miracles happened and the deliverances came, God's people faced hunger and thirst; they trudged through hot, dry deserts and faced giants that caused them to tremble in fear. They were confronted by selfish political leaders and hostile armies in bloody conflicts.

As I learned more, I realised that witnessing miracles or listening to great Bible teachers and preachers did not automatically grow faith. My faith would grow when I trusted and obeyed God and relied on Him in the midst of uncertainty and adversity. Difficult circumstances, feelings of inadequacy and facing opposition when sharing about my relationship with Jesus were all opportunities for my faith to grow and flourish. My attitude would determine the effect these things had on me. Instead of allowing them to overwhelm me, I could choose to take positive steps of faith and see God work in and through me. This was quite a revelation to me, and it gave me much to think about as I worked.

My new job on the large dairy farm was pressured. I realised how laid-back life had been before. The days were long and the work tiring. We milked twice a day, and in between we had to make and cart hay, construct new fences and repair damaged ones. In summer time we had the added task of shifting irrigation pipes every four hours. But I was not afraid of hard work and was fully aware that the extra responsibility and experience would be useful when I owned my own farm.

It was great to be around my family more and I was so grateful for our simple but solid Christian upbringing. My parents and siblings loved me and valued me as an important part of their lives. In our home we were taught that each of us was created by God as a unique person with specific gifts and abilities, and this gave me a deep sense of security. It helped me to know my life had meaning and purpose and aided in making important choices. During these young adult years, I had a lovely sense that God's hand was on my life, just as it had been on young Joseph's in Egypt. God seemed to bless whatever I put my hand to. The people I worked for appeared to prosper too while I was there.

Living away from home had helped me develop a greater dependence on God. My walk with God was steady and my life a quiet witness. My workmates knew I was a follower of Jesus, but I was shy and felt guilty that I did not share more freely with them. I knew He had a plan and purpose for my life. My desire was to seek Him and discover what that plan was.

Chapter 7
A fork in the road

South Australia
1966–1967

In my daily time with God one morning, I read, 'Call to me and I will answer you, and will tell you great and hidden things which you have not known' (Jeremiah 33:3 RSV). I was calling on God to show me His plan for my life. Little did I realise just how quickly He would answer my prayers, nor could I ever have imagined what my response would be to these 'great and hidden things' which the Father was about to reveal to me.

***

By 5.30 am each morning, summer and winter, rain, hail or shine, I had to be up to milk the cows. After a hearty breakfast I would set off down to the farm and work hard throughout the day, then be back again to round up the cows for the evening milking. Life revolved around milking the large herd and there was very little time in the week for anything else. On Sunday mornings I would rush to finish in the dairy in time for church.

Each Saturday I would hurry home after the evening milking, shower and grab something to eat as I rushed back out the door. With a rare sense of freedom, I would jump in the car, spin the wheels on our gravel road and head down to Adelaide to a Youth for Christ meeting, or whatever other event happened to be on that week.

I was 20 and a bit of a loner, but I was beginning to long for some deep, meaningful friendships with young people my own age. Some female ones would be good too! These casual outings kept me in touch with some of the young people I met, but I was disappointed that they did not provide opportunities for prolonged contact or for anything more than fairly superficial conversations. To stay awake on the drive home, I would turn up the radio and wind down the window so the cold evening air rushed in.

Missionaries would come to speak at our home meetings sometimes and they all emphasised the need to reach the unreached peoples of the world—those who had never had the opportunity to hear of God's love. I wanted to do my bit, so I began regularly sending money to help support two missionary families. Slowly but surely I developed a genuine personal concern for people who were yet to hear of God's wonderful plan of salvation.

The dream of one day becoming a top Illawarra stud dairy farmer still burned in me. I leased a small farm close to where I was working. I bought heifer calves to raise at home, then turned them out to graze on my little farm. A deep contentment settled over me—I was well on my way to realising my dream, was busy and fulfilled earning my living, and was enjoying my relationship with Jesus. A verse from the Bible sat well with me: 'This should be your ambition: to live a quiet life, minding your own business and working with your hands … As a result, people who are not Christians will respect the way you live, and you will not need to depend upon others to meet your financial needs' (1 Thessalonians 4:11 NLT). I felt my life reflected this. I was happy.

***

Then one night after our missionary meeting, my world turned upside down. It came like a bolt of lightning, but I knew without a shadow of a doubt that God wanted me to go to live and train at the WEC Missionary Training College (Worldview) in Tasmania.

My heart was thumping. I should have been ecstatic—this was an immense privilege. Instead, I threw up all the excuses under the sun.

God, I can't do this. No way! I'm just a shy, quiet farmer without any particular gifts. Your cause would be far better off if you sent doctors and nurses, or teachers—those with better qualifications. Send those who have the 'gift of the gab'; I could never stand up in front of people.

I'm already doing my bit by supporting missionaries. What about my dreams? Where do they fit in?

And what would other people think? Most people spend their lives seeking success, wealth and health, leisure and pleasure. They'd think I was crazy, maybe even a religious fanatic! Who knows where this path would lead me? Can I leave the familiar and head out into the great unknown?

As I listened to myself and the fears and anxieties which threatened to engulf me, I felt I must have got it wrong. I admired missionaries, but could I actually be one? I knew in my heart that this 'call' was not just for a six-month experience. To obey meant a life-long commitment. It would be a radical change of direction.

I was soon to discover the truth of Proverbs 16:9: 'Many plans are in a man's mind, but it is the Lord who directs his steps' (MLB).

The next morning, just as the sun was coming up, I rose to have my usual Bible reading. Despite my protests, excuses and rational attempts to convince God that He had the wrong person, the conviction in my heart had not gone away overnight. I didn't want to disobey God, but I hesitated to open my Bible, afraid a verse might stand out, might speak to me and confirm what God had said the night before.

I decided to read in the Psalms since I had never heard a missionary testify that God had called them from the Psalms. A safe book—or so I thought.

I began reading Psalm 73. Coming to verse 26 I read, 'Though my flesh and my heart fail, God is the strength of my heart and my portion forever' (MLB). God had just turned up the volume of his call. It rang loud and clear in my spirit—no mistaking it! I knew this was God's specific word to me. He was concerned, not with how much ability I did or didn't have, but rather whether I was willing to lay aside my own plans and walk in obedience to His will. He promised me that even though I felt weak, He would strengthen and enable me to do all He asked of me.

But this first step seemed *huge*! When Jesus talked about the cost of discipleship in Mark 8:34, He said, 'If you want to be my follower you must give up your selfish ambition, shoulder your cross and follow me' (NLT). I wandered down the backyard and sat under the clothesline, weeping as I wrestled with God. I struggled to come to terms with all this would mean for my future.

In the past I had made my own plans and then asked God to bless them. Now I realised just how much I had always wanted to be in control. In Sunday school I used to sing with childlike enthusiasm, 'Follow, follow, I will follow Jesus/Anywhere, everywhere I will follow on'. In my present situation, following Him had just got a whole lot more demanding and challenging.

Eventually I struggled to the summit of that mountain of excuses, and triumphantly exclaimed, *Yes, Lord! I am willing to give up my personal ambition and follow your leading. I submit to your Lordship, and I'm willing to trust you to enable me to do it.* Suddenly it felt like blinkers were removed from my eyes and I could see clearly the way ahead. Peace and joy flooded my heart and mind. Yes, I had just made a commitment to serve God in missions. But I recognised that it was more than that—it signalled a significant turning point where I gave up my small ambitions and chose a different fork in the road, one that would align me with God's plan and purposes.

Romans 12:1–2 suddenly took on new meaning for me: 'I beg you to offer your bodies to [God] as a living sacrifice, pure and pleasing. That's the most sensible way to serve God. Don't be like the people of this world, but let God change the way you think. Then you will know how to do everything that is good and pleasing to him' (CEV).

When I went back inside the house, Mum was busy, but not too busy to notice that something was different. 'You've seemed troubled, Graham. Do you want to talk about it?'

'I've just been wrestling with God,' I said, 'and He won! I'm going to train to be a missionary.'

'That news doesn't surprise me at all. I've been wondering if God might have something like that in store for you. I'm sure you'll find it challenging, but we'll be right behind you.' Her words were reassuring as she reminded me of one of her favourite verses:

'Trust in the Lord with all your heart, and lean not on your own understanding; in all your ways acknowledge Him, and He shall direct your paths' (Proverbs 3:5–6 NKJV).

***

From that point on, my commitment to God and His good plans for my life became more intentional and steadfast. Apart from some minor ups and downs, my hunger for God deepened. I became bolder in sharing my faith, and I had a strong desire to trust and obey, moment by moment, day by day.

I quickly found that when God takes the lead, He often steers us into places and situations where our weakness and frailty are exposed. My faith and commitment were definitely tested, but I could also see the Father's care and faithfulness demonstrated.

During the process of applying to Worldview I had to have a medical examination. My doctor suspected I might have Type 2 Diabetes. A specialist confirmed this and prescribed medication, but we needed some time to see if tablets could control it. I received a letter from the college, which I read aloud. 'We advise that your application has been deferred until the medical condition discovered in your examination is controlled and stable.'

I had been keen and ready to go; it felt like such an anti-climax.

But this time I did not fight with God. I had learned my lesson well—His ways are higher than my ways, His thoughts higher than my thoughts. During this time of waiting, I realised that faith in Almighty God connected my weakness and frailty with His strength and sufficiency.

I was amazed when my current boss, after hearing my news about having to defer, offered me a raise if I would stay on. Then, just when it looked like there was no alternative to having insulin injections for the rest of my life, the doctor had another thought. He recommended one last combination of tablets, and this time my sugar levels became stable.

When a letter from the college arrived confirming my acceptance for the next intake of students, I whooped for joy. During the unexpected year of waiting and working, I had saved enough for two years' fees. I handed in my resignation from work and received my last ever salary payment.

I was eagerly looking forward to what lay ahead, but a little apprehensive about 'living by faith'. What would that look like in real terms?

Chapter 8
Carrots and a ukulele

Launceston, Tasmania
1967/68

1967 was a significant year around the world. China's Cultural Revolution was in full swing. General Suharto took power in a military coup in nearby Indonesia. Ghana was adjusting to military rule after its revolutionary first president, Kwame Nkrumah, was ousted in a dramatic coup 12 months before. Before the end of that year, the Australian Prime Minister, Harold Holt, was reported missing, presumed dead. Demonstrations against the war in Vietnam were gaining momentum in Australia.

It was a significant year for me, too. On December 29, 1966, I had turned 21. I was eligible for compulsory national military service. Every morning I checked the mailbox, waiting for the one letter that could change the entire direction of my life. Kevin, a friend from church, received his call up. He left our small community in combat dress to serve in Vietnam.

Finally, the long awaited envelope arrived. With trembling hands I tore it open, but the short message simply stated that my number had not come up in the national ballot. Relief flooded my body. My life could continue as planned.

***

When I arrived at Worldview in January 1967, I soon discovered that living in community was not just a prolonged camp. It had its own particular challenges. Up until then I had only had a few Christian friends my own age, but suddenly they were all around me. My shyness compounded all the new experiences I was facing.

Worldview was similar to many other Bible colleges, but it had the specific aim of training and preparing people for overseas missionary service. During our orientation, Evan Davies, a staff member, explained the routine.

'We all rise at six in the morning and have one hour set aside for a daily quiet time. If you form healthy practices here, it will be a good foundation for your future.

'Breakfast is followed by rostered duties which change fortnightly. You'll learn new skills and gain practical experience, often working in teams. Members of staff don't receive a salary but trust God for their support. Your help with practical tasks enables us to keep fees lower than most other Bible colleges.

'A fellowship time, lectures and study periods take up most of the day. Late afternoon the college community enjoys a time of volleyball or other sports to ensure we all keep active. There are other periods for practical duties twice a week that help with the running and maintenance of the college. Ministry assignments on weekends include Sunday school teaching, leading youth clubs and preaching.'

There were numerous rules governing lifestyle, including a dress code, how we related to the opposite sex and set times for waking and lights out. While we were hopeful some of these would be relaxed in the future, conforming to the rules and expectations was not difficult for me; it suited my personality to have clear guidelines and boundaries.

Living with others at close quarters was a different matter. We slept in dormitories of eight, shared practical duties in teams, studied and even relaxed together. Such close interaction had the potential to become a breeding ground for misunderstandings and conflict. Sometimes my reactions and words both surprised and disappointed me.

My turn came to be on the vegetable preparation team. One day, while we were peeling carrots, the team leader called out insistently, 'Come on! Move it, guys. We only have 10 minutes to finish these.' There always seemed to be a rush to get everything done in time for the morning fellowship. I fumed as one guy peeled very slowly and meticulously while the rest of us powered on. A trivial thing, but it burned me up inside. I hated to be late for anything. I allowed it to become a big issue and it robbed me of my peace. We arrived two minutes late, with me still stewing over what had just happened. My usually calm spirit was agitated and I found it hard to concentrate on the devotional message that morning.

Afterwards, as the Spirit of God spoke to me, I realised that this other guy was not the problem—I was! I confessed my bad attitude and asked God for forgiveness. Peace reigned again. Proving God's grace and sufficiency in the little things, not just the big, was an important part of my spiritual growth.

Learning to accept others and their differences was an integral part of our training for future ministry, and this was emphasised in the teaching we received. Most of us would find ourselves working as part of a team, most likely a multicultural one. It was important for us to learn how to handle conflict in relationships. Many people are surprised to discover that interpersonal conflict is one of the biggest difficulties missionaries face. It sends many home prematurely.

Martin, a young man in my intake, received his call-up for compulsory military service in Vietnam and felt right about going. It was a fresh reminder of just how close I came to having to go and fight in this war. *Thank you, Lord. You are sovereign over world events, and at the same time you are working out your purposes for my life. I am so glad I've committed my future into your hands. Keep leading me please.*

The staff members, both academic and practical, frequently reminded us, 'As you prepare for missionary service, you need to be RFA—Ready For Anything!' I was acutely aware that I still had much to learn, in both biblical knowledge and applying it practically in daily living.

The students at Worldview had come from many different Christian denominations and with a variety of experiences and spiritual encounters with God. We were all there with the same desires: to know God and His word more fully, to learn ways of communicating the truth of His Word more effectively, and to touch the world with Jesus' love and compassion. A few students were very vocal about particular spiritual experiences they had had, and felt it was their responsibility to exhort others to seek these same experiences. At times I longed for and prayed for a more demonstrative experience, but Jesus challenged me about my motives: *Be sure you are seeking after Me, not an experience. What I want is for you to become more like Me. I want you to talk with Me; to walk with Me as a son would with his father. I live in you and you live in me. Remember that the One who began this good work in you will bring it to completion.*

The Bible warns us of the deceitfulness of our hearts, and sometimes it was not easy to discern my motives—to discover the difference between what *I* wanted and what *God* wanted. Our principal, Stewart Dinnen, would teach, in his broad Scottish brogue, about our union with Christ. 'Understand that your old life, with its selfish desires and ambitions, has been crucified with Christ. You are now united with Jesus, so allow Him to live His life through you.'

I could understand and embrace the fact that 'in Christ' my sinful nature had been crucified (put to death) and its power over me broken. But the reality was that 'the flesh'; my capacity to live life in my own strength, was still there. It had not been done away with, removed or improved. The difference was I no longer had to obey its impulses and demands. I am a new creature in Christ, under new management, and no longer have to obey the old master. I have freedom to allow Christ to live his life through me.

Knowing who I am in Christ is fundamental, but counting on that and acting on it became part of a growing experience including transformation through the renewing of my mind.

Over time, as these deep truths were reiterated, I began to truly understand and believe that 'Jesus is all I need', 'In Jesus dwells all the fullness of God, and I am complete in Him' and 'I am blessed with everything I need for life and godliness.'

***

As we lived, studied and worked in practical ways so closely with one another, it was not too difficult to discern those who really 'walked the talk'. They were the ones who humbly followed the way of the cross and demonstrated what it was to be 'Christlike'.

I soon discovered it was easy to see others' weaknesses but not so easy to admit to mine. Naturally reserved, I didn't like others knowing where I was vulnerable. It had always been important to me to keep up appearances. I had yet to realise that I was only fooling myself by trying to build up my own self-esteem and reputation.

With the faithful teaching of the Word of God, and as I watched godly people around me, cracks began to appear in the façade. I prayed, *Lord, please help me to be real and transparent. Help me to see myself as you see me. Thank you that you haven't given up on me. Please keep transforming me into your likeness.*

The Father did not need a second invitation. Some painful and humbling experiences soon tempered my youthful enthusiasm and pride.

Impressed by those able to lead singing, I bought a ukulele and had some private lessons from my friend, Geoff. I thought I was doing reasonably well as we played along together. When the time came for teams to go out on three weeks' mission, I volunteered to help lead the singing in the afternoon children's meetings. We began the first meeting with singing. I started playing, but my timing was all wrong. The singing sounded terrible. I got even more nervous and sweaty. The ukulele playing got worse. The kids did their best to keep going, but it was a nightmare.

The following day, during our team meeting, someone highlighted the problem with the singing. Our leader, Ross, suggested, 'What about Kevin playing the old organ?' Everyone nodded in agreement, which was not surprising. Immediately the singing improved, and the children's enjoyment was obvious to all.

This very public experience dealt a huge blow to my pride. Yet I also saw that even though it was not pleasant for me, God was answering the prayer I had prayed so recently. Jesus was the potter at work—breaking me, moulding me and making me into a vessel He could use.

I was very impressed with the gifts and abilities of some of the senior students. By comparison, I felt inadequate. However, I soon learned that gifts alone, without integrity and maturity, are not sufficient for effective Christian service. A graduating student I admired had to gain some pastoral experience before the mission could accept him. Within a few months, we heard he had run off with the church secretary's wife.

This reinforced to me that college was like a spiritual hothouse. Lessons we learnt still needed proving in the realities of everyday life away from such a loving, supportive community.

Worldview was a tremendous place for spiritual formation. The staff's desire, and the subject of many of their evening prayer times, was to see transformation in students. Faculty members did not want their classes to be solely content based; they longed for the subject matter to come alive and lead to changed lives. For me, these years were a gift and I wanted to make the most of them.

Being willing to walk the 'way of the cross'—to walk humbly and simply and at times endure suffering—was frequently emphasised. From a young age, I had yielded the ultimate direction of my life to Christ. The challenge now was to surrender all areas of life to Jesus on a daily basis, to stop striving and to allow Jesus to live His life through me.

Towards the end of each term, students became a bit nervous as, one by one, we went in for a PI (Personal Interview) with two staff members. They usually began the interview by asking how we thought we were doing, then shared the staff's perspective, followed by words of encouragement and guidance as needed. Their genuine concern and heartfelt prayers were touching, and we usually left feeling encouraged and strengthened to keep 'pressing on'.

At the end of my first year, I returned home for the Christmas holidays keen to put into practice what I had been learning. I was appointed second-in-charge of a two-week Scripture Union beach mission outreach at Port Lincoln. I had absorbed a lot of Bible knowledge in a short concentrated time at college; now it was great to experience the reality of God's grace and sufficiency in new ways and new contexts. We actively shared our faith with holiday-makers on the beach and in the caravan park, and had great times with the children. Singing, games, stories, crafts and social activities packed our days and left us ready for bed at night.

I was particularly attracted to one of the young women on our team. We seemed to click and enjoyed each other's company. Back in Adelaide, we met a number of times at different events. My feelings grew, but as we chatted about the future, I was dismayed to hear that she had no immediate plans for involvement in missions. My inner peace disappeared, and as I restlessly tossed on my bed, I cried out, *Lord, what is going on? I've been longing for someone to love, to share my life with. There is potential for us to develop a relationship, but my whole being seems agitated, out of kilter.*

In the darkness of the night, it suddenly became clear we were heading in different directions. It hurt, but I had to make a choice. Without disclosing the struggle going on in my heart, I said goodbye to her. This was yet another opportunity for me to submit to Jesus, to delight to do His will, whatever the cost.

I prayed very sincerely, *Yes, Lord, wherever, whenever and whatever you want me to do. Guard my affections, Lord, and if you have a special person for me, I trust you to show me.*

Chapter 9
Caught rather than taught

'Graham, how can we pray for you?' a number of people asked. After a restful holiday in South Australia with family and friends, I was about to fly to Tasmania for my second year of studies.

'Well, I have a number of assignments from last year still to complete,' I replied. 'I struggled to keep up. Now I'm really trusting for God's help to catch up and to keep pace this year.'

It felt so much better returning as a second year student. I knew what to expect and enjoyed helping the new students adjust. Meals around the tables were jovial as we recounted stories of our holidays and got to know one another.

Towards the end of the first term, we had a major, college-wide Bible Survey exam. I worked hard revising the material and felt I should do well. I had kept pace with the studies this term, but with my goal of catching up on the previous year's studies, I turned my attention to the uncompleted assignments. I felt this would be more useful than continuing my Bible Survey revision merely to see my name higher up the list of results.

As I concentrated on the backlog of essays, I trusted God for His enabling. There was quite a hubbub one morning-tea break when the results of the Bible Survey exam were posted on the noticeboard. A couple of students congratulated me: 'Hey, Graham, you topped the college! Great work!' I rushed to check the results for myself. For the one and only time during my training, my name was at the top of the list.

Friends had prayed. I had worked hard and God had blessed the effort.

Personal lessons like this were very precious. Gaining knowledge and understanding were integral to my training, but experiencing God in personal ways in my life overwhelmed me and helped increase my trust in Him.

***

When I was home during the holidays, some of the young people told me they were daunted by the idea of training in Tasmania, feeling it would be too cold and was too far away. I tried to understand their thinking, but for me residential missionary training was a wonderful experience. Being totally apart from family and friends for this period enabled me to concentrate on study and growing spiritually.

Brother Lawrence's book, *The Practice of the Presence of God*, was popular reading and I delighted to put into practice what I read—seeking to dwell in the presence of Jesus moment by moment, no matter what other activity I was involved in.

In our daily interaction with staff members, we saw them modelling the life and maturity we aspired to. Most had field experience, and we loved hearing about their exploits in other lands. They spoke of both the joys and pitfalls of missionary life and were not afraid to share with us the hard lessons they had learnt. This greatly added to the effectiveness and value of the training.

One area I continued to struggle in was praying in large groups. I was used to praying with others and had no trouble praying aloud in our small home meetings. Yet in our frequent communal prayer times, I was hesitant. Often, just as I was about to pray, someone else jumped in first. My quiet attempts were overshadowed by louder, more confident prayers.

This inability to pray became an issue for me, and I wondered what others thought of my feeble attempts. The Lord revealed to me that pride still dwelt in me—that if I was preoccupied with my reputation and continually concerned about what others thought, I would miss opportunities to be a blessing to others. Once I confessed this, and stopped worrying, I felt a new release and freedom in praying.

These times of prayer were different from any I had previously experienced. We were encouraged to pray for the matter at hand with short, specific prayers. One person followed another, praying about different aspects of the same topic. Finally, there came an almost tangible rise of faith; we sensed that we had 'prayed through' to a place where we could believe for an answer and confidently leave it with God. Often that sense of confidence was strong enough to thank God for what He would do, even though there was nothing yet visible to show our prayers had been heard.

We experienced many dramatic answers to prayer. We saw much evidence of God at work—provision of finances and other personal needs, healings, friends, neighbours or family members coming to faith in Christ. We also prayed for the current, specific needs of the college. Some requests were for finance, others for personnel. I learned that my going to Worldview was a direct answer to times of prayer for new students to apply. My faith grew enormously.

Learning to wait on God, discern His will and pray confidently in faith, expecting rather than just hoping for answers, was all good preparation for ministry and became an integral part of my life. It would be crucial later when there would not always be an 'on the spot' community to pray with.

In the 1960s, resources for studying missionary principles were still very limited. Yet the studies prepared us well for missionary work in a cross-cultural situation. Even more strategic and beneficial to me was the privilege of absorbing spiritual truths, many of which related to the 'exchanged life' of Galatians 2:20: 'I have been crucified with Christ; it is no longer I who live, but Christ who lives in me; and the life I now live in the flesh, I live by faith in the Son of God, who loved me and gave himself for me' (RSV).

***

Years later in 2000, the WEC Australia annual conference was held at Worldview. After morning tea one day, the principal, Ron Perschky, asked us all to meet outside B Block, the building which had been the men's dormitory.

'Graham, as WEC Director, you have the privilege of being the first person to deliver the initial blows in the demolition of this building. I know it holds many memories for you and others; many transactions with God have taken place right here. Just as you have moved on, it is now time for this building to go in preparation for a new education block on this site.'

As I looked at all the cracks in the walls, I couldn't agree more; it was indeed ready for demolition. But I was not prepared for the emotional impact this moment had on me. Memories came flooding back.

With eight in a dorm, it was inevitable that we played lots of practical jokes on each other. We short-sheeted beds, placed tightly-blown balloons strategically beneath the beds of students out late on a ministry assignment, or turned their beds around to confuse them in the dark.

There was the constant struggle between those who wanted the windows open and those who preferred them closed. There was no central heating in those days. If the windows were shut, we were warm, but endured the odour of eight bodies and smelly shoes. If they were open, the blankets were almost frosty in the morning. I much preferred the fresh air.

Each week before homiletics class, some budding preachers would stand on the end of their beds, practising on anyone who remained in the room. One day I joked, 'Brian, it's my turn to preach today. I'm going to give an appeal, so could you be ready to counsel, please, just in case the principal comes forward!' Such bravado and frivolity quickly disappeared when my turn came to preach. The fact that there would be constructive criticism of my attempt made it quite daunting.

I returned from my reveries and, with great delight, swung the sledgehammer as hard as I could. It made just a tiny indentation on the corner of the building, but a few more blows chipped the corner away. It was a small beginning in the process of developing a new education block. It reminded me of my training all those years ago—the old character traits being chipped away and replaced by the new.

***

The large dormitories have long since been replaced with smaller, more comfortable heated units. Missionary training, too, has changed significantly. The emphasis on 'rules' has diminished. The rules were designed to guide us towards developing a life of integrity and godliness. But now there is a greater emphasis on each student learning to discern and apply godly principles to each situation. The desired outcome is the same, but methods have changed with the times.

***

In October 2012, on another visit to Worldview, I was asked to lead the college in a day of prayer. It was so good to see that this strong emphasis on prayer had continued down through the years.

I began the devotional time by referring to a problem Worldview had in 1966. There was a shortage of male students, so staff and students joined in believing prayer for more men for the following year. They sent an urgent request around Australia and New Zealand, asking people to pray and believe for more men. The following year, there was a record intake of men—twelve of them from all parts of Australia and New Zealand. Only five women applied that year. People had taken up the challenge to pray for more men and God had answered. I said, with tears pricking my eyes, 'I was one of those twelve men, and amazingly, after 45 years, five from our intake are still actively involved in missions.'

Later in the day, we prayed together for a number of specific college needs, including the need for more Australian students to apply for the coming year. At that time, Worldview had a good number of international students, but together we trusted God for more Aussies. A number of students commented that my testimony had built up their faith to believe for this.

The next morning, as we shared morning tea together, a bell rang in the dining room and Denise, the Registrar, announced, 'While we were praying yesterday, I had a phone call from a young Aussie lady enquiring about studying next year. Then this morning I had a phone call from a man here in Launceston asking for application papers. When I asked what had prompted him to phone today, he said he'd had a dream the night before in which he felt God prompting him to apply.'

A cheer went up through the room as we heard of these immediate and specific answers to our prayers.

I left Worldview encouraged that staff and students were still embracing a life of faith and dependence on God. Some things are definitely caught rather than taught. This aspect of college and Christian life, more than any other, has impacted me and held me steady on my journey with Jesus.

Chapter 10
God still speaks today!

Tasmania
1967/1968

'Does God still speak to us today?' My own experience proves that He does. God communicated His will to me at a very significant time in my life. Despite that, was I really prepared to launch out and have the courage to do what He revealed to me?

***

During our course at Worldview, we were all assigned various ministry responsibilities. Some were weekly commitments while others were occasional in response to particular needs or opportunities. I enjoyed teaching a regular Sunday school class with a local Baptist church. The children interacted well and kept coming back each week. They taught me as much as I taught them.

One Sunday I was to preach in the large Memorial Baptist Church with a congregation that had gradually dwindled. The pulpit was high—half-way to heaven, it seemed to me, the congregation was so far away. I was nervous—so nervous that I mixed my words and did not express myself at all well. I felt sorry for the congregation having to endure this bumbling first attempt at preaching. Afterwards people were very gracious, but despite their genuine warmth and encouragement, I went away devastated, reminded of how weak I really was.

The old demons of fear and inadequacy rose to the surface and dominated my thinking. All I could do was cry out to God, *Lord, if I am to accomplish anything for You, it will definitely have to be You working through me.*

***

During the following week, as I mulled over the experience, I reminded God that I had told Him right from the start that I really could not do this. Later that week, as staff and students met together for the weekly afternoon of prayer for local and international needs, we specifically asked God for the release of a plot of land on which to build a radio studio in Ghana. Previous attempts to obtain a plot had been unsuccessful because of the refusal of corrupt officials to release it without a bribe. I felt burdened to pray for a breakthrough in this situation.

The next morning, during my quiet time, I again prayed for the land. As I did, an inner voice whispered, 'This is where I want you to serve.'

I was still feeling discouraged after my attempt at preaching, so I set about bargaining. *Lord Jesus, if this really is Your voice and direction, You need to make it very clear. I can't see myself going to Ghana. My own resources and abilities are not enough. Please help me learn to live in dependence on You.* I was yet to fully embrace the fact that Jesus' commission to 'go' carried with it the promise of His enabling.

I was reading through the book of Isaiah at the time and was up to chapter 6. God's question to Isaiah, 'Who will go for me?', and Isaiah's ready response, 'Here am I, Lord, send me', challenged me greatly. I felt I could not trust my own feelings and asked God for a further sign. *Please do something objective over which I have no control. Have Mr D [as we called the principal] talk about Ghana today and I will believe that this is really Your will.*

Our principal, Stewart Dinnen, had recently visited a number of West African countries. The previous day he had told us about Senegal, saying he would speak about Cote d'Ivoire the following day. When we gathered for our morning fellowship, he said, 'Yesterday I told you I would share about the countries in the order I visited them. This morning, as I prayed and prepared, I felt it would be more beneficial to share about them in the order of the level of church development, so today I am going to talk about Ghana.'

I could not believe my ears. I was awe-struck in the truest sense of the word. The God of the whole universe had just spoken to me personally.

My heart was full of gratitude that my heavenly Father had not left me in my stubborn disbelief but had patiently allowed me to accept His guidance at my own pace. It had come, first, through the inner witness in my heart, then through God's Word, and now through specific circumstances. It had taken time, but I could no longer doubt His clear leading. I bowed my head and humbly accepted God's purpose for my life. I sensed He had a smile on His face.

From this point on, I testified openly that God had called me to serve Him in Ghana. Once I believed this was God's will for me, there would be no turning back.

***

One day, later in the year, the whole college met as usual for our afternoon of prayer. We were told of the need for a replacement Farm Manager at Worldview. The farm helped to keep fees as low as possible and provided us with fresh fruit and vegetables, as well as all the milk and cream we could use. However, the current farmer planned to leave early in the New Year.

As one of the few students with a farming background, I was often asked to work with the Farm Manager. This need touched my heart. I was just about to pray when I hesitated, wondering if I might be the answer to my own prayer. I knew I could fill the position, but I was confused because I was now heading for Ghana.

Then I recognised God's voice speaking to me again. At the end of the prayer afternoon, I quickly went to see Mr D and told him, 'I feel God is asking me to be willing to join the staff for three years before proceeding to Ghana.'

Mr D responded positively. 'That could be a wonderful answer to our prayers, Graham. We would welcome that. But there is a problem. You won't finish your current course until December, and the Farm Manager wants to leave in January. Before you can join the staff, you need to do the WEC Candidate Orientation, which takes six months. It is a requirement for everyone wanting to join WEC, no matter what Bible college you attend. I will have to discuss it with the WEC leaders.'

I did not stress. I was learning to trust Jesus' guidance. A week later

Mr D informed me, 'The leaders have agreed that you can proceed to Candidate Orientation early, even though you have only completed five of the six terms at Worldview. When you return to manage the farm, you can complete the unfinished subjects part-time.'

Going through the formalities of applying for Candidate Orientation, doctors discovered my sugar levels were low, so the diabetic tablets I had been taking for the previous two years were discontinued. My levels returned to normal, and I proceeded to the orientation without any need for medication.

Agreeing to attend orientation now meant I would not have the joy of graduating with my classmates. On the other hand, after so much concentrated study, it felt good to be on the move. I found some time to go down to the paddocks to pray. Lying on the green grass, I drank in the sights and sounds and smells, and entrusted myself to God yet again. His thoughts were higher than my thoughts and His ways higher than my ways.

But the end of term was not far away. I knew where I would be going and when, but how I was to get there was still a mystery.

Chapter 11
Learning to live by faith

Launceston, Tasmania
1968

How was God going to provide for me in these coming weeks, months and years? Since leaving the farm in South Australia, I had not received a salary. People might support me if I was going to Ghana, but I wondered whether people would think that, by staying in Tasmania at the college, I was not a 'real' missionary and therefore not in need of money.

I was a little apprehensive, yet also intrigued to see where my support would come from in the three years ahead.

In 1967 I had arrived at the college with enough savings to pay my fees for the two-year course. I was careful with my money and became annoyed with some of my fellow students who used their resources more freely—in my view, carelessly. When they struggled to pay their fees, they would ask us to pray for them. I really wanted to be a good steward of my finances.

Intertwined with my studies, I learned through experience what it means to live by faith. What did that look like in real life?

During my second year, God challenged me to give to others who had particular needs. How could I pray for God's provision for them when I had the means in my bank account to be part of the answer? Yet if I gave to them, how would I pay my own expenses?

Graciously the Lord encouraged me. He reminded me of Matthew 6:33, which had always been one of my favourite verses. I was intentionally 'seeking first His kingdom'. Would He take care of all my other daily needs? He had promised He would.

I knew I had just enough to cover a dental bill due at the end of the month. However, I felt challenged to give what I could towards the urgent needs of a missionary. That left my bank account almost empty—just the few dollars needed to keep the account open. I had even cashed in my Life Insurance policy. Now, for the first time in my life, I had no alternative but to put my trust fully in God to provide for all my needs.

It had been easier when I knew there was a little reserve I could fall back on. Now I had absolutely no reserves. My journey of living by faith was taking me to yet another level of trust.

Wonderfully, before the end of the month, an amount double what I had given away came in the mail. I was blown away by the kindness and generosity of my loving heavenly Father, who knew my needs even before I did. A week before, He had prompted someone to give and that person had been obedient. What an incredible encouragement!

I also needed funds urgently to travel to WEC's Candidate Orientation in Brisbane and Sydney. I had to book a flight across Bass Strait to Melbourne and a ticket on the *Overland* train to Adelaide. It would be good to see my family briefly before travelling north for the orientation.

With just one week left before I was due to travel, I still did not have the money needed. *This could be very embarrassing for me, God, if You don't provide in time. I will be going to my church for the last time on Sunday. Surely someone will give me a farewell gift.*

By the weekend, however, I was quite sick and could not go to church.

Now, with just days to go, I was worried. People phoned to thank me for my input into the church and assured me of their prayers as I went—but there were no gifts! I knew God was Jehovah-Jireh, my provider, but learning to look to God alone and not to people, was harder than I ever imagined. Here I was again, trying to work out how God might provide instead of trusting Him to do it in His way, in His time.

On Monday afternoon, at the 'eleventh hour', one of the elders of the church came to say goodbye. As he left, he handed me an envelope. Thanking him profusely, I politely saw him out to his car. Once he had driven away, I rushed back inside and tore it open. It contained enough money to cover all my immediate travel needs.

Father God, forgive me for trying to second-guess You. Your Word says You are faithful to all your promises. I am such a slow learner. Thank you for being patient with me, and for showing Your faithfulness in such a tangible way. I want to really experience a confident rest in You, and look forward to the next stage in my journey with You.

This was a crucial lesson in preparing to join WEC International. I needed to experience God's provision for myself. Those joining the mission embraced the principle of living by faith, looking to God alone for provision of their needs. We were not to make our needs known. The WEC policy of trusting in God's faithfulness and His ability to provide, without giving hints or appealing directly to those who might be able to give, was a serious commitment.

My dependence was on God alone. I had always been encouraged by testimonies of how God had wonderfully provided—not just finance but also guidance for the future, enabling in difficult circumstances, empowering in ministry and wisdom in leadership responsibilities. Being totally out of my depth and with my resources at an end was potentially a scary place. Yet seeing God answer prayer in unbelievable ways built my trust and my understanding of His loving character. I could not imagine living any other way.

I was impatient for orientation to start; I wanted to get to know WEC and WECers more intimately. Arthur and Lillian Davidson were the prime movers in setting up WEC Centres in a number of Australian states. Testimonies of God's provision of these properties, without any public appeals, inspired me. I was eager to learn from these 'giants of the faith'.

I had asked a number of new workers, 'What was the most significant factor in your joining WEC?' Their responses were almost the same: 'The people—their maturity, integrity and vibrant faith; and a strong sense of being family.'

I wanted to know more.

Chapter 12
The green light

Brisbane and Sydney
1968/1969

'Why do you need more training, Graham? You've already trained at Worldview.' Kevin, like many of my friends at home, had difficulty understanding this next phase of my journey.

I tried to explain in a way he might relate to. 'Worldview is only a department of WEC—the training arm of the organisation, if you like. It's not the headquarters. Prospective workers come to WEC from various Bible colleges. All who join the mission need to understand the ethos of WEC and how it functions. It's a bit like a game of football—it's not enough to know the field you'll be playing on. It's important to know the game plan, the strategy and the members of your team—those you'll work with.'

'Makes sense when you explain it like that.'

'Yes, it's important we develop a positive relationship with our leaders. That will facilitate good communication when we're out on the field.' I surprised myself with how much I knew about the reason for it all.

Arriving a month late to begin my orientation would not normally have helped my prospects of acceptance into WEC. However, during the application process, I saw clearly that the leaders of WEC in Australia were guided, rather than bound, by structure and policy. They were willing to hear from God and be flexible—solid at the core and fluid at the edges.

In 1968, the WEC Australia Candidate Orientation took six months. The time was normally divided equally between the Brisbane and Sydney WEC Centres. But I was to spend just the first two months in Brisbane. There were just four of us taking the course.

***

The morning of my departure from Adelaide, I woke early and was keen to get started on the long train journey that would take me first to Sydney, then Brisbane. Family and friends came to see me off, and there were a few teary farewells as the train pulled away from the station.

Travelling alone overnight, I appreciated the opportunity for some personal space and time to reflect on the fast-paced events of recent months. After changing trains in Melbourne and travelling all day, I was glad to get off in Sydney for a few hours. Even then my body felt like it was still rocking with the movement of the train.

At the Sydney WEC Centre, Arthur Davidson, the director, met me with a smile and a firm handshake. 'This morning I received news from Ghana,' he shared with me. 'The government's quota for WEC missionaries is full. No new workers can proceed until further notice.'

We rejoiced together at the amazing way the Lord had orchestrated the unfolding plans for my life. *God knew this all along.* He had specifically led me to join the staff in Tasmania for the next three years, knowing I would not be able to proceed to Ghana at this time. Understanding that God's timing is always right, and that nothing catches Him by surprise, was a fundamental lesson for me. Not only did God have a perfect plan for my life, I also needed to trust implicitly in His timing.

The orientation in Brisbane was at a large property in up-market Clayfield—one of those wonderful provisions of God. In the first few weeks, I still found myself questioning: *God, is it still Your will in the long term for me to go to Ghana? There are twelve prospective missionaries on the waiting list held up by the quota. Some have been preparing longer than I have.*

The morning after I prayed specifically about this, a letter arrived from a worker in Ghana. It had taken six weeks to reach me. In the letter was written, 'Don't worry about the quota situation, Graham. If God wants you here, He will make a way!'

My deep sense of God's calling to Ghana was confirmed yet again. Being sure of this would be important later when I was confronted with difficult challenges in Ghana. The knowledge that I was right where God wanted me gave me a deep sense of peace, and a confident assurance that I could trust Him for all that was to come.

I really enjoyed the Candidate Orientation in both Brisbane and Sydney. I met new people, including some who had prayed over many years for Australian WECers. These dear people became friends as well as faithful intercessors. They certainly honoured their promise to pray for us in the years ahead. Later, when we returned to Sydney and spoke at various Prayer Forces, they asked, by name, about our colleagues and Ghanaian church workers.

We also had many opportunities to share in meetings, both formal and informal. I loved speaking about the challenge of mission, and the way that God had been leading me.

***

'Ruth, we're not spending as much time as I anticipated on the practical aspects of living and working cross-culturally,' I said to a fellow candidate. 'It seems like we spend an inordinate amount of time helping the staff with the practical running of the Centre. What do you think?'

'Well,' Ruth replied, 'I guess that as we work side by side with staff members, it gives them the chance to observe both our character and how we cope under pressure. It also gives them some idea of how we might cope in a cross-cultural situation.'

I was not fully convinced, but one thing I was sure of: I loved the strong sense of fellowship that was evident in the WEC community. The spiritual maturity of the staff members and their cross-cultural experience gave credibility to their advice and input.

In Sydney, one event was particularly memorable. A staff member came to chat with me. 'Graham, all of the staff are attending some special meetings this afternoon. We'd like you to remain behind to welcome the International Director. He'll be dropped off here. Please look after him and show him to his room.'

Len Moules was British and had been a major in the army. I imagined him as a conservative, rather stern gentleman, probably wearing a suit and tie. I was still shy and not sure how I would get on making conversation, but I had lots of questions I wanted to ask him.

I needn't have worried. Len jumped out of the car and with a broad, sincere smile said, 'You must be Graham. How are ya goin', mate?' He had obviously done his homework. His casual attire, with open-neck shirt, and his friendly disposition drove away any concerns I had. He was down-to-earth, fun and easy to relate to. We spent a very enjoyable afternoon together, and I revelled in his stories of trekking in the Himalayas. I could hardly believe I was spending time with the International Director. It reaffirmed that lovely sense of oneness I felt with the WEC 'family'.

***

The whole orientation experience was a positive one for me. I felt some of it needed revamping, but I was now absolutely sure that this was the mission God had called me to. I had a great appreciation of its principles and practices. WEC emphasises Holiness, Sacrifice, Faith and Fellowship—the 'Four Pillars' which, together with prayer, undergird all that WEC does. More recently they have been expressed as:

- We fervently desire to see Christ formed in us so that we live holy lives.
- In dependence on the Holy Spirit we determine to obey our Lord whatever the cost.
- We trust God completely to meet every need and challenge we face in His service.
- We are committed to oneness, fellowship and the care of our whole mission family.

January 19, 1969 was Acceptance Day—a serious occasion for a serious commitment. I was nervous as we were to be interviewed by the Acceptance Committee in the presence of the whole Sydney staff. Yet I was quietly confident of being accepted. While we were waiting to be called in one by one, I joked with the other candidates that I would be accepted because the leaders recognised my potential! In reality, I knew that Stewart Dinnen, the principal of Worldview, who was a member of the committee, did not want to milk the cows himself. That fact alone would probably count in my favour!

Finally it was my turn. I testified to a conviction in both my mind and spirit that it was right for me to be joining WEC. I shared God's leading about the way ahead. I answered some probing questions about my health and the visa situation in Ghana. For a short time, they discussed my situation among themselves and then called me back in. Their smiles told the story. After some words of encouragement, they each gave me the 'right hand of fellowship'. Excitedly, they gathered around, laid hands on me and prayed for God's blessing on me.

Suddenly, the light on the starting grid was green. I couldn't wait to see what lay ahead of me on this wonderful journey in missions.

Chapter 13
Finding a life partner

Launceston, Tasmania
1969–1971

It felt a bit weird to be returning to Worldview as a member of staff. Some of the students teased me, giving a mock bow as if showing deep respect. It was great to be back, enjoying once again the warm and friendly atmosphere. I realised I had genuinely missed people.

In my role as Farm Manager, I would live and work closely with the students. Along with other staff members, I would also share responsibility for some other areas of college life and ministry. We sought to be transparent and authentic in our relationships with one another and with students, modelling for them a Christlike attitude in words and actions.

One of the students was a young woman who was also from a farming background.

'Welcome back, Graham. No doubt you've heard that the government quota for WEC missionaries in Ghana is full.' Marj's interest was more than casual—but in Ghana, it appeared, not in me. She continued, 'I'm keen to hear what you think about that. What are the prospects for potential new workers?'

Marj then disclosed a fact I had not known and which surprised me. 'I feel God is calling me to Ghana, but at present there doesn't appear to be an opening for me.'

She told me later (too late!) that she hoped I would not get any ideas; she fully intended to serve God as a single missionary. But having admired her sunny character and outgoing personality for some time, my mind began to wonder whether the fact that we both felt called to serve in the same country was more than a coincidence.

***

Marjorie Winchcomb grew up in Johanna in the Colac district of Victoria. She was the eldest of six children, though her brother Malcolm was later killed in a shocking tractor accident. Marj's parents, Steve and Bobby, owned a mixed farm, but primarily ran dairy cows.

Her sister, Johanna, related some stories to me much later. 'Marj, being the eldest, took responsibility for looking after and bathing her younger siblings every evening while Mum was helping Dad milk the cows. I remember Marj had an enquiring mind and a simple faith from a young age.'

Marj herself wrote, 'I entered my turbulent teens, searching for purpose and meaning in life. I asked questions like, "Why are we here? Is God real?" One day, while studying a cross section of a blade of grass, I came to recognise God as the Creator, although I didn't yet know Him personally.

'While still a teenager, and before I became a Christian, I heard an audible voice calling me to missionary service. As preparation for that, I did nursing training in Melbourne. During that time, I told God I was tired of running my life my way and wanted to submit everything to Him and His plan for my life. I accepted Jesus as my Lord and Saviour, and from then on my desire was to follow and serve the Lord—wherever, whenever.'

After time as a staff nurse back in Colac, Marj moved to Sydney to do her midwifery training. A fellow nurse, Pam Whitley, became a good friend and invited Marj to attend services at Narwee Baptist Church. Marj appreciated very much the ministry and friendship of Pastor Rowland Croucher and his wife, Jan, who welcomed her into the life of the church and took time to mentor her. It was here Marj really grew in her faith.

One year at Narwee's annual missionary convention, Stewart Dinnen was the main speaker. Marj responded to an appeal and offered herself for missionary service. Everything moved quickly after that. She applied to Worldview and was accepted for training.

I first met Marj on board a flight from Melbourne to Launceston. She was arriving for her first term of study and I for my second year. A number of us were returning students and had seats on the plane close together. We were all very excited after the holiday break and were quite noisy. When we realised that Marj, who was sitting near us, was a new student, we felt remorseful. In our exuberance, we had not set the ideal example. She soon joined in the fun, however, and it was good for her to arrive at college actually knowing some other students.

***

Life as Farm Manager settled into a steady rhythm. I felt deeply contented; yet there was a longing within for a life partner, and I began to pray about this more earnestly. Recognising that we had similar backgrounds and interests, I continued to wonder about Marj. There were strict guidelines regarding relationships at college, so it was not easy to get to know the female students in depth.

I had returned as a staff member during Marj's second year, and after lots of praying I had a growing assurance that it was God's plan for Marj and me to serve Him together. We had not even been on a date or discussed the possibility of a relationship together.

One day I decided to confide in my friend Len Harvey, who was on staff with me. When I mentioned the name Marj, he became worried. I had no idea that he was also praying about marrying Marj—another Marj, a recent graduate, also a nurse, and also from Victoria! A smile of relief creased his face when he realised we were talking about two different women, but he didn't share his secret until some time later.

I did not approach Marj until later in the year. I wanted her to be free to concentrate on her studies without the distraction of a man in her life. There was no need for me to be worried about someone else getting in before me. I was fully convinced that it was God's will for us to be together, and that she would still be available when the time was right to approach her. I conscientiously abided by the rules, but when October came, I arranged for an official time to meet and talk together.

I had been very careful not to show my interest in her or my growing feelings, so this came as a real shock to Marj. Her immediate response was 'No!' She explained, 'I had a crush on someone last year. It affected me emotionally and distracted me from my studies. So I have very deliberately determined to focus on training and service.'

There was not the least bit of encouragement for me in this encounter. I could hardly tell her I knew it was God's will. I just had to leave it with God, and continue to pray that in some way God would make it clear to her too.

The college year finished. Marj stayed on during the first weeks of the holidays to care for the large vegetable garden. Passing by on my way down to the farm one day, I asked her, 'How are you feeling? Has there been any change?'

Her reply left me reeling. 'Well, as far as my feelings go, you may as well be a bar of soap!'

Phew! That was one way to get the message across loud and clear.

Stunned and totally disheartened, I wandered down to the farm to change the irrigation pipes. My thoughts kept flying to the bar of soap I showered with each day, and how little attachment, if any, I had to it. Was that all Marj thought of me? I had nowhere to turn but to my heavenly Father. *Lord, I am sure of Your leading and I trust You to make a way where there seems to be no way.*

A week later, Marj sought me out and asked if she could share her thoughts with me. I was pleased she had taken the initiative; however, I still felt hurt and not ready for any more of the same treatment she had meted out to me the previous week.

She saw the expression on my face and said, 'I'm sorry, Graham, I overstated things. I really am open to the possibility of a relationship. But I'm waiting for God to show me clearly what His will is in this. Until I know that, I can't commit myself to anything or anyone. I need to listen for His voice rather than be guided by my feelings.'

A few days later, she received an unexpected cheque in the mail. *Lord, I don't really need this. I haven't got any bills. What do you want me to do with it?* Immediately she had a strong assurance that it was for her to travel with me. I had shared that I was going home on holidays and that this would be a good opportunity to meet my parents if she felt right about it.

Everything changed so quickly. Once Marj realised God was

confirming our relationship, she was totally committed, and we made plans to spend the holiday time visiting both homes and meeting each other's parents. We phoned our families and warned them to expect an extra visitor.

I was leaping inside. Even though I was sure about Marj, we needed this opportunity to get to know each other informally and give time for Marj's feelings to grow.

Our parents were welcoming and accepting of us both. As they listened to our story, they were curious to know what our plans were for the future. It had all happened so quickly, we were not sure of the details ourselves.

We did know that I would return to my responsibilities at Worldview. Marj, already clear about joining WEC, had applied and been accepted for the February orientation course. Our paths were leading us together, like two tributaries becoming a stream. For the next few months when we would be apart, we vowed to write to and phone each other regularly. We were both excited to find out what God had planned for us in the long term.

But although we were eager to see each other again, we were not sure when that might be.

Chapter 14
Opposites attract—or attack

Marj was a warm, joyful, friendly person and a delight to be with. I was attracted to her positive personality and down-to-earth approach to life. Though different in many respects, we had similar backgrounds and interests. She was mature, dependable and well-liked by all the students and staff. I appreciated her strong commitment to Jesus and her vibrant love for Him.

In 1974, Marj wrote an article in WEC Australia's *Worldwide* magazine[1] outlining some of the lessons she had learned while at Worldview.

A lesson in Faith:
'Consider your bank account closed and rely on Me to supply your needs.' God is speaking to my heart. I believe nothing is impossible with Him. Am I willing to prove Him now? I step out in faith. The first expense is $50. My heart leaps. Then I remember it is God's responsibility, not mine. I remind Him and wait. The next day a cheque for $50 turns up in the mail. How thrilled I am to know that the money was in the post before the bill arrived. Since then all my resources have been used up, and God has provided all my needs. Sometimes it is beforehand, at other times after waiting several weeks, to teach me perseverance in believing.

A lesson in Prayer:
I learnt to pray early in my Christian life, but on entering Worldview, I encounter prayer in a new dimension. Staff and students take God at His word, and praise Him for the answers—before they come; even in the realm of spiritual warfare.

My first experience is during a prayer meeting. A student

prays, 'Lord, there are people whose lives are bound by Satan. In Jesus' Name, I claim deliverance for them on the basis of the victory You gained on the cross.' Many others join in. I am staggered. Never before have I heard such authoritative praying. For weeks I have been oppressed by Satan. I feel like I am under a heavy cloud. Now, as I silently claim victory for it, the cloud lifts, allowing the light of God's presence to flow in. Prayer in Jesus' Name is powerful.

A lesson about Self:
My constant desire is that Christ, not I, will be seen in my life. Yet the more I try to be like Christ, the more 'self' is evident. I become completely exasperated and defeated. God's answer is, 'You have been trying to live the Christian life with your own resources; they will always fail. I have placed all my resources within you, in Christ. Allow Him to live His life through you.' Following this initial step, I learn to walk each day appropriating this fact in faith.

***

In some organisations, the husband has a position and his wife assumes a more home-based, supportive role. One thing we both love about WEC is that both husband and wife carry ministry responsibility. In leadership positions, they work as team. Thus, in orientation, both are accepted on their individual qualities, and on the basis of being a right fit with WEC.

Marj needed to follow the same Candidate Orientation process I had been through. She began in early 1970. We really missed each other when apart. We consoled ourselves with letters and phone conversations.

Part way through her orientation she was invited to be bridesmaid at a friend's wedding back near her home in Victoria. I was invited to attend, so we had an unexpected opportunity to be together again. One night I surprised her and popped the question. The next morning, when I asked Marj's father for his approval, he told me, 'I've just given approval to Frank to get engaged to Marj's younger sister, Bebs. They're going to announce it in Saturday's paper.'

I asked him not to let on that we knew, and we put our own announcement in the *Colac Herald* the same day. When Frank and Bebs got the paper on Saturday morning, they quickly looked up the engagement column. Reading down the announcements alphabetically they came across 'Winchcomb–Bee' and exclaimed, 'Oh no, they've got the names wrong!' As they read on, they realised it was our engagement, followed by their own, 'Winchcomb–Buchanan'. We enjoyed surprising everybody. Marj's sister Johanna announced her engagement the following week!

Marj joined the Worldview staff in August of 1970, and it was wonderful that we could be more relaxed in our courting. We made plans to marry on January 2, 1971. We had a simple yet beautiful ceremony in the Colac Baptist Church in country Victoria, the area where Marj grew up. My friend Len married his Marj on the same day in Tasmania. Unfortunately, this meant we could not be best man at each other's wedding.

There was a critical shortage of accommodation for married couples at Worldview, so we shared a house with staff members Evan and Jenny Davies. Towards the middle of our first year of marriage, a request came from Ghana. The field leader wrote, 'Because of a particular need here, we are allocating the next available quota place to you. We would like you to come and fill this need as soon as possible.'

We had jumped the quota queue. Our mix of gifts and training, it seemed, fitted what this position required. According to the quota system, a couple only counted as one quota place, the same as a single—a real bonus for us and for WEC Ghana.

Marj was already pregnant, so we made plans to go the following year. This gave time for our baby to be born and for Worldview to find replacements for us. It also allowed us more time to adjust to married life before we confronted the challenges of living in another culture.

There are different theories about compatibility in marriage. Some say opposites attract while others say they attack! We found both to be true, and those early months definitely had both their joys and their challenges. It was only much later, when we did the Myers Briggs personality type tests, that we realised just how different we were. According to the results, Marj was an ENFP, and I came out as an ISTJ—opposites on every count!

With a growing comprehension of how we each 'ticked', we came to understand our differences and learned over time how we could complement one another. We both believed we were meant for each other and desired to serve God together, so even when challenging times came and our personality differences were magnified, we were solidly committed to each other. We both came from families that didn't show much affection, so we also needed to learn appropriate ways of expressing our love for each other.

The year on staff as newlyweds was a valuable time of growing and maturing, both individually and as a couple. We developed a 'big picture' view of WEC—the countries the mission worked in as well as specific ministries and personnel. We felt as though we knew many of those for whom we prayed. This worldwide perspective later helped as we prayed for other WECers from our 'small corner' in Ghana.

The day finally came when the college released us to prepare for the move to Ghana. Those three years on the staff were a wonderful foundation for the path ahead; we really felt part of a worldwide 'family' and knew the staff and students would continue to pray for us in the years ahead. They would always be in our thoughts and prayers too.

GHANA: THE KPANDAI YEARS

(1972 – 1983)

Marj & Julie

Graham, Paul, Julie, Merilyn, Marj

Pris Irvine, Barb Price and children (SIL), Marj, Julie and Graham

Elizabeth and Afua and twins

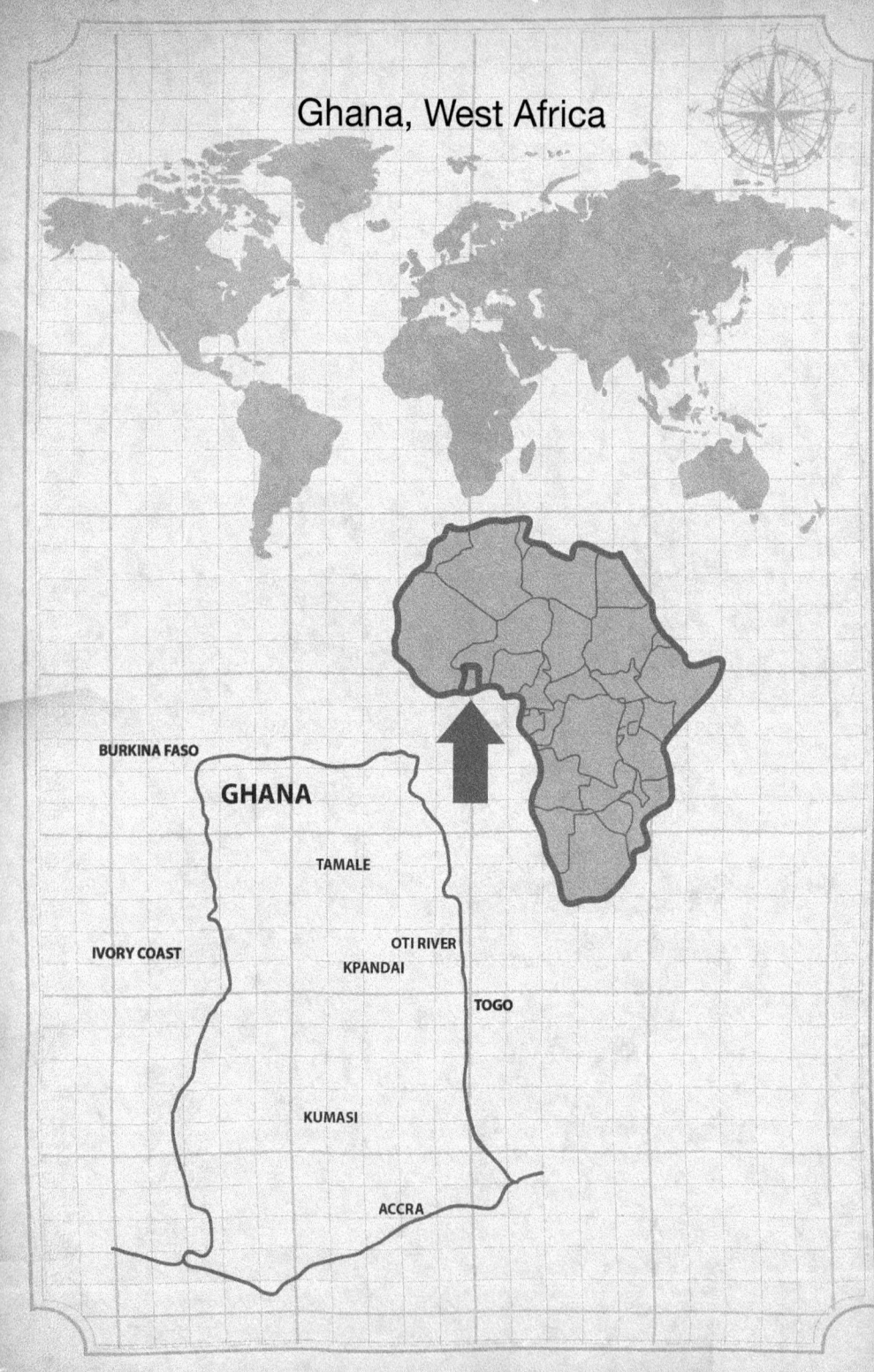

Chapter 15
Good price, just for you!

Today is the day! Marj and I pack excitedly in the tiny cabin of the Polish cargo boat that has carried us south-east around the West African coast. We are also trying to prepare our minds: a new country, a different culture and many unknowns.

'Will there be anyone to meet us? What will we do if there isn't?' asks Marj.

'I have no idea, but let's wait and see,' I reply. 'I did notify them of our travel arrangements. I can only hope the message got through.'

Mid-morning we pick Julie up from the floor of the cabin, where she has been happily playing, and clamber up on deck for our first sight of Ghana.

***

My journey with Jesus is about to enter a new phase, and instead of simply reporting what happened, I invite you to come with me. Rather than observe like a fly on the wall, hang on tenaciously to my back and experience with me the pain and disappointments; jump with joy at answered prayer; be amazed as you see God at work in my everyday life. Gather some of the sweetness for your own enrichment.

***

It is July 19, 1972 as the ship enters the port of Tema. The years of preparation, the struggles in learning to walk with Jesus and follow His leading, have all been part of my journey to this point. It has been six long weeks since we took those significant steps up the gangplank in Sydney. We are here at last—in the country where God has called us to minister.

Relief. I recognise a familiar face among the small group on the dock. Heather Tyler, who is also from South Australia, is there with a colleague to meet us. We have longed to pack away our sea-legs and put our feet on solid ground again, though strangely it seems to rise up to meet us every few minutes. We struggle to keep our balance.

'Heather, you've no idea how glad we are to see you.'

'Likewise,' she replies. 'It has been such a long journey for you, and we're so glad you've arrived safely. Oh, isn't Julie gorgeous? Let me hold her while you bring your belongings. Then I'll help you negotiate customs.'

Waiting for our luggage to be unloaded and cleared through customs is tiring. 'The journey was not relaxing and the whole cruise ship experience not what I hoped it would be,' I tell Heather. 'But that's behind us, and the experience in Abidjan reminds me of God's promise that with Him all things are possible. Though ill health plagued me on the journey, spiritually I feel alive. I have confidence that the Lord will prepare the way for us and show us how we can partner with Him in bringing hope to people in Ghana.'

Julie is hot and grizzly. It is great to have help. Thankfully, customs officials only select a couple of our 44-gallon drums and a few boxes, at random, and inspect them. We open them and check through the contents with the officials. Itemising all the contents had seemed tedious when packing; now we are glad we did. The random search proves our lists are accurate and the customs officials stamp our documents for clearance. Wandering through numerous sheds we eventually find the right office to pay the appropriate charges.

What a relief to have all these formalities completed. Heather helps me hire a truck to transport our luggage to nearby Accra for storage. Once we arrive up north, we will arrange for a local truck to collect our goods on a back-load arrangement after it has delivered yams to the Accra markets.

This driver's initial asking price is exorbitant. In a persuasive voice, he says, 'But I'm giving a good price, just for you, sir.'

Unused to bartering, I feel it is hardly worth wasting our time with a starting price like that. Whispers of experience from Heather encourage me to persevere. In the end, we agree together on a reasonable price.

With a great sense of relief, we climb into Heather's vehicle and follow the truck to make sure all our luggage is safely stored before driving north. Then we wind our way for four hours up to Kumasi, Ghana's second largest city. Many new and interesting sights, smells and sounds assault our senses along the way. We experience 'fast food' Ghana-style from a roadside stall. Buying yam chips with chilli sauce served on banana leaves becomes a favourite part of all future travel.

Kumasi is where the WEC field leaders for Ghana, Greg and Eileen Francis, live. After communicating by letter with them so often, we enjoy getting to know them personally. Greg's Australian sense of humour makes us feel right at home. We are taken around the completed radio studio, for which I had prayed so earnestly in my Worldview days. So many people pray and only hear about the answer to their prayers. It is such an encouragement to see the actual building and hear programs being recorded for broadcasting across West Africa on Radio ELWA.

We spend a couple of busy days attending to visas, driver's licences and other official documents. We are told to 'Come back tomorrow' a number of times. I am learning not to display my impatience or frustration. Instead, we use these waiting times as opportunities to shop for food. The lack of variety in processed food is quickly apparent. We stock up on the basics—tinned milk, tinned margarine, flour, sugar and yeast powder. Other essentials are tinned corned beef and 'tinapper' (small tins of mackerel, which need to be opened with a tin opener).

A visit to the doctor confirms I have pleurisy. Now that I have medication, I am hopeful I can quickly throw off the persistent cough and chest pain. I need good health to cope with all that lies ahead.

***

On our fourth day in the country, in the darkness just before sunrise we leave for the long drive north to Kpandai, where we will live and work. Greg, driving an older model diesel engine Mercedes Benz, turns out of the driveway and onto the bumpy suburban street. Marj tries to keep Julie comfortable and occupied in the back seat.

'You think this is bumpy. Wait until we cross the rice swamp later on,' laughs Greg.

By sun up, we are already well on the way.

'We want to make sure we catch the first ferry across the top end of the Volta Lake at Yeji. This way, we should miss the worst of the tropical sun.'

We make it onto the ferry. Greg tells us there are often long delays here. Thankfully, today the ferry operator gives priority to the few private cars and then loads up with as many trucks as he can fit on. Some of those trucks have been waiting all night.

The one-hour ferry trip is an opportunity to get out of the car and stretch our legs. It feels good to relieve our aches and pains before facing the worst stretch of road. We notice the different dress of those in the north of the country and hear languages that we do not yet recognise. We try some more local 'fast food' and watch, intrigued, as a few enterprising market sellers pressure the captive audience to buy their wares.

It is an interesting but uneventful ferry ride. Julie certainly benefits from this temporary freedom from the confines of the car, and she proves to be a magnet for the local people. They coo over her and pinch her cheeks, laughing as she starts to cry. On the next stretch of road we leave behind the rainforest area, and the savannah plains stretch out before us as far as the eye can see. The wet season is under way. The roads have already begun to wash out, and the road crossing the rice swamp is partly flooded.

Greg shares his strategy. 'I think it is best to go reasonably fast so that the car hits the top of each bump in the road without time to reach the bottom in between.' While on some roads there is truth in that, by mid-afternoon we arrive with both sore heads and sore bottoms—no seat belts to restrain us here. Marj has worked hard to keep Julie safe and moderately happy.

***

We have been assigned to work at the Oti River Leprosarium, founded and operated by WEC personnel in Ghana's Northern Region. As we arrive, people stream from every direction to extend a very warm welcome. They have heard about the Bees and are eager to meet us. Visitors are rare so far north in Ghana. They are genuinely excited that a foreign family has come to live among them.

Julie draws the most attention. White babies are an uncommon sight out here. Like the people on the ferry, the locals here ooh and aah over her and pinch her chubby cheeks. We shake hands with the staff but will have to wait until tomorrow to meet the patients. We enjoy customary cold drinks and head for a quick shower. Refreshed, we begin to unpack and settle in.

We are desperately tired from the journey, so after a healthy dinner we stumble into bed under the prerequisite mosquito net. Before falling asleep, though, we hold hands and pray, giving thanks to the Father for His protection on the journey, and His presence with us in this time of newness.

The next day, a local Christian helps arrange for our luggage to come north. We are grateful to have his experience in bargaining.

'That's a ridiculous asking price. We can only offer half that,' he tells the driver. 'Although there are many pieces of luggage, they don't weigh very much. Besides, your truck will be taking a load of yams to market and would otherwise be coming back empty. This load will be a bonus for you.'

'But the price of diesel has gone up. You will be ripping me off.'

The bartering continues until, finally, they agree on a price. We thank our new friend. 'The price is higher than we hoped for, but not outrageous. The fact you know the driver well, and know he can be trusted, is important. After transporting our luggage so far, we don't want to lose it now.'

Each new experience helps us understand local cultural practices, but I feel it will take time and skill to learn to barter like the locals.

***

The Oti River Leprosarium has 200 inpatients and more than 1000 outpatients within a 40-kilometre radius. 'I'm glad the numbers are not quite as high as they used to be,' I say to Marj. 'As it is, I feel like I've been thrown in the deep end.'

She nods in agreement. 'It's a big enough challenge with this number let alone more, but God will help us through.'

'It's good to have the benefit of Pris Irvine's experience, too,' I add, referring to the head nurse 'She's obviously loved and respected by all. We're going to need lots of advice in negotiating with the government regarding the future of this place.'

The current administrators, Norman and Betty Singleton, are due to go on home leave in four months' time. They have been patiently hanging on for us to arrive. They need a break. Our first priorities will be language and culture learning, but we also need to get a handle on the running of the leprosarium before they leave.

Chapter 16
That first handshake

Oti River, Kpandai, Ghana
1972/73

There is no time to waste. Language lessons start immediately. Pastor Che, who once had leprosy, is our language teacher. Other recently arrived missionaries have learnt the Twi language, which is spoken by a large percentage of the population. However, since I need to be ready to assume the administration role in a mere four months, we are instead advised to learn Hausa, an easier language. We will need to be extremely disciplined since in Ghana, a former British colony, it is possible to a certain extent to get by with English.

***

Living in this well-established community gives us a gentle introduction to life in Ghana. Moving straight into a mud house with a thatched roof in one of the surrounding villages would have been much more confronting. Here we have solid block houses, galvanised iron roofs and a plentiful supply of fresh water.

Just below the scarp on which our houses are located is the Volta Lake—the largest man-made lake in the world. Water from the lake is pumped up into storage tanks and run through a water treatment plant. All we have to do is turn on the tap. However, to be doubly sure, we run it through our own household filter. A generator operates for a few hours each evening, but otherwise we use kerosene to run our fridge and lamps.

We are very comfortable, but nagging away at me is the prospect of shaking hands with the leprosy patients. I am unsure how to relate to them. The effects of the disease are obvious—disfigured faces and hands with only the stumps of fingers remaining. I am fully aware that since biblical times those with leprosy have been ostracised and required to keep their distance from healthy people. Many believe it is quite contagious, so the stigma continues, and with so many living in this isolated community, it appears not much has changed.

***

After our first language lesson, we have a quick tour of the extensive property and facilities. We begin our tour at the 12-bed hospital, where the more serious cases are treated. We learn that often it is the consequences of infections and burns, resulting from damaged nerves in hands, feet and face, that result in the disfigurement, not the disease itself. We move on to visit the separate housing quarters of male and female patients, followed by the staff houses in a separate area of the property.

Finally I pluck up courage and talk to Pris Irvine, the head nurse, about my concerns.

'How should I relate to these people? I know Jesus touched leprosy sufferers when He healed them, but what if I get leprosy?'

Pris reassures me. 'Leprosy is not as contagious as most people think. Within two weeks of commencing treatment, the infectious period passes. There is no need to be alarmed, but it is always wise to wash your hands whenever you return to your house.'

Jacob, the headman among the patients, turns up. Pris gives him a hearty handshake and introduces me. Encouraged by her advice, I use the Hausa greeting I have just learned and warmly shake his hand.

***

Taking over as administrator is daunting. I am only 27, and with just my high school education and farming background I feel unprepared for the task. I ask the Father for divine wisdom and understanding to do the work well. It is a great opportunity to grow in dependency on Christ, and to daily draw on all the resources Christ promised I have in Him.

My responsibility is to oversee all the staff and the practical running of the leprosarium. This includes final responsibility for the accounts, which are audited by government auditors. Ensuring supplies are on hand to feed everyone grows more difficult as the economic situation deteriorates. Pris is a tremendous support and gives lots of wise advice on how things function and what is culturally acceptable.

The Ghanaian staff members have been well trained and most are reliable. There are a few questionable practices: one carpenter each year, just before Christmas, receives a 'telegram' from distant family members informing him of the sudden sickness or death of a relative. Funerals are culturally very significant, so he is required to have time off to travel home. To us this sounds like a very convenient way to force the issue of Christmas holidays, but we can't do anything but let him go.

***

As a patients health improves and their leprosy is controlled, they are able to move out to live in the surrounding villages. On agreed days each month, the outpatients gather at various centres. In each place dozens of folk surround the Land Rover as it arrives and greet the clinic team with enthusiasm. Someone shares a simple gospel message while patients wait for their medicines. Minor ailments and sores are attended to first. Following this, patients are given the next month's supply of their leprosy medication. Thankfully a cure has been developed, but it still requires years of treatment.

The medical ministry is a practical demonstration of God's love and compassion for those looked down on by the rest of society. The regular teaching of the Word of God results in quite a number of people putting their faith in Jesus. Over time, this ministry has become the foundation of an extensive church planting ministry throughout the region, with churches and preaching points established in many of these locations.

***

WEC has sought to run the leprosarium with a minimum of missionary personnel. Training of local people to handle many of the practical jobs is necessary to keep it running effectively. One of the rules is that healthy staff should not have sexual relations with patients currently undergoing treatment. The policy is made clear to all.

On one occasion, months before we arrived, this rule was violated and the staff member was dismissed. He complained to his trade union, which then tried to insist that, since there had been no problem with his work, he should be reinstated.

It became obvious that it would be difficult for the mission to continue to maintain moral standards. There were also fewer overseas medical personnel offering for service. The mission made a strategic decision: this work, together with the property, would be handed over to the Government Leprosy Service and WEC staff relocated elsewhere.

The practical details for this are now part of my responsibility, in collaboration with government officials. During the year, we finalise typed inventories of all equipment and agree on the timing and processes for the handover. The decision is strategic and necessary; however, Marj and I both know we will miss this ministry. We have made many good friends among the patients as well as the staff. I chuckle to myself, remembering my unfounded fears in facing that first handshake.

Everything is in place for a June 30 handover. Pris has booked her passage home to Northern Ireland on a ship departing two weeks later.

***

We have packed up and are surrounded by our boxes and crates, all ready to leave. But nobody comes to take over! We can't go until we know what is happening. A four-hour drive to the northern capital, Tamale, reveals that Ghana Leprosy Service personnel are on standby to come but are waiting for the authority from Ministry of Health officials in Accra.

The only thing we can do is make arrangements for our staff to continue while we head south as planned. Now we will also need to include a visit to the Ministry of Health HQ to discuss what will happen and when.

We drive via Kumasi so that Pris can say her goodbyes there. The next day we continue the long, bumpy journey to Accra. After taking Pris to the port and her waiting vessel, we head off to enjoy our first annual holiday. What an eventful year it has been!

I feel a bit daunted by the prospect of dealing with top government officials. I need not be, as they receive me warmly. After outlining the situation at hand, they inform me, 'We have not included the leprosarium in the budget for this year, so you should continue for another year. We will make plans for next year.'

By now my heart is pounding. 'I'm sorry, but that is not possible. I've just put our head nurse on a ship to return home to Northern Ireland. My wife and I have been transferred to another town. We have no budget for the leprosarium for the year ahead either.'

No doubt they sense my frustration. The arrangement between us has been made in good faith. They seek to reassure me, and ask me to wait outside the office while they discuss the situation among themselves.

I can assure you, my prayers during this waiting time are very fervent! My mind conjures up all kinds of possibilities, but I choose to focus on the verse, 'You will keep him in perfect peace whose mind is stayed on God.' After 40 minutes, to my great relief, they call me in and inform me, 'Workers will come 10 days after your return from holidays. There will be an agreed joint handover period and then you are free to move on, as previously arranged.'

In hindsight, I recognise this as a last ditch attempt to try to force the mission, which is so highly regarded and respected, to continue to run the leprosarium. On the new agreed date, 10 workers arrive to replace the three of us who are leaving.

***

The decision to hand over the leprosarium to the government turns out to be a very strategic one on the part of the mission. The leprosarium has been a significant part of the overall ministry of the field. Much finance and many personnel have been invested in developing it. Without doubt, the handover was not an easy decision for some. But it has freed up future mission outreach for greater relevance in the changing times. It is not always easy to recognise when it is time to move on, and we are grateful to those who sensed God's direction and timing in this.

On the other hand, though the decision that we should learn Hausa has been helpful in the short term, it proves detrimental to our long-term ministry. Hausa is a Nigerian trade language. It was spoken widely in Ghana in years gone by, but we discover that although it is still spoken in market places, it is not spoken fluently by many of the people groups responsive to the gospel. By the time we realise this, we are already too busy in ministry to start learning another language. We try to make sure that others coming out after us are advised from a long-term perspective, rather than on the basis of short-term needs and emergencies.

In the early days of ministry in Ghana, direct evangelism was slow and often discouraging. Later, outreach was greatly enhanced by the work of the Oti River Leprosarium and WEC's Kpandai General and Midwifery Clinic (which later became the Kpandai Health Centre.) News spread and sick people came from the surrounding countries for treatment. This loving and caring ministry to those looked down on by society has had a wonderful and positive impact on the lives of hundreds of people.

***

In the first four years after our arrival on the field, eleven WEC workers leave. I don't think it is because of us! Nor is it because they know us well enough to have confidence to leave the work to us. It is simply that a number of the pioneers have served their time—four of them for 37 years each!

While we think the current situation is very challenging, it is nothing compared to the challenges they have overcome, by God's grace, in seeing the first WEC-related churches planted across the country. What a firm foundation they have laid, and what an example to us they have been. Now the baton has been handed on to us.

Chapter 17
Tractors, tyres and tithes

Northern Region, Ghana
1973–1976

'Graham, I'm really looking forward to living on the edge of town. We can be much more involved with the local community than we could in the isolated settlement of the leprosarium.' Marj is always eager for new experiences.

Our new home in Kpandai township will be just 10 kilometres away, but the change for us will be significant. 'It will be a very different context to minister in,' I reply. 'The chief and elders of the town are all Muslim.'

'And I'll miss all the facilities and resources we've enjoyed here at Oti,' sighs Marj. 'Yes, I'm sure being part of a larger community will have its challenges.'

We have no illusions about those challenges. The most difficult is the multiplicity of languages. In addition, the majority of residents are Muslim or follow traditional animistic beliefs, so there is strong resistance to the gospel.

Not too much has changed since our first workers came here. On November 25, 1942, Don Theobold and Eric Christie arrived in Kpandai. They were the first of many WECers to minister in this region. They quickly discovered that a major problem was the number of languages spoken.

Don wrote, 'Hiring labourers to help clear the first three-acre allocation, we discovered that only one out of nine speaks Gonja.' He continued, 'There were three Konkombas, one Bassari, two Moshie, one Kusasi, one Dagomba and one Fra Fra … Judging from what one reads and hears of other works, this must be one of the worst parts of Africa … as there is no common denominator.'[1]

Despite the language problem, and the difficulties in getting buildings erected in those war years, they made steady progress in the work, and laid a good foundation for those of us who followed. Now we do have a church to work with and local Christians to train and encourage.

***

I am greatly relieved to be free of the responsibility for the leprosarium. We have been assigned to develop and expand the agricultural ministry into the surrounding areas. Marj is beginning to show her excitement about the move.

We visit the local Gonja chief, a Muslim, and negotiate with him for the additional land we will need to extend the work. We are able to obtain an area between the existing mission property and a small plot on which our tractor shed stands. Our busy General and Maternity Clinic already functions just over the road, helping more than 200 patients a day. It treats general sicknesses, assists local women with antenatal classes and under-five care, and its midwives deliver babies both night and day. A small Bible school at the back of our property trains 10 students.

It feels good to be working in a team with a holistic vision—demonstrating the compassion of Jesus in practical ways, as He did, and maintaining the priority of pointing people to Jesus, who is 'the Way, the Truth and the Life'. Keeping a balance between the practical and the spiritual emphasis is not always easy, but very important.

***

Local farmers have already benefitted from a tractor hire service offered as a sideline of the leprosarium in Oti, but the demand is growing. One tractor is relocated with us, and later we purchase a second with proceeds from the work. We train tractor drivers and a mechanic is sent away for training. We take on apprentices at regular intervals so that more locals can learn to drive and gain proficiency in other practical skills. The primary aim is to help local subsistence farmers enjoy a better standard of living for their families, and in the process demonstrate God's love for them.

Traditionally, cultivation of the land is done by hand using a small hoe. This back-breaking work is physically demanding. It is limited by the individual capacity of the farmer and his family. For a reasonable fee, we aim to plough one acre for as many farmers as possible. We are willing to plough up to four acres for any one individual as time and pressure of demand permits.

A small team of local people carries out most of the work. I help with the direction and oversight, the financial records and some of the repairs. At the same time we continue with Bible teaching, training and other evangelistic outreach. Life is full, but encouraging.

Our assistance with the ploughing and harrowing means farmers can plant a larger area. They can use their energies in the weeding and harvesting of their crops—usually yams, corn and rice. Once the months of cultivation are past, the tractors and trailers can be hired out to help with transporting the harvest. Some are given the help on credit to be repaid at harvest time. We also arrange cooperative selling of the harvest on their behalf when the local market is over-supplied.

We assist Christian and non-Christian farmers alike. This is greatly appreciated even by those who have employment as salaries are insufficient to feed families. Everyone has to farm to survive. I start a farm myself to identify with the people and to demonstrate alternative types of crops. Our fervent desire is that the help given will demonstrate God's love and concern for them. We long that some will put their faith in God and begin attending church, though this is not a requirement for them to get assistance.

***

We teach and encourage Christians in the use of their tithes and offerings. We hope a better income will mean they have more to give to the church for supporting their pastor better.

At one of the regular Church Area Conferences, two elders share how they have been helped by the project.

'At the end of the last year's harvest, I separated out my tithe ready to give to the church,' says Jacob. 'But then I thought, if I keep this to plant next year, I will have even more to give to God. Well, I had a very good yield. With the help of my sons, I harvested and stacked the rice ready for drying and winnowing. Later, as my sons were beating the rice to separate it from the stalks, they were attacked by a swarm of wild bees. In an effort to drive off the bees, they lit a handful of rice straw to wave at them, but some of the hot ashes fell on the stack and the whole harvest was lost in an instant. There was nothing they could do. So, my friends and fellow leaders, do not be tempted to withhold your tithe!'

Salifu agrees and shares his own story. 'I was blessed last year with a good batch of both chickens and guinea fowl. I tithed the guinea fowl, but, tempted by the hope of breeding more chickens, I decided not to tithe them until their numbers increased. Later that year, sickness struck. I lost nearly all my chickens, but the guinea fowl flourished!'

Although there are many frustrations, we feel privileged to have input into the lives of many who are seeking to grow in their faith and witness. We are building on the sacrifice and loving service of many who have worked and persevered here before us.

***

Maintaining the tractors and equipment in good working order is a constant challenge. Without heavy bulldozers, farmers have to clear the bush and prepare the land by hand. Not all of the stumps are removed properly. Despite careful prior inspection, there are often hidden stumps whose foliage has been cut off just below ground level. Sometimes the drivers only discover this when it is too late—after a tyre has been punctured.

New tyres are in short supply, so we have become adept at sewing in rubber sleeves to repair the gaping holes. There is a limit, though, to how many times you can repair one tyre. At a critical point in the ploughing season one year, we finally have to discard one of the large tyres. I travel the length of the country visiting tyre stores, urgently seeking a replacement.

The salesmen don't offer me any hope, and one is very frank. 'That's an oversize tyre—no new ones have been imported for 18 months.'

An old man also trying to purchase spares echoes, 'No, haven't seen any for years.'

Disappointed, I slowly begin the long drive home. *God, how can we help all the small farmers who land on our doorstep every morning at 5 am? They have families to feed, and it won't be long before it will be too late to plant crops this year.*

One glance at my empty pick-up or at my face and the workers know the outcome of my search. 'I don't have an answer; we will have to keep on praying,' I exhort them.

A short time later, a local agriculturalist suggests we check out an agricultural project over 100 kilometres away. 'I know they had some tractors about that size,' he says. It is worth a try. We are desperate. There, away in the bush, God has his answer—an almost unused tyre that has stood idle for several years because the tractor could not be repaired. It is the exact size tyre we need, and apart from some minor surface cracks in the tyre wall, it looks good.

For our small team of local workers who have not experienced such a dramatic answer to prayer, this is a real encouragement. They begin to pray for other needs more earnestly.

***

In addition to our own agricultural ministry, we are part of a team consisting of both expatriate and national workers with the task of facilitating evangelism and church planting in the area surrounding Kpandai. Thanks to the pioneering work of earlier missionaries, a number of fledgling churches and preaching points have already been planted. A Bible school has been established and local pastors are being trained and sent into the work.

As well as caring for Julie, Marj is also vitally involved in the ministry. She teaches in the Bible school and uses her nursing experience to help in the clinic when needed. Many local women come seeking her help, not only for medical reasons, but also for her wisdom related to family and practical issues.

The availability of leprosy treatment is one of the reasons many people moved here from more distant areas and neighbouring countries. They settle in well and happily call Kpandai home. At one Kpandai church service, we ask people to indicate which language group they are from; 23 different people groups are represented. To ensure that everyone present is able to understand the message, the church has a preacher plus two different interpreters ('interrupters') up front. In addition, there are a few other people 'turning the talk' for a small number who do not understand any of the three languages used up front. We understand the difficulties the early workers faced with this literal Babel of languages.

Kpandai church was pastored initially by Pastor Sanna who was followed by Pastor Njabi. To help them with training their members, we run Sunday afternoon Bible teaching sessions for church leaders. Mostly Marj does the teaching in Hausa. The following Sunday, after the leaders have given further thought to the material for that week, they teach adult groups in their own languages. That way, despite the diversity of languages, most receive teaching in their own mother tongue.

We often think about heaven, where there will be some from every nation, tribe, people and language gathered around the throne (Revelation 7:9). We long for many of the community we interact with on a daily basis to be there alongside us, worshipping the Lamb. That is the reason we are here.

***

Many adults have not had a formal education. It is a challenge for them to remember any teaching apart from stories. One worker was disheartened and frustrated by the numbers in a church who had still not broken fully with the traditional worship of spirits. Another young missionary, on hearing this, declared, 'Oh, all they need is more teaching!' He was offered the opportunity to take over and teach them. Soon afterwards, this young man also became discouraged, and when someone else offered to give him a break, he jumped at the chance!

The Konkomba people, like many in the area, come from a strongly animistic background. In the face of family pressure, many find it too difficult to stand firm in their new faith. The pressure on them increases whenever a child gets sick as the extended family pushes them to return to traditional ways of healing rather than trust in Jesus. Despite this, we are overjoyed to see many stand firm and give a vibrant testimony to God's faithfulness and protection.

Syncretism is rife; some folk try to follow both ways at the same time. They may hide a protective charm in the roof of their house while giving the appearance of trusting in Christ. Having been taught the taboos and fear of the spirits all their lives, following Christ is not just a mental assent to new teaching. It involves breaking free from the fear and control of the spirits that have bound them. But once they realise the need for a complete break with tradition in order to follow Jesus, they destroy their charms. We celebrate each of these victories. They are hard won.

***

We have heard that when the very first missionaries prepared to go to West Africa, they packed their belongings in a coffin for transportation to the field. They were 'Ready for Anything' on a continent described as the White Man's Grave. Many gave their lives in service.

The numerous attacks of malaria we have suffered have already made us aware of the dangers we face, even though we are so much better off than they were. We hope not just to survive, but to thrive.

Chapter 18
Wonderful people, terrible roads

'Welcome back to Ghana! How was your trip?' The border officials engage us in conversation while they process our visas. It is good to be back.

Returning from neighbouring countries that were once French colonies, we notice a sharp contrast in attitudes. The people there seem less jovial and much more serious in their approach to life. By comparison, Ghanaians are warm and amicable. When we bargain to buy something here, we often end up developing a friendly relationship with the seller. It usually results in both parties coming away happy, despite mock protests as to how ridiculous our first offer was. As the work develops and our network of friends and contacts expands, we have a growing love and appreciation for the people of Ghana.

We are amazed at how generous Ghanaians are, despite the little they possess. Often, when staying in a village for a Bible teaching weekend or conference, we are the recipients of a specially prepared meal. The meat in our bowl is often as much as the whole family would normally eat between them.

***

During our early years in Northern Ghana, we are surprised that people constantly talk about the heat. We have come from Australia where there are similar temperatures. However, as time goes by, we realise that the frequent cool changes we are used to do not arrive. The constant heat and humidity drains us and eventually wears us down. Locals have adjusted to this—so much so that after Christmas, when the Harmattan wind blows off the cool night-time Sahara desert, locals don coats and stand around shivering when the morning temperature drops only a few degrees lower than normal.

We now understand the slower pace of life here, especially when we observe how profoundly people are at the mercy of the weather and the frequent delays in obtaining things. A common response to a request for help is 'You go come!' In Ghanaian-speak that means, 'Come back tomorrow.'

***

Market days are held every six days. There is no need to look at the calendar; from early morning, streams of people wend their way past our house loaded with produce to sell. The men stride out in front while the women follow, carrying the heavy load of produce or firewood. Often they also have a child on their back. There is much friendly bantering and calling of greetings as farmers and gardeners converge on the market. Dogs, goats and chickens add to the noise and smells.

We enjoy these forays into market life when we can buy food for the next few days. Unfortunately, we quickly discover that markets are not good places for our small children. Out of curiosity, people who have not seen them before pinch their white skin and tug on their long fair hair. Consequently, until they are older and more able to handle the attention, our children are apprehensive about going.

In the dry season, as food stocks run down, people bring in *dowa-dowa* to sell. This is made by boiling and pounding large seeds from the pods of the *dowa-dowa* tree into a thick, black paste which is then rolled into small balls to sell. Like durian in Asia, its smell is overpowering for those not familiar with it. Add this to the pungent smells of dried fish, over-ripe tomatoes and fruit, and entrails hanging in the sun, covered with flies, and market shopping is definitely not so enjoyable. At these times, we laughingly dispute which of us should go quickly for the essentials.

***

In 1974, the Ghanaian government decides to change from driving on the left, as the colonial British did, to driving on the right, as all the neighbouring countries do. 'Ghana drives right' is a government plan to educate and prepare people for the changeover. Special editions of stamps are produced. Extra first aid stations are established. People discuss ways to minimise the number of accidents that will no doubt occur.

One well-meaning person writes into the *Daily Graphic* newspaper suggesting that 'things should be done gradually rather than rushing into it'. He proposes that 'cars should start driving on the right in the first week and the trucks the next week'. Thankfully, the changeover begins all on the same day and with much less drama than anticipated.

Driving in Ghana is challenging. Village folk see roads as their pathways to walk on and do not have an awareness of traffic, so we are always on the alert for the unexpected.

One Sunday morning, while driving through the centre of Wulensi, the road is crowded with people. A celebration is underway. Hearing my vehicle approaching, the crowd separates to both sides of the road. However, as I pass through slowly, a small child suddenly realises she has been separated from her parents. Without looking, she makes a sudden dash for the other side of the road. Marj screams as I jam hard on the brakes. The brakes lock but the momentum carries the car forward on the gravel road. Just as the car skids to a standstill, there is a loud thump. The child slides forward on the gravel. We fear the worst.

We jump out of the car and rush to see how the child is. A crowd gathers. Our hearts are pounding from the shock. Then fear grips us. Here, the driver is always at fault, especially a foreigner!

Carefully examining the child, we are relieved to see she is all right. She has bad bruising and skin grazes, but nothing more serious.

A tall old man steps forward. 'There is nothing you could have done to avoid this. We all saw what happened, Mr Bee.' Being known in the area helps me.

'You are not to blame; it was my child's fault,' her father unexpectedly agrees. 'With the crowd lining both sides of the road, there was only just enough room for you to pass through. Had you swerved into the crowd, the outcome would have been far worse.'

'Thank you, I appreciate your honesty. I will take you back to our clinic for your daughter to be treated.'

We forgo our trip and return to our home with the girl and her parents. For the next two days, the nurses at our clinic care for her and she makes good progress. Before leaving us, she receives a new set of clothes from our humanitarian aid supply. Everyone is happy.

We are grateful to the Father for watching over us all. It could so easily have turned out otherwise—for the girl and for us.

***

The roads are often in bad condition, especially during and after the wet season. On one of the main roads, we are following a big bus when suddenly it almost disappears from sight. It has followed the road down into a 'pit hole' so deep that all we can see is the back window. Amazingly, it emerges on the other side to continue the journey.

On another long trip, aching from the constant jarring and bouncing through potholes, night falls before I reach a bridge. There is just 18 kilometres to go. Through the darkness I notice that recent torrential rain has flooded the river and water is flowing over the bridge.

Blow! What will I do now? Thankfully the torch I carry for emergencies like this is working. Wading onto the bridge, I weigh up the situation. The current is not strong and the water is just over my ankles. There are no rails to show where the edge of the bridge is, but I can easily see the wooden planks. I can probably drive slowly across.

With no one else to talk it over with, I have a conversation with myself. My brain tells me, 'Don't do it, Graham. There's no one here to help guide you or assist if there's a problem. Marj and the children want you home in one piece.' My body disagrees. After driving all day, I am exhausted and aching all over. The alternative is a two-hour detour and more pain. 'Just do it!' my body snaps at me. Body wins over brain.

It is not very wise, especially in the dark, but I take the risk. Thankfully, I am alive to tell the story.

***

There is another reason we have to be constantly alert as we drive, particularly when passing through towns and villages: the goats and sheep sleep in the middle of the road. It doesn't matter whether it is day or night. Generally, the goats will hear the car coming and run off. The sheep, on the other hand, despite the danger, remain sitting calmly until you get very close and blow the horn loudly.

An intriguing local legend explains why …

Chapter 19
A bowl of rainbow soup

'One day a sheep and a goat go on a journey together …'

We are sitting on stools, listening intently to old Ninkab. He, like all traditional elders, has a wealth of stories to explain why things are the way they are. We find local cultural differences and traditions intriguing, and often amusing. On this hot, dusty afternoon, he is regaling us with a story about sheep and goats, and the reason they react differently to oncoming vehicles.

'When the sheep and the goat reach their destination, the goat gets down and runs off without paying. The sheep, on the other hand, does the right thing and pays his fare. Unfortunately, the driver is distracted. Forgetting to give the sheep his change, he drives off.

'Now, when the goat sees see a car coming, he presumes it is the driver coming to get his fare, so he runs away. But the sheep keeps waiting patiently for the driver to give him his change.'

***

In seeking to understand the culture by observing and asking questions, we recognise that the fact this is different from our own culture does not mean it is wrong. We need to understand our own culturally biased worldview and behaviours and be willing to learn new customs just as we learn a new language. Sometimes it helps to laugh at ourselves—to see the funny side of our efforts to communicate in the local language and culture.

Many in the local community struggle to survive and provide for their families. Unemployment is high, and for those fortunate enough to have a job, wages are low. Whatever their occupation, most people still need to grow some of their own food. Women and girls walk long distances twice a day to water sources, and return carrying heavy pans or buckets full of water on their heads. Children carry their own stools to school, often walking long distances to get there. Despite the fact that teachers already receive a salary, children are expected to work on their teacher's farm one or two days a month.

Although they have so little, we generally find people more content with their lot than Australians, who sometimes go on strike for more pay. We in the West have no idea how the Two-Thirds World lives and how little it takes to be happy.

Weddings and funerals are always big occasions. Relatives and friends travel from near and far to attend. Often it takes a year for family members to save up enough to host a wedding. We are shocked a little by the wailing that follows a death. Traditionally, if a person you know dies, you are expected to wail and demonstrate your sorrow so that you will not be accused of causing their death through witchcraft.

Sickness and death are very much a part of everyday life. In our area, approximately one-third of babies die before the age of five. Our clinic at Kpandai establishes an under-five program and starts a vaccination campaign. We are all thrilled when this results in a greatly reduced mortality rate.

While we Westerners have been taught and accept that sickness is a result of germs, many Ghanaians have been taught that it comes because they have offended the spirits. Education can help them understand and improve hygiene practices and diet in order to prevent some common sicknesses. Simply straining their drinking water can filter out minuscule eggs or larvae and prevent problems with Guinea worm developing months later.

***

Teaching health and hygiene is something we all try to do. Changing traditional ways, though, is a slow process, particularly as people have such limited resources.

Marj encourages the village women, 'Use what you have to improve the diet of your children. Nearly everyone raises some chickens. Eggs have high protein content. They are beneficial for the health and growth of your children.'

'But my children don't like them,' objects one woman.

Marj tries to understand why some children do not want to eat the eggs. She asks the woman, 'How do you prepare them?'

'Well, after the hen sits on the eggs for three weeks, the chickens hatch. Then we collect the leftover eggs and boil them.'

Marj rolls her eyes in disbelief.

***

We also discover different attitudes to the discipline of children. At times we send Julie to her room for disciplinary reasons. Knowing she can attract the attention of people living nearby, she cries at the top of her lungs.

The locals think we are terrible for disciplining a child so young. They voice their concerns, but then look on in amazement when Julie obeys us.

One particular day, Julie wanders down to the tractor shed, where I am helping the workers repair one of the tractors. After a while she starts to grizzle and cry. 'Please go home to Mummy, Julie. You're very tired.' The look of amazement on the Africans' faces is priceless as they watch her turn and obediently follow the narrow track home. This provokes a lot of discussion, and together we are able to reflect on how local children are allowed to virtually run riot for the first few years of their lives.

Very young children are carried on their mother's back or that of a young relative. They have little stimulation or encouragement to learn and are generally given what they need to keep them quiet and happy. When they are weaned, it is a different story. Often, out of anger and frustration, parents deal harshly with them. It is punishment rather than training.

Some of those who work with us observe the ways Marj and I handle Julie, and learn new ways to discipline their children more effectively. Mind you, we have our own challenges as ours grow older, and we certainly don't claim to be perfect parents.

***

Our greatest concern is for the spiritual condition of the local people. Every part of their lives is affected by the fear of evil spirits. They have to live in such a way that spirits will not interfere with their desire for a happy life.

Traditionally, if they get seriously sick, it generally results in a visit to the fetish priest. He will often prescribe the sacrifice of a chicken or other animal in order to appease the spirits that have been offended.

Africans know there is a creator God, but generally they view him as being far off. An elder explains to me one day why they relate to spirits more than to the Creator God. 'One day a woman was pounding the evening meal, and as she lifted the pestle high, she hit God under the chin. God was offended and moved far away. Now, he can only be reached through the spirits.'

Another language group has a slightly different variation. For them, 'The woman preparing the evening meal ran out of ingredients for the soup. Worried she would not have enough to fill the bowls, she cut off the end of the rainbow to use instead. God became angry and moved far away, leaving us at the mercy of the spirits.'

My mind boggles at the thought of a bowl of rainbow soup, but this is real for these people, and here you accept rather than question what you are told.

The need to offer sacrifices is a real burden. These additional costs mean there is little chance of people being able to improve their lot in life. Even after some decide to follow Jesus' way, it is a real battle for them to do away with the fetishes they have trusted for protection. To overcome their lifelong fear and to trust God for healing when their children get sick is a real test of faith, particularly when there is pressure from family to go to the fetish priest.

Yet what a privilege it is for us to bring them the good news of salvation and freedom in Jesus! It is a thrill to see the transformation of their lives and their growth into spiritual maturity when they are able to break free. Finding Jesus as the answer to their needs and seeing demonstrations of His power at work encourages them enormously.

The church in Lungni, a small village about five kilometres north of Kpandai, and their elders become known and respected in the district. A number of women, previously unable to conceive, soon become pregnant when prayed for. As women unable to produce children are regarded as wasting their husband's money, this is an enormous relief to them. Many people experience wonderful answers to prayer and, seeing God's power, decide to break with spirit worship and follow Jesus.

***

Life is simple and the hardships many, but the warmth of the people is what makes this country such a special place to live. I now recognise that seeds of appreciation for peoples of different cultures were planted back in my childhood and are now bearing fruit. Friends back home are concerned about the hardships we face, but for us it is a real privilege to be able to come alongside Ghanaians and help where we can.

Just around the next corner of our journey, Marj has some news that grabs our attention.

Chapter 20
Double trouble and twice the pleasure

1974

'I am convinced this is not a normal pregnancy,' Marj says with a tremor in her voice.

'You're joking, I hope!'

'No! Come and feel here, and over here.'

***

Marj is a trained midwife. When she realises her pregnancy is growing faster and larger than a co-worker's, who is a month ahead of her, she realises there must be a reason. In this remote area medical facilities are limited—definitely no place for a complicated pregnancy.

Kpandai is 100 kilometres from the hospital in Yendi. The rough, washboard gravel road to get there is enough to bring any pregnant woman into labour, so we hope no emergency forces us to make that trip. With the benefit of Marj's training and our encounters with many of the local 'bugs', we can recognise symptoms of sickness and often treat ourselves. We try to avoid hospitals if we can. Even the locals prefer treatment at our clinic to being referred to a hospital. Hospitals may have more equipment, but often their supplies of medicines are inadequate. Pharmaceutical items are frequently sold through the back door to local vendors, who then inflate the prices for a handsome profit.

I press and prod her growing bulge. 'I'm not sure I can feel what you feel, Marj, and I'm not sure I want to either. Let's ask the nurses.'

Our mission clinic is just across the dusty road from our house. Later that day, when clinic consultations are over, Marj goes over to talk to one of the midwives. Janet listens and at first is also not sure.

Marj guides the placement of the stethoscope and hears Janet exclaim, 'Yes, there's a second heartbeat. Congratulations! You're going to have twins.'

Although our friend and colleague is excited, we are at first concerned. 'Marj, how will we cope without all the mod cons enjoyed by mothers back home?'

Marj hesitates for a moment as she comes to grips with this latest news. 'I know we only planned to have two children, and we're not prepared mentally just now for two at the one time. But we'll adapt. With the heat, clothes won't be too much of a problem—they won't need to wear much more than a nappy.'

'My concern is that there's no electricity, no washing machine and no disposable nappies here,' I reply. 'We'll have to find a reliable girl we can pay to help with all the washing.'

After the initial shock, we get used to the prospect of having twins and begin to look forward to their birth. Word goes out through the grapevine and our supply of nappies is bolstered by gifts from missionaries down south who no longer need theirs. We write home to family to share the news and include them as best we can. It is during times like these that we feel the distance and separation most keenly—especially the separation from our parents.

'Marj, you'll need to go to Kumasi for the birth,' our nurses recommend. 'We can't take responsibility here with our limited facilities. Down there you'll have access to a well-equipped hospital and all their facilities.'

I agree wholeheartedly with them. 'I can't imagine what we would do if something went wrong. We'll need to leave early to be sure.'

We make an exploratory trip to Kumasi. To our delight, we are able to arrange with a hospital and qualified gynaecologist just 30 minutes from the WEC guesthouse. This means we will be able to stay in the guesthouse with people we know while we wait for the birth.

Thankfully, all goes well during the pregnancy and soon it is time to make the journey and prepare for the babies' arrival. Heading south over the same bumpy roads we braved on our first trip north, I try to drive as carefully as possible. Having just missed Julie's birth, I am determined to be present with Marj for this delivery. Other family members are a world away and I want to be there for her. The weather is extremely hot and humid and the last weeks have been very uncomfortable for Marj, but check-ups reveal everything is proceeding normally.

The due date passes and the gynaecologist decides to induce Marj. It is good to be right beside her in this unfamiliar environment. She copes well through the pain, and her relief is evident as the second twin is born. We are overjoyed and amazed to see our two new treasures— but as the doctor looks up, she notices I have gone extremely pale.

'You'd better go and sit outside in the fresh air for a while,' she orders. 'We'll clean up here and look after your healthy son and daughter.'

***

After the birth, the Ghanaian nurses immediately place wristbands on the twins with names for those born on a Tuesday—Kwabena and Abena. Later, we choose the names Paul and Merilyn. We know their grandparents will be over the moon and I write to let them know the news; it will still be some time before a letter reaches them. We are reminded of the cost it is to all of us to be so far apart.

The news eventually reaches Australia. Don Jamieson, a close friend and deacon at Narwee Baptist, Marj's home church, waits until everyone is seated for the Sunday morning service. Struggling to contain his joy, he runs up the aisle calling out, 'The Bees have swarmed in Ghana!'

***

Our arrival back in Kpandai causes a buzz around our town too. Like bees in search of honey, neighbours, friends and even people we have never met come to visit.

'White people have twins! We have never heard of such a thing, let alone seen this before,' chorus our local friends. 'Can we see them?'

We have a constant stream of townspeople and their visitors coming to see Paul and Merilyn to validate this unbelievable report. One by one, they each give us a small silver coin—their traditional practice on the birth of twins. Big sister Julie is very proud and happily shows off 'her' babies.

It is a lovely point of connection with the local people. Seeing our twins helps them understand to some degree that although we may seem different in many respects, in reality we are just like them. We hope that our message and our methods of sharing will now be more readily received.

***

With her experience as a nurse and mother, Marj is sought out by many women who want her advice. A local mother of twins is struggling to feed her babies, and despite the clinic providing supplementary help, the twins continue to be sickly. Marj takes one of them and cares for him for a week until he improves and regains some strength, but then we discover the other one has gone downhill. The babies are swapped over. After a few weeks, they are both well enough for the mother to confidently look after them on her own again. So many babies die before they reach five years, and the chances of twins surviving without additional help are even lower.

***

Their outgoing personalities and smiling faces ensure our twins are greatly loved and very popular. We are grateful that tinned milk powder is still available for purchase locally. They need supplementary feeding. Amazingly, almost as soon as they graduate to solids, it disappears from the market. The economic situation within the country is critical.

We are thankful for God's goodness and faithfulness in providing for our children's needs. Knowing, as Psalm 139 tells us, that He formed them and planned their days gives us strength and courage as we parent our three little ones.

As every parent knows, though, there are many challenges in parenting, and a big shock catches us by surprise. In fact it very nearly overwhelms us.

Chapter 21
Paul's brush with death

1976

'Graham! Come quickly!' Marj screams from the bathroom.

'What's wrong——?' I start to ask. But realising the urgency in her tone, I jump up and start running.

We reach the children's bedroom together. Paul, writhing in his cot, is already starting to turn blue. He is frothing at the mouth and every muscle in his body is convulsing.

What is happening in his little body?

***

Paul is now 18 months old. Earlier in the day he seemed off colour. He didn't eat much and then suddenly vomited up his breakfast. Despite our encouragement to rest, he wandered off to the Bible school to play with his friends. He seemed okay, but throughout the day he was just not his normal bubbly self.

In the evening, he didn't want to eat much again. He was quite happy to be bathed and put to bed. Obviously he was not well! Yet there were no strong symptoms to make us suspect anything serious.

While Marj is bathing the other children, I am working in the office at the other end of the house. When she hears some strange noises coming from the children's bedroom, she thinks it is our cat impolitely belching. When it continues, she realises something is wrong and calls out to me.

We find Paul in a terrible state. As I pick him up, we realise he has an extremely high temperature. Could he have cerebral malaria? We have heard of other children being affected by it, often with tragic results. We have been hoping we would not experience it ourselves.

We rush Paul across the road towards the clinic, shouting towards the nurses' house as we pass for someone to come. Panicking, I struggle to get the words out, but they get the message—it's an emergency! After a day treating hundreds of patients in the debilitating tropical heat, they are tired. Yet they come, as they always do, not knowing what the problem is, or how many babies there will be to deliver later this evening.

I keep running while carrying Paul. At the same time, I cry out to God for His help. The terrifying shock has our hearts racing.

Fearful but hopeful, we fling open the clinic doors.

The first injection fails to stop Paul's little body convulsing. Our hearts are thumping. We lay hands on him and pray. *Lord, our son is in your hands. We are desperate. We cry out to you for healing; please touch him and stop the convulsions. We know you are well able to heal, and we trust that you will!*

As we finish praying, we suddenly realise the heat inside the clinic building is stifling. We push open the shutters to let any breeze in. We sponge our tiny son and frantically fan him, trying desperately to get his temperature down. One and a half hours later, after another injection and some more anxious moments, Paul stops convulsing.

Thank you, Lord.

Shaken, we take him back home to care for him. We take it in turns to sponge him and fan him by hand day and night. The nurses re-emphasise, 'It is very important that we keep his temperature down to try and avoid further convulsions.' We do all that we can, but as the saying goes, 'It is easier said than done'. We have no electricity, so no oscillating fan or air conditioner. We have just a kerosene fridge struggling to keep us supplied with cool water. It has seen better days and both the heat and the humidity limit its effectiveness—at this time of year, it is not even able to make ice.

Paul is literally in intensive care; at least one of us is with him at all times. For the next four days and nights, he lies virtually motionless. We don't know if he will live. Even if he does, we wonder if he will have brain damage as a result of what he has been through. It is a terrifying thought.

We struggle to cope, particularly during the long nights. We have to wake each other up to take turns fanning him. 'Marj, I'm sorry to disturb you. Can you have a go? My arm is aching and I'm struggling to stay awake.' Physically and emotionally, it is taking its toll on us. We are both exhausted and emotionally drained.

During these days of caring, we pray constantly and often read in the Psalms to encourage ourselves in the Lord. We examine our hearts and try to hear anything God might be saying to us. At one o'clock in the morning on the fifth day, we are wrung out and desperate. Together we talk to the Lord, laying bare our hearts.

Lord, we know Paul is a gift You have given to us. We have examined our hearts, and we know that, despite the loss and grief we will feel, if it is Your will to take him, we will continue to serve you. As we have been reading Scripture, we have been struck a number of times by the words 'I am the God who heals you'. So despite the bleak outlook, we ask you for a sign by 6 pm today that you are going to heal Paul. We need some encouragement.

At 5 pm, Marion, one of the nurses, comes to the house to see how he is doing. (She later tells us she feared he might already have died.) After praying with us and for Paul again, she says, 'I'm going now, Paul—bye bye.' For the first time since his convulsions, Paul opens his eyes slightly and struggles to lift his hand to wave.

This turns out to be not just a sign but the beginning of a dramatic recovery. Later that evening, he is much better. So much so that we are able to leave him in the care of the nurses for the night. Exhausted, we both sleep soundly.

Although Paul had been walking quite well before this incident, the trauma he has suffered sets him back. He reverts to crawling. For the next three months, he won't let his mother out of his sight. Amazingly, apart from this temporary effect, he develops normally.

This has, without doubt, been our fiercest testing time so far. 'I'm not sure I'd like to go through an experience like that again,' I confide to Marj.

Looking back, though, we are both thankful that we were able to examine our hearts and tell God in the midst of the crisis, 'No matter what the outcome is, we will continue to serve you.' We feel we have had a little insight into how Abraham must have felt in offering up

Isaac. The difference is that Abraham voluntarily obeyed, whereas our situation was thrust upon us. There was no choice. Nevertheless, God was equally with us.

We are relieved and thankful. What a joy it will be, taking three healthy children home to see their grandparents for the first time. The alternative would have been so sad.

***

Despite many attacks of ordinary malaria ourselves, we try to stay out on the field for four and a half years. This will mean Julie can have her first year of school in Australia. At this time the usual missionary term is four years. We are so glad it's not seven years, as it was for earlier missionaries.

However, three months before we are due to leave, Marj and I both contract hepatitis. Even the thought of a drink of Milo is more than our stomachs can cope with. Nauseated and weak, we need the nurses to help care for our children.

We share the situation with our leaders, and they readily agree that going home to a cooler climate will aid our recovery. We make plans for the long trip home and only mention the prospect of home leave to the children just a few weeks before departure. From then on, almost every day the questions come: 'Are we going today? Why can't we go now? What will it be like?'

We too have questions running through our minds. Everything will be so different. How will we all cope? Where will we live?

Chapter 22
No House. No Money.

Adelaide, South Australia
1977

'Will I have to wear shoes?'

Marj nods.

Julie frowns and screws up her face. 'All the time?'

'All the time we're out in public, Julie.'

'Where will I go to school?' Julie continues. 'And where will we live?'

'Will all our grandparents come to meet us?' asks Paul. 'I can't wait. I want to see what they really look like. I've only seen their photos.'

Merilyn chimes in, 'But what about my friends, Dad? When can I see them again?'

We are about to board a plane—the first of a number of planes—to begin our journey home. Home for Marj and home for me but not yet home for the kids. The questions keep coming. I don't have all the answers. Our concerns are more immediate: how are we going to keep them occupied for 26 hours on the flight from Amsterdam to Sydney?

***

We appreciate the flexibility and understanding of our leaders. They give us three months of sick leave and then the normal year of home leave. This will accommodate Julie's schooling needs and give us the opportunity to be fully restored before commencing a normal program of ministry.

Our monthly support has only just been enough to live on in Ghana. Our shopping trips there have been quite a contrast to those of our well-supported Swiss colleagues. We just buy the essentials. Now, back home in South Australia, we wonder how we will survive without Ghana's cheap local produce. Costs have risen dramatically here. Inflation is soaring. Interest rates have reached 10%.

Although it does not affect me directly, my farmer friends tell me, 'Farm milk prices have fallen. In order to remain competitive and viable, we have to purchase larger farms. But now interest rates are killing us and we're struggling.' I have to admit that God has saved me from all those concerns. And to think I struggled so much to give up my dream! Had I insisted on my own plans, today I would have been heavily in debt, with increasing overhead costs but diminishing returns. Instead, I am enjoying a life of purpose and a joy I could not have imagined back then.

***

One of Julie's questions keeps coming back to us. 'Where will we live, Dad?'

I honestly don't know. Renting a house seems beyond what we can afford. Our WEC South Australia representatives make some enquiries and tell us the good news.

'We've arranged for you to rent a house close to the HQ. It belongs to Christian friends. They've offered it for half the current commercial rate.'

'That sounds great to us! We'll be glad to move in after our stay with Marj's parents in Victoria.'

But it falls through. Not long before we are to move in, the phone rings. 'There's been a complication with the property. It's no longer available to you.'

It is too late to make other arrangements so, for a number of weeks all five of us end up sleeping in one bedroom of my parent's home in the Adelaide suburb of Christies Beach.

One day Marj looks at me. 'We can't do this for very long, Graham,' she says. 'It's not fair on your parents.'

'Yes, I know. They're very gracious, but I've already noticed Dad getting a bit anxious for some of his ornaments.' The children are curious and not used to being cooped up in a suburban house and yard.

But nothing seems to come clear. Further enquiries and checking out other possibilities bring us no joy. We trust God, but nothing works out. Our prayers don't seem to be answered.

God, this is not the refreshing leave we hoped for, I complain.

A lady who lives on her own in the Adelaide Hills mentions she is going away for three months. We are invited to live there and share with her when she returns. We are excited. Then someone takes us aside. 'She's got a heart of gold, Graham, but she has real problems coping with children.'

I look at Marj and I know what she is thinking. Our three children have been used to the wide open spaces in Ghana and are always lively and full of energy. When we go out for meals, the children of host families usually sit quietly while ours want to be quickly up and active. It just won't work.

We are on our knees again.

Then, at church on Sunday, our friends Phil and Julie come up with an impossible idea. 'We think you should get a home of your own,' Phil says.

Our jaws drop. 'With what, Phil? You know we have very little money.'

'God has laid it on our hearts to help,' Julie says. 'But don't get too excited. We don't have that kind of money either. So let's pray and see what God will do.'

The next day, Phil phones a friend—Geoff Mills, a Christian real estate agent. He tells Geoff what has transpired.

'Oh,' Geoff laughs, 'I know Graham and Marj Bee. Graham was groomsman at my wedding!' Then he gets serious. 'You know, I was praying for them this morning and I felt God urging me to help them in some way. If this is what God has laid on your heart, Phil, I'll be in it with you.'

They ring me. 'We suggest that you visit some banks, Graham. Tell them you have $5000 deposit and see if they're prepared to give you a loan.'

This is new territory for me. Living by faith, I am used to spending only what God has already provided. I am not keen on having a mortgage back in Australia; it could detract from my focus in Ghana. But the more I listen to Geoff, the more I realise that God is in this. He has brought our friends together with this 'impossible' idea.

'OK, Geoff,' I say, 'I'll give it a try. Let's see what God will do.' I put the receiver down, take a deep breath and dial for an appointment with the manager of a local bank.

***

Banks build their business on managing risk. The manager is nice enough, but he rolls his eyes when I respond to his question, 'And Mr Bee, what is your annual income?'

'We are missionaries,' I explain. 'We trust God for all that we need. He usually provides through the gifts of interested friends and churches.'

'And how much would that be?'

'Well, it fluctuates from month to month. We're never sure how much we'll receive.'

That's when the bank manager puts his pen down and, with a few platitudes, shows me to the door. I am not surprised. It is hard enough for Christians to understand how God provides for us, let alone a security-conscious banker.

Bank manager number two is just the same. It is all strange to him. He mumbles, 'We do have our shareholders to protect, Mr Bee.' He politely shows me out.

Bank manager number three talks more about times being tough for banks too. 'With a lack of security and high interest rates, there would be too much risk. If you failed to meet the regular repayments, you could be worse off and lose the lot.' I've heard it all before. I feel humiliated. I cut the conversation short, rise and head for the exit.

On the way home, I have a serious talk with God. *This is crazy, Lord. What bank would ever take us on?* There is no answer. Then I think again about my friends. *OK, God. I believe you've spoken to my friends. I can't dispute that. I'm willing to try one more bank. If this is unsuccessful, I'll take it that this is not your will afterall.*

Entering the fourth bank, I am very defensive—certainly not confident or forthcoming. The bank manager keeps drawing me out.

I tell him what we received last month and say, 'This is the highest we've received yet. We got some extra one-off gifts to help us get settled.'

Encouragingly, he says, 'Well, write it down.'

In the end—more because of my character, I think, than my financial situation—he smiles. No doubt, whether he knows it or not, God has been prompting him. He agrees to accept the application.

I can't believe it! We'll find a house and get settled before Julie starts school.

'Thank you, sir,' I say, 'and when will the funds be available?'

'Twelve weeks,' he says. My shoulders slump.

'That's quite normal these days, Mr Bee.' Then he leans forward. 'But if you can put down a deposit of $6000, the loan will be fast-tracked. You'll have it in six weeks.'

I can't wait to ring my friends and tell them the good news. I am excited by the prospect of buying a house, but I still have no money.

My friends say, 'OK, leave it with us.' They soon ring back. 'We can help with $2000 each and that will leave you to trust God for a further $2000.'

Putting the phone down, I share their response with Marj. 'They are marvellous, Marj, and I am so thankful, but we still need another $2000 from somewhere.'

'Look, Graham,' she says, 'the Lord has brought us this far. If he supplies this final amount, it will be a clear indication that we should proceed and that He will continue to look after us.'

It's times like these that I'm glad I married a woman of real faith.

The money does come—but from an unexpected source. Years ago, when I went to Bible college, I gave my car to my sister Heather. 'You need a car,' I said, 'and don't even think about paying me for it.' Now, she hands over a cheque for $1000. Then some smaller gifts arrive.

'Only $500 to go,' I tell Julie on the phone. As I put down the receiver, it immediately rings.

'Graham, we'll see you on Friday night,' a friend says. 'We want to give you a gift. Do you want it in cash or a cheque? It's $500.'

We celebrate. God is doing the impossible.

***

Now the challenge is to find a house in a good location within our budget. I talk to the owners of the house next door to Mum and Dad's place. It is run down. Their marriage has broken up and they are planning to sell. It seems like a perfect provision. The only problem is that they can't agree whether to renovate and sell, or just sell. We are hoping for the latter, but the time for Julie to start school is fast approaching. We need to know where we will be living—and soon.

We pray, asking God for an answer by the Wednesday before school starts.

By Thursday morning, nothing has happened. I am discouraged, and tell God so. Suddenly I have the thought, *There's no doubting God's ability. He could have prompted them to come with an agreement, but He didn't. Therefore, it must not be His will.*

I spark up and look in the Advertiser newspaper for other possibilities. My eyes fix on a relatively cheap house in a nearby suburb. The ad states, 'It needs some TLC.'

I ring the real estate agent who responds, 'It is only advertised for this one day and the viewing times are almost booked out.'

'If possible,' I say, 'we'd like to see it. Can you please fit us in?'

There is a pause, and I can hear papers being shuffled. 'OK,' he says, 'we can squeeze you in at four o'clock. You'll be the last people through.'

It is a simple three-bedroom house. Paint has peeled off the window frames down to the bare timbers. The large front lawn is full of weeds higher than my knees. Marj takes one look and wants to leave.

'Hold on, Marj,' I say. 'Look behind the initial appearance. You can see the structure is sound. I'll have time between speaking engagements and can do the renovations myself during the year. A bit of scrubbing, painting, lawn mowing and gardening and you won't know the place.' She relents, and with some guidance from the agent, we make an offer.

Next morning we hover near the phone, waiting for a call. Finally it rings.

'It's yours, Graham,' the agent says. 'Come in and sign the papers.'

I put the phone down and we dance around the kitchen table, giving thanks to God. As always, Mum and Dad are as excited as we are. The children, hearing all the excitement, interrupt their play and come in to see what is happening.

'We want to see it! Can we go now?'

On Tuesday, I enrol Julie in the nearby primary school and go around to talk to the real estate agent.

'We are wondering about being able to rent the house for the six weeks until the loan is processed. Is that a possibility?'

At first he frowns and discourages me. Then a car pulls up outside his office and the house's owner steps out. The agent suddenly changes his tune. He hustles me to the door and says quietly, 'You go and leave it with me.'

Later he rings. 'It's done, Graham. You can move in on Saturday!'

It's amazing.

We settle the family in the house just nine days after seeing it advertised. Furthermore, it is within walking distance of Julie's school. Now I am free to take our only car and travel away to distant farming districts for the next two weeks, sharing about our work in Ghana.

***

At the end of the year, it is time to return to Ghana. Geoff, our Christian real estate friend, offers to take responsibility for renting out the house and overseeing the maintenance.

'When you plan to come home again, Graham, let me know well in advance. Then I can arrange for it to be vacant for you.'

Not only has God provided the house; He has provided a carer for it while we are away. And the miracle goes on. The rent we receive is $48 per week and our mortgage repayments are $45!

This home is such a blessing and we have really enjoyed living here during this first home assignment. We know of other missionaries who live in a different rented house each time they go home, but now we have the security of knowing that each time we return, 'we are going home.' No longer will Julie ask, 'And where will we live, Dad?'

***

God has done the unbelievable. He has provided a house for people who had no money. But we are going to need the fullness of His grace in the next few weeks to cope with some devastating news.

Chapter 23
The accident

Adelaide
1977

His eyes bulge and his mouth waters. He lunges forward and takes hold of the biggest cream-filled butterfly cake. 'Yes! These are my favourites.'

'And what would you like to be when you grow up, son?' asks one of the men.

Hurriedly, the boy tries to swallow the remaining crumbs and clear his throat. Then, without a moment's hesitation, he replies, 'I'd like to be a missionary on furlough!'

The young boy has noticed that whenever there is a meeting with a missionary speaker, the ladies seem to make a special effort to put on a good spread. What a life, moving from one meeting to another!

***

I have seen many come and go; now it is our turn. This being our first 'home assignment' (as furlough is now called), we don't really know what to expect. In the years we have been away, church attitudes, like those in society at large, have changed. Churches used to ring up mission organisations and ask, 'Do you have any missionaries available to come and speak?' Now when a mission representative rings a church to inquire about an opening for a missionary, the usual response is an awkward silence. Then, 'We do have a full program. I'll discuss it with the other leaders and get back to you.'

The pressure on church leaders has increased. The expectations of their congregations have changed too. We understand that. We are going to need God's help.

Together Marj and I pray, 'Lord, we know there's still a lot to be done here in Australia. But we also know of many towns and villages in other countries where there is not even one person to tell them of the love God has for them. How can we help the Aussie church catch your vision for the unreached in our world?'

***

We need to base ourselves near the city for deputation purposes so it is not possible to regularly attend my original sending church in country Strathalbyn. This means we will need to find a new church home. We also need spiritual input and encouragement in our own lives. When not out and about taking meetings, we will need a fellowship to be part of and to identify with.

There are quite a number of churches in the area where we live. My parents attend one of them: Noarlunga Church of Christ.

'Mum, I'd love the extra contact we'd have with you if we attended Noarlunga——.'

Before I can finish, she interrupts. 'You know many of the people already. I'm sure they'd love that.'

'Yes, I know. But I sense God might have a different direction for us,' I reply. 'We'll make it a matter of prayer.'

Uppermost in our minds is the knowledge that as Christians we are blessed to be a blessing. Salvation is not just for our own enjoyment. As both individuals and local churches, we can easily become self-focused and reluctant to give of ourselves. Many churches do not have a vision for missions, and we see this as an opportunity to be personally involved with one of them. We would love our presence to help people gain a wider vision for God's kingdom purposes.

While praying about this, we receive an invitation from a deacon of a church 20 minutes closer to the city. 'Edwardstown Baptist is a large church with little exposure to missions,' he explains. 'I feel that your presence, and our contact with a real live missionary, can be a blessing to the church.'

Marj and I visit. We are warmly welcomed and feel at home. We have peace in accepting that this is God's direction for us. Later in the year, we are given opportunities for service. We lead a Sunday morning adult Bible class. This helps us in developing deeper relationships with some of the members and assists our integration into the church. Eventually we become members.

***

The phone rings. We are still just settling into our new home and church.

'Hey Marj, it's Bill Chapman calling!' Bill is our Ghana field leader.

'You'd better sit down, Graham,' Bill says. 'I have some tragic news.'

I sink into the chair and wait, frustrated by the delay in the international connection.

Bill continues, 'There has been an accident.' There is a further pause. 'Your brand new vehicle is a write-off.'

My mind goes into overdrive. New workers from Australia, Keith and Jill Beasley, had taken over our responsibilities for the year.

'What about Keith? Is he OK?' I ask.

'I'm sorry, Graham. Keith's gone. It was a bad accident.'

Choking up, I ask, 'What happened, Bill?'

'Keith drove to Tamale with James Bavoh [our mechanic] for business. As they were returning, there was an accident. The front wheel of an oncoming Bedford bus came off. The driver lost control and his vehicle crossed the road. There was a head-on collision. Keith was killed instantly. Thankfully James wasn't hurt, but they were in your car and, as I said, it's a write-off.'

After reassuring me that Jill is OK and being looked after, Bill hangs up.

We slump back into the lounge chairs, reeling from shock. The silence is deafening. Finally, struggling for words, we share our feelings.

'Marj, I can't believe it. I feel so sad and helpless. We're so far away.'

'I know what you mean,' Marj says. 'My heart goes out to Jill, widowed with two young sons so far from home and family.'

'It's very hard to understand,' I continue. 'They spent years preparing. They tenaciously endured setbacks when others might have given up. It doesn't make sense. I can't think of any reason why God might have allowed this to happen.'

Our struggles deepen as the realisation sinks in that this affects our future too. We have lost a brand new vehicle which we have not even seen. Talking and praying together, we agree there are no simple answers to our questions. We have to trust God's Father heart of love.

***

Our previous vehicle, an older Datsun pick-up (ute), was given to us. Once there were five of us in the family, it was no longer big enough. We considered our options. All the second-hand vehicles for sale had been run into the ground. Most were constantly overloaded and frequently used on bad roads as passenger vehicles. With very few parts available for repairs, they were too much of a risk. The only realistic option was to buy a new one.

So we sold the pick-up. With the proceeds from the sale plus some extra gifts, we ordered a new vehicle from Japan. It was shipped directly to Ghana for us—the only way of obtaining a new vehicle there. We asked Keith, 'Would you please collect it when it arrives? Then you can use it for the rest of the year until we get back.'

Because of corruption in the country and little prospect of getting anything out of an insurance company, most people do not insure their vehicles. We didn't either. The wreck was later sold for the value of the engine.

***

We work in a remote northern area of Ghana where a vehicle is essential. We need one, not only for our own transport but also for carrying bulk supplies for both personal and ministry needs.

Lord, it's like climbing Mt Everest. It's huge, and obviously beyond us. First we were trusting you to supply our fares back to Ghana. Now we need thousands of dollars extra for a replacement vehicle. But we're committed to not appealing to people. We're trusting you and waiting to see what you will do.

***

Our children adjust well to life back in Australia. Wide-eyed, they are amazed at the affluence all around them. They thoroughly enjoy and appreciate the many presents they receive from family members. Our families have missed so much of their early lives.

There are new things to get used to too. Julie runs around to the back of the TV to try to see the man reading the news! They grow accustomed to wearing shoes. They love being able to relate to their grandparents, whom they had previously only heard about.

Because we are living in South Australia close to my parents, each school holidays we make the long journey to visit Marj's parents in Victoria. After one of these trips, Marj remains in Melbourne to speak at a number of meetings. I set out to drive back home to Adelaide with the children. We need to get Julie back into school after the holidays. The children are at the age of asking many questions. Passing through the outlying suburbs of Melbourne, they start chorusing, 'Are we nearly there yet?' *Groan. This is going to be a long day. There are still more than 700 kilometres to go!*

Out in the middle of nowhere, surrounded by bush, the children ask for an urgent stop. Getting back into our older model vehicle, I am keen to be moving again. But when I turn the key there is no response. I get out, fiddle with the battery wires and connections, and try again. There is no response at all. The engine is lifeless.

My concerns grow. My mind begins to flood with all kinds of possible outcomes. My prayer for God's help intensifies. I can cope myself, but how will I cope with three young children out here?

I get out again and check everything I can see and think of, but I cannot find any obvious problem. I get back in and turn the key again in desperation. This time the engine springs to life.

'Praise the Lord! We knew it would start this time, Dad,' the children excitedly tell me. 'While you were checking the engine, we prayed and asked God to help us.'

God has used a problem to test and grow our young children's developing faith. I am greatly encouraged. Living in an undeveloped area in Africa has not disadvantaged them. By living and praying with us, they too are learning that God answers prayer. Not only is He real, He can be trusted.

***

We travel in a number of Australian states, sharing about the work in

Ghana and reconnecting with those who pray for us. We are encouraged by the depth of their commitment to standing with us.

One of those people is Janna. When we were getting ready to go to Ghana five years before, we met her at a small country church. There were just 18 people there. Janna and her husband, Grant, came specifically to hear us.

As I finished packing up our display, Marj was busy trying to answer all Janna's questions. 'What will you be doing there? How will you cope with your baby there?'

They talked together for just five minutes before I needed to interrupt. 'Our hosts are leaving.'

'Just two more minutes,' Marj called out.

Since then Janna has corresponded regularly with us and is one of those truly committed pray-ers. Meeting up with her and Grant again, we are amazed at just how much they know about our work and the workers.

'How is Joseph doing? ... It was so sad to hear about the death of Pastor Boye ... Has the new church at Ekumundipe continued?' Their questions and comments clearly demonstrate the depth of their involvement.

We are blessed by many people like them—people who identify with us and are such a vital part of what God does in us and through us. The devil would like to sideline us from what God wants to do, but God answers their prayers. He protects us and keeps us focused.

Communication is not easy from Africa. Letters take six weeks to reach home, and it takes another six for the answers to come. At times, writing letters is an extra pressure on top of everything else we do. But we are reminded again that relating to our prayer partners is an important and vital part of our work.

By year's end we are renewed in health. We are encouraged by the interest and support of so many and overwhelmed by God's loving provision. Edwardstown Church agrees to contribute towards our support, and, amazingly, God provides us with enough finance to order a new vehicle. His ability to do what seems impossible continues to astonish and inspire us.

It is time to return to Ghana for our second term of service. But recent reports from the country have not been encouraging. Spare parts for the tractors are in short supply. Will we be able to continue? Does God have an answer for us? We will have to wait and see.

Chapter 24
For such a time as this

Kpandai, Northern Ghana
1978–1980

The tropical heat slams into us as we step down from the air-conditioned plane. We arrive back in the country with deep concerns for the future of the work. On our minds are the reports we received before leaving home: 'The tractors are beginning to breakdown frequently.' 'The service to farmers is being limited as a result.' 'Economically, the country continues in a downward slide.'

The dark clouds of uncertainty hang ominously over the future of the ministry.

***

On our return to Kpandai, it is blatantly obvious that the work cannot continue like this for long. The tractor problems are frustrating everyone—farmers, mechanics and missionaries alike. Something needs to be done.

But what?

We spend time seeking God and His direction. *Lord, what are you saying in all of this? Should we close down the agricultural work? Should we change our emphasis and strategy?* Our small team of local helpers eagerly joins us in prayer. They have good reason to be concerned: their jobs are at stake.

Personally, we are open to the possibility of change. While I love using my farming experience to help local people, agricultural work is not my top priority. My primary desire is to see the Gospel shared and embraced. Helping to meet pressing physical needs is part of why I am here, but seeing local people freed from fears and the control of ancestral spirits and the fetish priest is another important reason for living among them. When a person does become a Christian, they describe the experience as being like the lifting of a heavy burden.

We try to hold all aspects of the work lightly. We can do many other things than agriculture to assist the local people.

Yet we have a growing assurance that it is right to continue. We have no idea how. The older tractors can give supplementary help, but they cannot be relied on to do the bulk of the work anymore. We begin to pray specifically, *Lord, we need a new tractor. We have absolutely no idea how you will provide, but our trust is in you.* The assurance we are to continue enables us to pray expecting an answer rather than just hoping it will happen.

Two weeks later, a worker with Summer Institute of Linguistics (SIL) in a village 18 kilometres away contacts us.

'Please come over and use our two-way radio to talk to a Canadian businessman in Accra. His name is Harry Norris; he's a Christian working with the World Bank on a hydro project in southern Ghana. He's seen a new tractor waiting to be collected in Accra for another mission agricultural project, and he asked if we knew of any similar work. I told him about yours. Now he wants to talk with you to see if he can use his connections to help meet any needs you might have.'

Harry's enquiry has come without any prior knowledge of our work, just the prompting of the Holy Spirit. He believes God has brought him to Accra for such a time as this. The result is that our project is blessed not just with a tractor, but with a plough, harrow and trailer as well! Two years later a second tractor arrives, which wonderfully enables the agricultural ministry to continue.

Harry and his wife, Barbara, travel north to see the work and the new equipment in action. They become dear friends.

***

Economically, Ghana continues to struggle. The long queues of people waiting to obtain rationed commodities are evidence. These form whenever a limited supply of something becomes available. With exports in decline and rampant corruption in high places, the country is faced with a shortage of foreign currency to purchase adequate supplies of fuel and food for its people.

On one occasion in Kumasi, I spend two and a half days queuing in the tropical sun with my vehicle to get a mere six gallons of fuel—just enough, with what I have, for me to travel back to Kpandai. My car is number 166 in the queue! That night a thief steals a mission vehicle from the queue despite its being parked bumper-to-bumper with other cars.

Strangely, while it is difficult to get a tankful of petrol for my car, I discover I can order a 3000-gallon tanker of diesel for the tractors. It is still not easy, but it is possible.

Whenever our diesel supply runs low, I make the minimum three-day round trip south to the refinery and place an order for a tanker load. The roads are dangerous and either dusty or boggy. Sometimes the ferry over the Oti River at Damonko is not working and I have to drive the long way around—an additional 150 kilometres.

After paying for the fuel in advance, I return home and wait and pray for it to be delivered. Due to extreme shortages, tanker drivers can sometimes be bribed en route to sell the fuel to someone else. Then we have to wait anxiously for another week for it to be delivered. How good it is to know there are many at home interceding on our behalf. They share the joy when they hear the supplies have arrived.

In time we are able to sell our car and buy a double-cab diesel pick-up. Now we can carry a 44-gallon drum on the back and utilise our bulk supplies. We have to do whatever we can to adapt to the trying local conditions.

The continued shortages keep us on our knees praying. This is also a great opportunity to include our workers in prayer. They know corrupt people can divert our supplies and their jobs depend on the diesel being delivered. They also share the joy of seeing their prayers answered.

***

Before starting the agricultural project, I visited Nigeria to investigate what we thought might be a more sustainable project using bullocks. However, with the prevalence of tsetse flies in our area, we learned it was not a realistic option to depend on cattle here.

We settled on the tractor project despite it being capital intensive. We are aware this approach will not be reproduced easily, but it does serve people in this area during a desperately tough economic period.

We anticipate that in coming years, as the economy improves, more local people will be able to buy tractors themselves. They will then be able to provide a similar commercial service for others who need it. Eventually our project can be phased out and missionaries will be able to concentrate more fully on the development of the growing churches. For now, though, ministering to their felt needs is a practical way of demonstrating Christ's love.

***

Eventually the economic crisis becomes so severe that it is tough not just for subsistence farmers but for everyone—including missionaries. We are all wondering: how will we survive?

Chapter 25
Coups and counter coups

1979

The situation in Ghana is continuing to worsen. Marj and I often find ourselves discussing the country's future over morning coffee.

'I wonder, Marj, how much lower the country can fall. Do you think anyone can turn it around? The government seems so impotent.'

'Well, since we arrived, it's been downhill all the way! People from neighbouring countries used to come here to shop; now we have to travel there to buy groceries. Something has to happen, but don't ask me what.'

***

Ghana gained its independence from Britain in 1957 under the dynamic leadership of Dr Kwame Nkrumah. It was the first country in sub-Saharan black Africa to achieve this. Expectations were high. With good economic reserves and ongoing export commodities, the country's future looked bright.

But finances were not managed well. The economic situation in the country deteriorated so much that in 1966 the military staged a coup and overthrew Nkrumah. The army planned to right the wrongs, but it failed miserably, as did the civilian government it eventually handed over to. Dr Busia's government devalued the currency by 44% and caused a massive spike in commodity prices. This move was deeply unpopular, opening the way for the army to take control once again.

A military takeover in January 1972, just as we were beginning preparations for travel to Ghana, was the first of a series of coups and counter coups (at least six) that occurred during our years in Ghana. During our missionary training, they told us to be 'Ready for Anything', but I am not sure how we could have prepared for this.

In the years after our arrival we have a couple of brief periods of civilian rule, yet each one is followed by another coup. Despite this (or because of it), the economic slide continues. Corruption and abuse of power become even more widespread. Much of the infrastructure deteriorates and equipment breaks down with no spare parts for repairs.

***

Now, in 1979, Ghana is at a crisis point. All the excitement and expectations of a prosperous, independent future have disappeared. When the military leaders took over in 1972, they promised to fix the economic woes, but corruption and profiteering in their ranks contributes to rampant inflation. The anticipated improvement in the quality of life has not happened.

Dissatisfaction spreads like gangrene among the population. Demonstrations, particularly by university students, escalate.

It is now seven years since we arrived in Ghana, and every year we have watched the economy slide irreversibly downhill. Where will it end? Most of the military activity during these coups takes place in the capital, Accra, and generally it doesn't directly affect us in the north. But there are some periods of real tension and uncertainty which affect us profoundly.

***

After a failed coup attempt in May 1979, the June 1979 coup is a violent one. Junior officers in the armed forces overthrow their senior officers. Ashamed that the reputation of the military has been tarnished, these younger members promise to try to clean up the mess and return the country to civilian rule.

In the weeks following, the Armed Forces Revolutionary Council executes eight senior military officers, including three who had previously been head of state. From July to September 1979, 155 military officers, former officials and wealthy businessmen are imprisoned in a 'house-cleaning exercise'.[1] Everyone in the country is gripped with fear.

Listening to the 6pm Ghana Broadcasting Commission news is unnerving, but nobody dares miss it. Government decrees are issued as part of the news. Nearly every day, people are named on the broadcast and told to report to the Gonda Military Barracks by 9 am the next morning. Each decree ends with the words 'without fail!' Given the recent executions, the warning is ominous, and everyone hopes their name is not the next one called.

***

One evening, at the end of the news, my ears prick up on a different announcement. 'All expatriates in the country must travel to their regional capital tomorrow. You must report and register your details.'

Marj is away, speaking at a Women's Conference, so I reluctantly jump in the car and drive the 20 kilometres of dusty, corrugated road to collect her. She is not keen to leave; however, we know that non-compliance is not an option, and we return home that evening.

We rise at five o'clock the next morning and eat a quick breakfast before picking up the local Catholic priest, who wants to travel with us. The journey takes four hours, and we are surprised to find we are among the first to arrive when the office opens. Initially, there is confusion about what we need to do. The officials are aware of the decree but are still awaiting instructions.

Just before lunch, we are each issued with an 'Aliens Card'. We will have to show this on specific occasions during the coming months. I smilingly reflect on the fact that the Bible describes Christians as 'aliens in a foreign land' and now the government regards us as aliens too!

***

A short time later, the following decree is broadcast: 'All NGOs must hand in your two-way radios to the District Police Headquarters.' This decree is given amid mounting tension and rumours of dissidents gathering in neighbouring countries. The government is afraid of a counter coup, so it seeks to minimise that possibility by confiscating the means of transmitting news or rumours.

Communication with our field members during this tense and uncertain time is very difficult as there is still no functioning telephone system. We wonder how we ever managed without the radios in earlier days. Three months later they are returned to us. We are relieved to be in contact with one another once again.

***

While most coups leave village people largely unaffected, this revolution purports to give power to the people. People's Defence Committees are established and soldiers are stationed in many rural areas.

This has far-reaching implications. The government puts a halt to university studies and students are sent into the villages to cart cocoa for export and to work on road rehabilitation, sanitary projects and political education in aid of the revolution. Soldiers use their new authority to frighten people into obeying their decrees. Often, they take action before checking out the truth of allegations.

The locals are divided on whether all of this is for their welfare or destruction.

***

During one of the attempted coups, we are down on the beach relaxing. We are about a mile from the Castle, which is the residence and seat of government. All of a sudden, we hear loud explosions from out at sea. We later find out that an attempt to overthrow the government has taken place using a naval vessel. We are glad that although they missed the Castle, they didn't miss by a mile!

***

Returning from one Home Leave, we step from the plane on to the platform at the top of the stairs. This time we hardly notice the tropical heat as we are confronted by the turret of an army tank pointing directly at us. The tank is parked on the tarmac just 200 metres from the plane.

The country is nervous and fearful of a counter coup. We are not surprised by this turn of events, but we are definitely concerned about the effect it will have.

***

Towards the end of our time in Ghana, while we are still living in Tamale, leaders of another organisation contact us. 'We are travelling away to a conference,' they tell us. 'Would you please keep an eye on a couple who are staying behind to prepare for their return home?'

We seek to cooperate with and assist those in organisations like ours wherever possible, and they do the same for us. We do not expect any complications, and we are mystified when we receive a summons to the Regional Secretary's fortified residence.

We discover the husband had decided to take some photographs to show folks back home. He did not realise how sensitive military government officials are about photography. He has been arrested and his film confiscated. 'Who can vouch for you and reassure us you are not a spy?'

He is grateful that after some 'sweet talking' on my part, the officials release him into my care without further incident.

Mission policy encourages us to have contingency plans in place at all times and to have a bag packed with essential items in case we need to flee or hide. We know that even though there are times of crisis in Ghana, on the whole we are respected and are not targets. At the same time, we cannot take risks and need to be ready, just in case.

***

After the violent coup, which has links to Libya's Colonel Gaddafi, I wonder what the future holds for the Ghanaian people and church. I start to pray against what is happening, but feel a check in my spirit. I reflect on the fact that in many places where people are comfortable and without stress, the church is declining. In other situations, where there is persecution, the church has grown.

God has His plans for the growth of His church in Ghana. I can rest secure in that knowledge and trust Him to bring about His own good purposes, even if it results in my being less secure and comfortable than I have been.

Times like this also remind us to continue to give priority to the training of local leaders. They will be the ones to continue to lead the church into the future. This will be especially true if there comes a time when we are no longer allowed to live and work in the country.

***

It is not until December 1992 that the leader of the 1979 coup, J.J. Rawlings, after resigning from the armed forces, returns the country to democratic rule and is elected president himself. He helps Ghana turn the corner economically, and eventually the country is praised by the World Bank as a shining example of economic recovery.

It is not until 2001, 11 years after we leave Ghana, that the first presidential change of power from one elected president to another takes place.

***

The uncertainty, anxiety and tension of these crisis years have provided opportunities for us to prove God's faithfulness. My trust in God has grown deeper. Had life remained comfortable, this growth probably would not have happened to the same extent. Still on my journey of faith, I am continuing to learn, and I know there will be more hills and valleys ahead of us.

Chapter 26
Sssspitting cobras

Northern Ghana
1972–1983

I loved the *Jungle Doctor* stories as I was growing up. I particularly liked the one entitled 'Safe as Poison', about the greedy snake that was caught after being tricked into swallowing a hard-boiled egg. Like all these stories, this one had a clear message: whatever we do in life has consequences for ourselves, and for others.[1]

Little did I realise I would have my own dramatic encounters with very dangerous snakes at various times throughout our years in Ghana.

***

The extreme shortages of processed food create an ideal seed bed for a thriving black market. The government introduces 'controlled prices' in an attempt to clamp down on it and hopefully reduce inflation, but this approach fails. Locals tell me, 'Every new decree like this is just a challenge to Ghanaian ingenuity to find a way around it!'

Kalabule, the illegal buying and selling of goods above controlled prices, becomes rampant. Food and other items are blatantly sold at exorbitant prices.

This makes it difficult for law-abiding folk like us who bring our support money into the country and change it at the official bank rate. This is only one-seventh of the black market rate, and this means many local items are now out of our reach. The temptation not to follow the decrees is enormous, especially when we are disadvantaged by doing so. Many people do make excuses and ignore them.

One way of overcoming the exchange rate problem is to grow our own food. So, for all of our time in Ghana, we raise our own chickens for eggs and meat. During this extremely difficult period, we also raise rabbits as another alternative to buying meat. We discover that this really is 'fast food'—when they escape from their cages, they are not easy to catch! They also multiply prolifically. A positive spin-off is that we are able to help some locals start their own rabbit farms. This provides an improved diet for their families.

Keeping chickens, though, has a negative side effect. They attract big black spitting cobras, which come looking for the eggs. We have numerous startling encounters with them.

***

One very hot day, perspiring profusely and drained of energy, we lie down for a siesta. This is normal here if you want to have some energy left in the evening. Our one-year-old twins are content to play on the floor under the open window near the foot of our bed. It is not quiet, but at least it is restful.

The twins become tired and grizzly so we lift them onto the bed with us. A few minutes later, a car passes by on the driveway, just outside our bedroom. I glimpse something dark flash over the window sill and down into the room. Intrigued, I get up to see what it is. There, right where the twins had been playing, is a venomous snake coiled up on the floor. It had obviously been disturbed and fled from the passing car.

I ask Marj to keep an eye on it while I dash out to get something to deal with it. We thank God for His constant protection over our young ones. It could have been so different!

***

On another occasion, around midnight, an unsettled nervous cackling in the chicken house awakens us. It is some distance away, but that noise on an otherwise peaceful night is so loud it disturbs us.

Realising there is an intruder there I grab a torch and rush outside. Marj follows. In my haste, the only piece of timber I can find is a large one. We dash up to the chicken shed. Sure enough, coiled in the back of the shed is a black spitting cobra.

To get at it, I have to go inside the shed. Holding the torch in one hand, I try to hit the snake with the timber I'm holding in my other hand. Its alarm bells go off and it looks for a way to escape. Now, with the snake moving and the timber too heavy to wield properly, I start to hand the torch back to Marj—I need to use both hands. Accidently I flick the torch switch off in the process. Aaaagh! In the darkness and gripped by fear, I drop the wood and make a hasty retreat backwards out of the door. Marj had a head start; she makes it first.

By the time I regain my composure and shine the torch again, the snake has seized the moment and made a quick getaway.

***

On another afternoon, after a busy day in the clinic, one of our co-workers, Janet Clarke, is searching in a dark corner of the storeroom just outside our backyard. She is checking carefully in case she puts her hand on a scorpion. She notices a putrid smell and makes a mental note to get someone to find the dead rat.

Then, without warning, a sudden splash of what seems like water hits her eyes.

She quickly realises it is the venomous spit of a cobra. Dropping what she is doing, she races home and rinses her eyes with milk and snake antivenin. Despite this, they swell so much that they close over and she is unable to see out of them for over 24 hours. Word spreads and there is much prayer for her. Thankfully, over the next few days, the swelling subsides, her vision is restored and there are no lasting effects.

Again we are thankful for God our protector and His angels watching over us.

***

In recounting what happened to her, Janet mentions that the strong smell in the storeroom that she thought was a dead rat must have been the cobra. Several months later, Marj smells a similar bad odour in the lean-to storage room built on to the bedroom of our house.

Just a curtain separates the rooms. Remembering Janet's experience, Marj keeps her distance. She reaches across and tentatively pulls the curtain to one side. A distinctive hissing sound confirms her fears and she rushes out and calls me. Initially I am a bit dubious, but just in case I cautiously begin a search. Then I hear the same sound, but I can't see anything. I guess the sun glasses I am wearing to protect my eyes don't help my vision!

It is almost time to walk to the evening church service, so we call some of the young men from the Bible school to help us check behind the storage boxes. They have a quick look but don't see or hear anything suspicious.

'To look properly, we'll have to shift all those boxes,' they say. 'That will take time, and we don't want to be late for church. But don't worry, we'll come back and look tomorrow.'

It's all right for them to say don't worry! With just the curtain between our bed and the snake, there is no way we will be able to sleep tonight.

The watchman, Kwaku, is on call at the clinic so we ask for his help. He brings his bow and arrow. Together, we shift the boxes and discover the cobra in the gap behind the slats of a large box. Kwaku tries to get above the snake and shoot an arrow down to immobilise it. He shoots and, at the same moment, quickly moves his head to keep his eyes out of direct line with the snake. In his haste, he misses a couple of times. As brave as he is, he is wisely not taking any chances. Finally he kills the cobra and takes it outside to bury it.

What a relief. We will now be able to sleep soundly—and not dream of snakes.

***

Early one morning on yet another occasion, I take feed up to the chickens. As I am returning for breakfast, I remember that I have forgotten to give food to the hen sitting on eggs in the side cage. Our children are eagerly waiting for the chickens to hatch.

Returning, I find a big black cobra in the cage with the hen. I grab a heavy stick, open the door of the small cage and prepare to strike it. The snake rears up and opens its mouth wide. I can see something white in the back of its throat. While I am trying to work out what it is, an egg pops out.

My heart is pounding as I try to kill it. At the same time I'm trying to look away to shield my eyes. In fright, the cobra spits out seven eggs one after another!

My mind goes back to the *Jungle Doctor* story I heard as a child. The snake in the story couldn't escape because the boiled egg, which had been put in the nest for it to swallow, stuck in its throat. This cobra is now trying to avoid the same fate.

The hen dies of snakebite. We lose the eggs. Our children are left disappointed.

***

Some people would no doubt be horrified by the way snakes are treated here. We have seen many local people come to the clinic suffering from snakebite. Antivenin is often in short supply. Those who have access to it through Ministry of Health stores frequently sell it to others, who keep it until there is an urgent need. Families are then prepared to pay almost anything to save the life of their relative. Some nights, if no antivenin can be obtained locally, we drive the patients 100 kilometres to the nearest hospital.

There are no snake catchers here and the local adage is 'the only good snake is a dead snake'. When a decision has to be made quickly, the snake always loses out.

***

The local Gonga chief is walking through our property to get to his farm one morning and we engage in conversation.

'Chief, we seem to be having lots of snakes around this year.'

'Yes, I've heard about some of your encounters. Let me give you some advice. Don't bury the next snake you kill. Instead, burn it right outside the chicken shed. The burnt smell will keep other snakes away.'

It sounds like what we would call an 'old wives' tale' so we do not take much notice. However, after another couple of night-time raids, we decide there is no harm in trying. Believe it or not, we are not troubled again by snakes for the next eighteen months.

I am not sure if we killed the last of the local colony or whether the chief's protection policy really works! What I am sure about is that, in the midst of the many dangers and challenges we face, there is great peace in knowing that our lives and times are in God's hands.

That knowledge is a great help for us as we make important decisions concerning our children's future.

Chapter 27
Jesus cares for our children too

South Australia
1981

'Simon says, stand up!' Following the rules of the game, we all stand up. This direction followed by a quick 'Sit down!' catches one of the children out. I repeat, 'You only do what Simon says.'

This nightly game in the hour before bedtime is a special time that the children and I enjoy before I head off to meetings. Sometimes we end up having pillow fights, despite warnings from their Mum that 'someone will end up crying'. We always finish with, 'Simon says, go to bed.' This prompts loud groans of fake disappointment and protest—they know the rules but always seem to delight in this nightly charade.

We pray together and then, after cuddles, tuck them into bed. As we see answers, the children discover for themselves the blessing of taking everything to God in prayer.

***

Our children do not find the home schooling we do in Ghana (using correspondence lessons from South Australia) very easy—and neither does Marj. We build a schoolroom out in the backyard so the children can physically walk to school, thinking that might help, but it is still a struggle. A volunteer teacher comes to teach them for the final year before we go on home leave, and this frees Marj up for ministry. Yet even with a dedicated teacher, it is still a challenge to get through schoolwork when there are so many enticing distractions in the community where we live.

We are all looking forward to going home and to the kids attending a real school. The children join us in praying, and we write about our plans for home assignment in our newsletter. A timely reply comes from a friend, Lois Moyle, who lives not far from our house in Adelaide.

'The local Baptist church has just opened a Christian school nearby,' she writes. 'Would you like me to ask if there is room for your children?'

'Yes, please!' we reply enthusiastically.

In a later letter Lois shares: 'My spine tingled from top to bottom when I received the school's response. "We are sorry, but we are fully booked for next year. Our policy is to give priority to siblings of existing students; all we can offer are three places for just the first two terms of the year. Other family members are due to commence at the start of third term." That was exactly what you were praying for, Graham and Marj. I believe this is the school for your three.'

It is true. Home for just nine months this time, we need three places for those exact two terms. What an amazing provision! As we follow the Lord's leading and timing, everything seems to fit together so perfectly. The Father is looking after our children too.

This is the beginning of a warm relationship that our family enjoys over many years with the staff and students of Southern Vales Christian Community School. Each time we return home, our children are welcomed and are able to renew friendships again. We reflect on the fact that when we first tried to buy a house in Christies Beach, that door closed, and the Lord led us to Morphett Vale, years before the school even began.

***

Back on home leave, we share in many groups and churches about our ministry and the challenges we will face on our return to Ghana. Working and living cross-culturally is tough. We need people who will pray with us for God's enabling.

The issue that sparks most interest, and the one aspect our listeners find most difficult to identify with, is what we will do about the children's schooling when we return to Africa. 'Will you have to send them away to school?' they often ask. 'I could never do that. It's the biggest hurdle that keeps me from agreeing to be a missionary.'

There was a time when we felt the same way. However, after three years of teaching our children in a village environment, we realise it would be far better for their education and general development if they were able to attend a good Christian school. There isn't one close to where we work in Ghana. The low standard of teaching, lack of resources and absence of moral standards means local Ghanaian schools are not really an option.

The recurring question of what to do weighs on our minds. Our options seem so limited. We agonise over it together. We love our children so much and struggle to be objective. Time is running out and we need to make a decision before we return to Ghana for our third term.

We reaffirm together the things we are sure of. We are still convinced that it is God's will for us to continue in ministry in Ghana. We also know that God has good plans for our children. Home schooling is not working, and we do not want their education to suffer because of our work.

The only viable option is the small WEC missionary children's school in Cote d'Ivoire (Ivory Coast). We have received glowing reports of VIS (Vavoua International School). 'They have lovely, caring house parents and teachers. The children can follow an Australian curriculum once they reach high school. The students love it and make good friends from all around the world.' It sounds promising.

Marj's mother's heart speaks. 'I don't know. It's a thousand kilometres away and there's a border to cross as well. It's at least a two-day trip.'

'I know. It's such a tough prospect to consider,' I empathise. 'Because of the distance, we would only see them for three months each year—one month at a time. We wouldn't even get to see them mid-term like parents who live nearby do.'

'What if they get sick? Communication between the two countries is so poor. It won't be possible to phone them, and letters take so long.'

'We've never been apart from them for long periods before, and they are so young.' Julie is nine and the twins just seven.

We both struggle to accept this as a realistic possibility. However, being a pragmatist, I can see no alternative. 'Yes, it will be hard for them and for us. But if we are to continue in Africa, and our children's education is not to suffer, this appears to be the best option.'

Marj and I continue discussing the implications of such a move long into the night. It will be difficult to be separated for so much of the year. And how will the children cope? Will it be a positive or negative experience for them?

Lord, if this is right, please give us peace in our hearts.

Gradually, the Lord melts our objections and dissipates our fears. He assures us that He is our loving heavenly Father and cares for our children even more than we do. We realise that if we entrust them to His care, He is able to do 'exceedingly abundantly above all we could ask or think' in loving them and caring for them—even more than we can. His promises and His grace strengthen us just when we need it.

Peace enters. We write to the school and begin arrangements.

Chapter 28
Twenty-two days[1]

1982

'How long did you say it will take to drop your kids off at school and get home again?' Our friends at home are caught between amazement and disbelief. 'That has to be some kind of record!'

My ability to joke with a deadpan face does leave some people unsure at times, but this time I am not joking. It will be a very long first trip to the boarding school in Cote d'Ivoire.

***

Heading out to Ghana again, we recognise life is going to be very different this time around. The promise of God's presence with us has not changed though. The Gaskin family from Australia, who are in Ghana for the year, decide to send their two children to school with ours.

To save costs, we make plans to travel together in one vehicle, a Datsun minibus borrowed from the clinic. Fitting in is not a problem, but comfort is. Those sitting in the back of the minibus on its makeshift timber benches have to face sideways rather than the direction of travel. There are no seat belts to stop us from swaying. Both the homemade seats and the vehicle springs are hard. At times like this, I wish I had a bit more padding.

The first day's journey to Kumasi is over 400 kilometres. All goes smoothly, apart from the frequent potholes in the broken-up bitumen that jar us to the bone. The extreme heat is a given. Our vehicle does well and we arrive safely.

Originally we planned to continue the journey the next day. Our wives, however, are tired after the trip and have already spent a lot of time preparing for the children's three months away. We decide to rest for one day.

During the night, New Year's Eve, there is a military coup. All the country's borders are closed. There is no indication as to when they will re-open.

Thankfully, we have good temporary accommodation and can stay as long as we need to. Feeding two families under the present circumstances is a different matter. With extreme food shortages throughout the country, it is a challenge every day to find enough to feed everyone. We have stocks of food at home, but there was no warning of this event and we are totally unprepared. We wait and pray for the way to open up.

Thousands of Ghanaians, home for Christmas, now need to travel back to the countries where they are employed. After ten long days of waiting, there is a government decree: 'Everyone who wants to leave the country, Ghanaians included, needs to go to the Accra Football Stadium to apply for an exit permit.'

Without delay Ross Gaskin and I drive south to join the thousands already queuing. The crush of people and disorderly lines remind me of trying to get into a major sporting event after the game has started. It is bedlam. We are packed in like sardines in the oppressive tropical sun and everyone is grumbling about the inconvenience.

While waiting in the queue, I am suddenly propelled forward from behind. I hang on tightly to my briefcase, trying to make sure it is not snatched from me. It contains our official documents as well as a substantial amount of cash. When the pushing stops, I discover I am much closer to the front of the line.

Dripping with perspiration, I receive my permit.

Relieved to be out of the crush, I search in my pockets for money to buy yam chips and chili sauce for lunch. As well as having an empty stomach, I discover dejectedly that my pockets are also empty. Obviously, I was distracted when pushed forward and became an easy target for a pickpocket. Some cash was stolen, but at least I was able to hang on to the briefcase. To lose that would have been disastrous.

Ross and I travel the four hours back to Kumasi and are welcomed with excitement. We pack and prepare to depart the next morning.

***

At 5 am, as soon as the curfew is over, we all climb into the Datsun and head for the border. It feels so good to be on our way again. The children are still drowsy from being woken so early and struggle to sit upright as we wind our way through the forest. We keep to the middle of road to avoid the jagged edges.

When we arrive at the border, we find everything still closed. The officials did not expect anyone through so soon. They have all gone to tend their farms. Their wages alone are not sufficient to feed their families, so they have made the most of this unexpected opportunity.

Now the children are well and truly awake, and hearing news of a further delay, they groan, 'What next?' It is frustrating, coming on top of everything else that has happened.

There is nothing else for us to do but wait while someone goes on a bike to call the officials from their farms.

The actual processing of our permits takes only a short time. Eventually we are on our way again. A few kilometres further on, we find the Ivoirian officials are there to process our visas. With a smile and an 'au revoir' we drive into Cote d'Ivoire.

The road through no-man's-land between borders seemed bad enough, but now we get another shock. In this area, the road leading away from the border is not being maintained. They have started constructing a completely new one. We can see it, but we can only dream of what it will be like to travel on it once it is finished. The current road, pitted with broken-up bitumen, is so dusty that those sitting in the back tie handkerchiefs around their mouths. Anyone seeing us might think we're transporting a group of cowboys! The handkerchiefs help to filter the air, but the dust collects on them as we breathe in and we end up looking like a group of bandits.

It is impossible to go fast—a blessing in disguise. The car begins to swerve and we pull over. Oh, no! A puncture in the rear tyre. The state of the road is terrible; it is too risky to travel very far without a spare. We stop at the next town to get it repaired.

Their method of repair looks a bit dodgy, but we have seen it done before. An old car piston has been fitted with a simple frame that enables it to be clamped over the patch on the tube. A small amount of some flammable liquid, probably kerosene, is poured into the piston and set alight. The heat melts the raw rubber patch, sealing the hole.

It is an archaic method but successful. This process takes an hour and a half, setting us back even further. We use the time for a refreshment break and try to minimise the children's disappointment. There is still a very long way to go.

Just before we get onto really good bitumen, the exhaust system falls off. We pick it up and stuff it in the back amongst all the baggage. It broke off close to the manifold, right up near the engine. Although the condition of the road improves, we now have exhaust fumes and un-muffled engine noise to contend with for at least the next five hours.

We have only a basic map and roads are not always clearly marked. Darkness falls, making it even more difficult to find our way through the towns en route. We drive slowly through the towns, trying not to draw attention to ourselves. The last thing we need is trouble with the police.

Finally, just before midnight, we roar into the schoolyard. We made it!!

We are surprised when the generator is started and all the lights come on. People appear from doors and windows and we receive a very warm welcome. After 19 hours on the road, we slump onto our makeshift mattresses and lie down to sleep. The only problem is that the roar of the car engine keeps ringing in our ears all night.

The next morning is the usual Sunday morning chapel service. Two of the senior boys at the school testify that on Saturday morning they went to the headmistress, Jean Barnicoat, and told her, 'We've prayed and we believe that although the "Ghana Gang" are two weeks late, they will arrive today.' We had arrived five minutes before midnight!

We are greatly encouraged by the spiritual maturity of these students. Our children will flourish in this environment. We stay for a few days while they settle in and we have our vehicle repaired. When we are ready to leave, the children are playing outside with their new friends.

We call out, 'We're going now.' They are already so settled and happy, they just wave and shout back, 'Bye Mum! Bye Dad!' We have to call them over for a hug and a proper goodbye. We know we will not see them for another three months. We drag ourselves away and, after one last wave, drive off.

The deep ache in our hearts reminds us of the cost, but we are grateful they seem to have settled so quickly. We are thankful, too, for the lovely way the Lord has lifted the burden we felt. We know we are leaving our children in His loving care and the hands of capable staff.

After the long drive home, we count the days this epic journey has taken—twenty-two!

***

After every three months away, the children return home for a one-month holiday. We find they just slot back into family life as if they have never been away. We love being a family again and treasure these times. Earlier we may have taken them for granted.

During one term, when Paul is 12, he contracts cerebral malaria again. He becomes so sick the doctor on staff fears she might lose him. With no phone contact, and letters taking up to a month to arrive, we do not find out about his sickness until after he has fully recovered.

The school has a policy that children write to their parents every Sunday afternoon. The problem is that the postal system is so very slow. We receive only the first few letters they write during the term, and then the others arrive while the children are home for holidays.

Overall the children really enjoy their experience. They develop friendships that will prove very long-lasting. Rather than missing out on things back home, as friends in Australia suggested, their lives and experiences are greatly enriched.

***

Thirty-nine years later, Paul's friend Lee encourages us when he says, 'Graham, I want to commend you on all three of your children. They've turned out to be beautiful people with lovely hearts. You must have done something right.'

Thank you, Lord!

Trusting God for ourselves is one thing; letting go of our children and entrusting them to Him is another. But it has proved to us once again that 'God is faithful'.

Chapter 29
Protection and provision

Jumping over barriers and quickly pushing past obstructions, soldiers storm into the airport terminal. They catch us all by surprise and we freeze with fear. Like everyone else, we turn to try and discover what is happening.

'Leave the airport immediately! Everybody! Now!' the commanding officer shouts.

My heart is pounding and my knuckles tighten their grip on my bag. Moving closer to one of the soldiers, I plead, 'I'm concerned for my three young children. They're on their own because they're travelling unaccompanied. They've just checked in and are waiting for their flight.'

Unmoved, the soldier points to the door with his rifle and sharply commands, 'Outside!'

At the end of the school holidays, our children are flying back to Abidjan, the largest city in Cote d'Ivoire. Saying goodbye for three months is hard enough, but now fear overrides my feelings of grief.

In situations like this, we usually try to stay calm and keep talking while hoping to find a way through. But the soldier leaves us with no alternative.

I whisper to Marj, 'We'd better go. I have no idea what's happening, but we can't afford to antagonise him.'

'Do you think this is yet another coup?'

'Surely not! Yet if it isn't, what's it all about?'

We start to move towards the terminal doors. As we lose sight of the children, we anxiously pray for the Father to watch over them and protect them from any evil.

Outside the terminal, as the doors close behind us, a soldier orders us to line up on the footpath. We are completely puzzled about what is going on. Will the plane land? Will the children make it safely to Abidjan?

Terry Lobb, our co-worker, manages to work his way to the back of the crowd and get close to the soldiers guarding the doors. Chatting to them, he is reassured to hear, 'It's an exercise to round up the young men who continually harass passengers inside the terminal. We've had complaints of people being ripped off.'

Before long, we are allowed back inside. We joyfully reunite with the children, who are not as traumatised by the event as their parents. Later we see 25 boys being marched across the tarmac to the barracks. I am glad I am not in their shoes.

The children's plane takes off without further incident and we return to a very quiet house.

***

This 'round up' provides temporary relief at the airport from the pestering of these young boys. However, before too long they are at it again. Sometimes, even as we are driving into the airport, they jump onto the back of our double cab pick-up to ensure they are the ones we choose to 'guard' our vehicle. We find it is better to pay a token amount than to offend them and risk damage to our vehicle.

On one occasion, as we are about to leave the airport, I am suspicious and look underneath the car. There I find the point of a spark plug jammed under our rear tyre. Had I not checked before reversing, the tyre would probably have burst.

***

J.J. Rawlings' first coup is on June 4, 1979. He allows planned civilian elections to take place, and in September hands over to Dr Hilla Limann with a warning that his government will be held accountable for its actions. Unhappy with Limann's performance, Rawlings stages another coup in 1981 and takes Ghana into a period of military rule that extends through the 1980s.

The country's economic woes continue. When Rawlings first tries to control rampant inflation by forcing shop owners to sell at government-controlled prices, many bury their merchandise in the bush and later sell it on the black market. The country's main export, cocoa, is smuggled across the border and sold for much higher prices in Cote d'Ivoire, limiting the export revenue coming in to fuel Ghana's economy.

The country struggles to meet payments for overseas goods and services. A Ghana Airways passenger jet is left stranded in London because there is no money to buy fuel for its return journey. Food imports drop dramatically and local prices remain very high.

Apart from keeping chickens and rabbits for meat, the only other options we have to beat the poor exchange rates are to purchase food items from the foreign currency shop in the capital, Accra, or to travel over the border to shop in neighbouring countries. The foreign currency shop, although located in Ghana, only sells to people with foreign currency, which it uses to import more goods. The problem is that it keeps only limited stock, and definitely not everything we need.

A shopping trip over the border is not a simple matter in these days before credit cards. We need to plan well in advance and arrange for money to be sent from Australia to a bank in the country where we plan to shop—changing currencies with local traders is both illegal and open to exploitation. As well, we need to obtain a Ghana exit visa, a re-entry visa, a visa for the country we are going to, an international driver's licence, an international vehicle permit and international car insurance! With limited communication options, it all takes at least two months to arrange.

We live 400 kilometres from the capital where all these things have to be organised, so it means we can only go shopping every three or four months. On these trips, we usually purchase goods in bulk for ourselves and such items for others on our team as our limited foreign currency allows.

***

Later, when on home assignment, we buy clothes in various sizes for our children for the next four years. At one shop, the woman at the checkout looks at the pile of underwear, clothes and shoes and asks Marj, 'How many children do you have?'

When we share about these challenges of daily life, people often ask, 'How can you live there and put up with that?'

We explain, 'Our focus is not on what we have or don't have. Our priority is to follow the path God is leading us on. Tomorrow is God's concern; He promises to provide what we need each day and tells us not to worry about the future. We take Him at His word. Worrying about it doesn't help one iota. In fact, we find that every problem is an opportunity for God to show His greatness.'

I sometimes ask people, 'What does buying bread from your local bakery or supermarket do to stretch your faith?' Bemused by the question, they usually reply, 'Very little; it's just a matter of choosing which variety to buy.'

With that as an introduction, we love to tell them about the time God provided our daily bread in Ghana.

Each afternoon, we as a team gather for a short time to pray for one another and for WECers worldwide. On one particular day, we discover that we have all come to the end of our flour supply. Bread is not sold in the town and since we do not have the necessary permits, we cannot go elsewhere to buy flour. Together, we praise the Lord and tell Him of particular needs, including flour. We trust Him to do what He did for the Psalmist and 'provide a table in the wilderness'.

The next day, prior to our scheduled morning contact via two-way radio with other WECers, we receive a message from SIL workers who share the same frequency as us. 'We've received an allocation of flour and after distributing it to our workers we still have one large 50 kg sack left. Does anyone in WEC need flour?'

You cannot imagine how we rejoice in this loving provision! As far as we know, it has never happened before. The morning after we prayed so specifically, our heavenly Father has literally provided our 'daily bread'. Rather than being a huge problem, running out of flour becomes another opportunity for God to demonstrate how faithful and creative He is.

Worry and anxiety put me on a downward spiral; resting and trusting lead to nuggets of treasure like this answer to prayer.

***

Years before, I decided to take God at His word when He said, 'Seek Me first ... and all the things you need will be taken care of' (Matthew 6:33, paraphrased). I didn't know then what the future would hold and how many times I would need to cling to this promise. Now, I experience profound joy and gratitude as I see God's miracles happening in everyday life.

Chapter 30
Hospital, hernia and hen's eggs

Kumasi, Ghana
1982

Start with a hernia, throw in extreme drought and rampant inflation, add a devalued Ghanaian Cedi and crippling shortages of food, stir in cheap government services and mix with two and a half dozen eggs. Let them bake together in 33° tropical heat and humidity for five days. Apply these ingredients to a man in hospital desperate to be stitched up, watched over by an anxious wife. The finished product is an extraordinary and never to be repeated experience. I hope!

***

Ghana is in the throes of a terrible drought—the worst that any of my friends can remember. There are acute food shortages right across West Africa.

The Nigerian government is pressured by its own suffering populace to expel 1.5 million Ghanaians. They have moved there because work and pay conditions are so much better. The Nigerian people start to take matters into their own hands. It is reported that angry mobs catch Ghanaians and put car tyres over their heads and set them alight. The government gives the Ghanaians a deadline of just two weeks to leave the country. Due to the abnormal demand, it is almost impossible for them to get transport home. Flights are booked out and convoys of battered vans snake their way across the intervening countries, clogging up the border crossings. It develops into a major crisis.

Finally, the Ghanaian government has to deploy some of its navy vessels to the Nigerian coast to bring its citizens home. Local newspapers show photos of thousands of people standing packed together on the decks of these vessels as they return to port.

Ghana is already in dire straits, and now it has no way of feeding the swollen population without overseas aid.

When we arrived in Ghana in 1972, the inflation rate was 10% per annum. The Cedi was C2.80 to US$1.00 or C20 on the black market. Now in 1982 inflation is 123% and the US dollar fetches C30 at bank rate and C120 on the black market. The economy is in freefall and no one seems to know how to turn the situation around. Now the drought and sudden increase in mouths to feed brings the country to rock bottom.

Our NGO does what we can to assist World Vision with the distribution of food aid in some of the towns and villages in the north. As the weeks go by, the shortage of local corn becomes desperate. This creates a major crisis for egg and poultry producers. It is almost impossible to get feed corn for their chickens, and consequently the cost of eggs soars dramatically.

***

I am in desperate need of a hernia operation. I had a couple of hernia repairs in Australia years ago, but now the pressure of too much lifting and straining in the agricultural work is more than my body can cope with. With our children in boarding school, finances are tight. We don't feel we can afford a trip outside the country to have the repair done.

We find a Ghanaian surgeon who has been trained in West Germany and he agrees to do it in the Kumasi public hospital. At the initial consultation, he tells me, 'As with most things, there is a shortage of medicines. I can do the operation, but you will need to obtain your own medical supplies before you come into hospital.'

We have heard horror stories of the power going off during operations and of operating theatres running out of oxygen, so Marj is concerned about me having it done locally. She only consents to the surgery when I agree to have it under local anaesthetic, where the risks of anything going wrong would be less.

A date for the operation is fixed. Needless to say, in addition to our preparations, we ask colleagues as well as family and friends back home to pray for a good outcome.

***

At the end of the school holidays, we make the long journey south to the capital Accra to put our children on the flight to Cote d'Ivoire. Marj and I walk out on the long viewing platform to wave them goodbye and watch as they board the plane. Once seated, they flash their window shades up and down—their usual signal to show us where they are seated. We give them one final wave goodbye.

The walk out along the platform and back is a struggle for me. I have to keep my hand firmly pressing on my hernia to hold things in place. It does not look good, though it's good for my pride! I make it back to the car and we travel four hours to Kumasi.

***

On the Monday of the operation, I fast and go in early to prepare. Marj stays with me until the nurses come to take me to theatre. Just after we say our goodbyes, suddenly a nurse runs after her without saying anything to me. She tells Marj apologetically, 'The surgeon has not come in today as he has not returned from holidays. Your husband can stay and wait until next Monday, or go home and come back.'

'I'll go home, thank you.' *That is the easiest decision I have ever made!* I am not sure how I will endure the pain and discomfort for another seven days, but anything is better than an extra week in hospital here.

The following Monday I return, and as I prepare, the nurse tells me, 'We have just received a new supply of medicine. You can leave yours in the bedside locker.'

'Well, things must be looking up,' I reply. I leave my supply of painkillers in the locker as instructed, relieved that the op is finally going to happen.

Down in theatre, the surgeon asks, 'Where are your medicines?'

'I was told I didn't need them now.'

'That is unfortunate,' he states bluntly. 'We will have to make do with what we have.'

The operation begins. I am dopey but fully conscious. As he makes the incision I am aware of a dull sensation like a knife cutting a block of wood, but I feel no pain. The surgeon places a tray of instruments on my legs, which, unlike my arms, are not restrained. As he stretches the opening to gain access, there is a sudden sharp burst of pain. My legs involuntarily shoot up in the air, sending the instruments flying in every direction. They administer more medication and the operation continues. As he is sewing me up at the end, I clench my teeth and feel my body tense in anticipation of pain, but it is bearable.

When Marj comes to see me in recovery, she is shocked. I do not need to tell her it has been a harrowing experience. The trauma of seeing how drained and wiped out I am results in her having a full blown case of malaria. I feel worse for her than I do for myself.

***

I remain in hospital for four days. One evening I am woken by a large cockroach crawling over my face. The next morning I notice that a vitamin capsule left uncovered in the top drawer of my bedside cupboard has tiny holes in it. Jokingly I tell the nurse on duty, 'I know where the cockroach gets all his energy from.'

Having a sense of humour and making light of the situation is more therapeutic than complaining about things. However, laughter for me just now is painful and not necessarily the best medicine!

When it comes time to pay, the amount I am charged is the same as the current price of thirty eggs. 'Am I hearing right? Five days in hospital with food provided, a hernia operation and accompanying medicines—all for the same cost as thirty eggs?' That is unbelievable! Where else in the world could I get a deal like that?

Not only is it very cheap, but it gives me yet another story to tell. Everything heals well. The end result is good, and I am thankful for God's protection over me. I know people at home are praying for me. I will have to take it easy for a while, but there are still many things I can do to help the church leaders.

Chapter 31
ECG on the move

'Well, what do you think?' Thirty pairs of eyes turn and look directly at me. Instead of giving my own answer, I reply with another question—two in fact. 'We all know the Bible doesn't talk about whether it's okay to marry under a mango tree, so what biblical and cultural principles do you think are relevant to this question? And how will any decision we make impact on the lives of the couple concerned?'

***

Two hundred years ago, missionaries were often accused of bringing their home culture with the gospel message. Local people often referred to Christianity as the 'white man's religion'. They viewed it as an imported set of practices that had little relevance to their daily life and struggles. These days, cross-cultural workers study subjects such as cultural anthropology and cross-cultural communication in a bid to make sure the gospel is shared in ways that are culturally relevant and personally applicable.

The issues are different for each culture. In Ghana, these are some of the dilemmas that come up for discussion:

- Is it OK to use xylophones in Sunday worship?
- Do we need to agree on what dances are allowed in the church?
- What about those tunes and instruments associated with spirit worship? They can stir up memories and feelings that may not be helpful, or may even be problematical for some new converts.
- What is suitable dress for a Christian wedding in northern Ghana?
- Should those who are under church discipline be encouraged to attend church but asked to sit in the back row?
- Who can be married in the church? And if someone does not

have a good testimony or is known to be living in sin, should they still be allowed to be married in the church? If not, what about marrying them under the mango tree at the front of the church property?

These are real questions faced by our church leaders across the country. What biblical principles and passages of Scripture can help make a clear path through the multitude of practices and traditional beliefs of the different language groups? Working through them is not always easy or straightforward. Sometimes emotions run high as we are all passionate about our own cultures.

***

In 1940, WEC's first missionaries to Ghana arrived after around 100 years work by other missions in the south of the country. They focused on the largely unevangelised northern region, in line with WEC's policy of going to unreached areas. In the years since then, many small churches have been started in rural areas across the country. The pioneers tried to avoid transferring church culture from home and encouraged the local church leaders to find culturally appropriate ways of worship and Christian practice.

In 1977, the WEC mission encouraged our Ghanaian church leaders to establish an official organisational and unifying link between the churches. They formed a denomination, with their own elected leadership and constitution, and chose the name Evangelical Church of Ghana (ECG).

At first there were tensions as the two organisations adjusted to operating as equals following the ECG's inauguration. Later, with more experience, a greater understanding of each other and leaders intent on cultivating a good working partnership, God's blessing became apparent.

The mission remains committed to a working partnership with the church and to supporting its leadership as best we can. Structurally, this involves missionaries being members of the church and attending church regional conferences while the ECG leadership attends WEC annual conferences and committee meetings. It is a healthy partnership.

***

Marj and I work for a number of years with the churches in the Kpandai area. Our main role is to teach, mentor leaders and encourage church members to be more involved in evangelism and not rely so much on missionaries to do the outreach.

During our first home assignment, we purchase a Gestetner duplicator and a modern typewriter with a view to establishing a bi-monthly newspaper for ECG churches. Our prayer is that the church will be 'On the Move' with the gospel and that becomes the title. The aim is to motivate us all to keep moving forward. The various editions encourage each of the ECG churches to set goals, which will help us all focus our prayers and evangelistic efforts. Testimonies are printed telling of God's blessing in various areas of the country. This is a real inspiration and motivates individuals and whole churches to desire growth—both numerically and in depth of walking with God.

Pastor Samuel Apeligaba shares how the church in Lungni has set a goal of ten new believers for the year. They reach it by July. Encouraged, they trust for another ten by the end of the year. They reach that too. Other churches read in the broadsheet what they are achieving and say, 'If they can do it, so can we.' Testimonies of an increase in the number of people coming to Christ start to flow in.

The Tuna Area Youth, on the western side of the country, compose a song, 'ECG on the Move'. For the first time, the church as a whole starts to be excited about this move of God, which they are experiencing as never before.

***

Due to a shortage of qualified missionary personnel in the Tuna area, I am asked to make regular supervisory trips there. This is primarily to check on their agricultural project, but it also gives me contact with the pastors in the area. I begin to sense that God is opening up a wider area of ministry to me, but in what capacity I have no idea. I do not see myself as a conference speaker and can't think of any other way it could happen.

I begin to see the Lord's plan and how He has been training me when the WEC Ghana field conference appoints us deputy field leaders. With the field leaders on home assignment, I have the opportunity to develop more in-depth relationships with the ECG leaders. This interaction grows even more after Marj and I become the field leaders. It is a joy and privilege to fellowship with church leaders across the country, to encourage them and to have input in the formative days of ECG. I am part of a committee set up to revise the initial constitution and produce a pastor's handbook. This will guide the leaders in the responsibilities of church leadership and help answer some of the pressing issues and questions of church life.

***

For the first time, ECG church leaders from across Ghana meet together and begin to examine the church's policy concerning the various cultural practices used in worship and church life in different areas of the country.

With members coming from a large number of people groups, it ensures there are many lively discussions. At times they have difficulty reaching agreement on some points and the debates are lengthy. The church leaders are intentional in agreeing on a biblical approach to each of these practices. The aim is not to prescribe a list of do's and don'ts but to have guidelines that will provide a biblical framework to assist the growing churches. The results of these discussions form the basis of the new pastor's handbook.

***

We also exhort the pastors to prayerfully consider moving from rural areas to the cities to establish churches there. We are losing our best young people when they move to the cities for education, training and employment.

It is a request they wrestle with. The pastors' salaries are insufficient to feed their families; thus, they are heavily dependent on their farms to support them. Moving to the city would be a huge challenge. Understandably, many find it too difficult to contemplate.

I thank God for the humble, godly Ghanaian pastors and leaders who are faithfully continuing the work of extending God's kingdom. They are a great blessing and encouragement to me. I value their friendship. It is not possible for me to name them all, but I do want to acknowledge two with whom I have enjoyed strategic cooperation in ministry: John Kipo Mahama and Samuel Apeligaba.

My partnerships with these two men flourished when Marj and I moved to Tamale, the capital of Northern Region, and into a daunting new role.

GHANA: THE TAMALE YEARS
(1984 - 1989)

Pastor Samuel and Miriam Apeligaba

Baptism of Dagomba man
Pastor Peter and Pastor Samuel

Chapter 32
New move, new ministry

Tamale, Northern Ghana
1983–1986

It is election time for the WEC Ghana field, when field members will elect new leaders for the next three years. We are travelling south to our annual conference where the elections will take place. On the way we meet up with colleagues Terry and Reta Lobb. We have barely greeted them when Terry surprises us with a proposition.

'Hey Graham, we think you and Marj should become our new field leaders. Can we nominate you?'

The question catches me off guard and I respond with a gut reaction. 'Whoa, hold on, Terry! We appreciate your confidence in us, but we can't take on anything else. We already feel we're too busy and don't have the time we'd like to give to people. We're struggling to cope with the pressure as it is.'

During the conference, the same question is raised again, and our response is a very definite 'no!' The regional director, Alastair Kennedy, who is chairing the meeting, encourages us to at least allow the field members to discuss the possibility. I reply, 'We have no problem with you talking about it, but the fact remains we are too busy and are already handling too much—we need less responsibility, not more.'

Alastair asks us to leave the room while they discuss options. For the next four hours, including a lunch break, we are left wondering what is happening. We should have been called back in long ago. Our questions are met with smiles rather than words. As the hours pass, we have a niggling sense that God is indeed asking us to take on the leadership.

Finally we are called in and given the news.

'Don't be worried that we spent all this time talking about you,'

Alastair assures us. 'We quickly and unanimously sensed from God that you're to be the next field leaders. We've spent all this time trying to work out how we can help you hand over your present responsibilities and take on leadership. Although we have no clear answers, we're asking you to become the field's first full-time leaders. To ensure you're free for leadership responsibilities, we're asking you to move to Tamale. It will be more central to all the workers. We'll pray with you to find the right people to hand over your present responsibilities to, and we'll help however we can. We do accept that you can't continue with your present responsibilities and leadership as well.'

This is an enormous challenge. The old feelings of inadequacy surface; I wonder how we will be able to help others while we are still trying to find our own way in ministry. My view of leaders as people who have it all together suffers a reality check. I am now one of them.

Leadership responsibilities begin as soon as the conference ends. The handover happens on the way home, when we pick up the filing cabinet with all the official files. We still have our existing responsibilities and need to find suitable people to take them over. Added to that, we will need to make frequent trips to Tamale to find a place to live.

The longer term plans are fine, but it's the interim challenges that weigh on me. Everyone else returns to their home and work and we are left with this huge burden. *Here we are again, Lord, out of our depth. We can't do this, but we trust that You can.* We are reminded once again of the words, 'The task ahead of you is never as great as the power behind you.'

***

Country-wide economic constraints limit the availability of cement. Consequently, with very few new houses built in recent years, there is a housing shortage. After looking in Tamale for six months without success, we are finally able to move into another missionary couple's home for six months while they are away on home leave.

Despite constant searching, we are unsuccessful in finding suitable property. Then one morning we hear the couple has arrived back in the country. Our neighbours, hearing of our plight, kindly agree to share their home with us while we continue searching.

Within a month a Ghanaian doctor comes to our door. 'I heard you are looking for a house to rent,' he says. 'Is that right?'

'Yes,' I reply. 'We've been looking for months. Do you have some news for us?'

'The organisation I work for is building me a house as an incentive for me to stay on. Many doctors are leaving the country for better pay in other countries. It is an investment in my future, so I am looking for an expatriate couple who will take good care of it for me.'

'Well, this is an answer to our prayers,' Marj and I chorus.

Amazingly, this house has all the features our family, including the children, have been trusting God for. Our number one desire is for a good water supply. Much of Tamale does not have piped water. Houses that do, like the one we are staying in temporarily, receive water in the pipes for about four hours every week or ten days. When it comes, day or night, we all have to fill containers and use it sparingly so it will last until the next supply.

In our new role we will need to host new missionary personnel for a month's orientation and care for visitors from time to time. It is essential we have a good water supply.

'Well, I am happy to tell you'—the doctor can't keep the smile off his face—'this house has one of the best water supplies in the city. We are connected to the main pipeline to the military barracks!'

With both parties keen, an agreement is reached quickly.

***

The first person I want to honour is Pastor John Kipo Mahama. Our time of leadership coincides with the ECG appointment of Pastor John to the position of general secretary. I work very closely with John and grow to love and appreciate him.

We are both invited to attend the international leader's conference in Kilkreggan, Scotland, in 1984. Here John gains a deeper insight into the way the mission functions, and the struggles and challenges missionaries face. It forms a sound basis for a good working relationship.

John is a Gonja and comes from the chief's clan. His father and mother both passed away by the time he was 14, so he spent his teenage years living on the WEC compound in Damongo. He gave his life to Christ and devoted himself to serving the Lord. He assisted our colleague Jeanette Zwart in compiling a Gonja primer and then the translation of the Gonja New Testament. His understanding of Scripture and his experience as a pastor in a local church equip him well to help ECG through many issues faced by the developing church.

Working with John is a privilege, and much credit is due to him for the great improvement in church/mission relationships. The easing of tensions makes it so much more pleasurable for us all as we work together in partnership.

***

This unity, combined with the church's fervour, an influx of new missionaries, and new mission strategies, results in the rapid growth of the church. It is truly harvest time. We are greatly assisted and challenged by the work of our colleague Ross Campbell and the Ghana Evangelism Committee's National Church Survey. This highlights the fact that many northerners are now living in the south of the country. Because of cultural differences, they are not being reached by the large southern churches.

The survey, together with a challenge from Patrick Johnstone, WEC's international director of research, to focus on specific unreached people groups, helps us as a team, and ultimately ECG, to embrace a new Ghana-wide strategy. Rather than focusing only on the northern region of the country, we begin to minister to northern peoples wherever they live. Together we aim at planting a string of churches along the main road north from Accra to Bolgatanga.

***

ECG begins to embrace the challenge of moving into the cities, and Pastor Samuel Apeligaba and his wife take a great step of faith in moving to Tamale around the same time that we move. I have already referred to Samuel as the pastor of the Lungni church; he is the second person I want to honour.

Before I knew him, Samuel lived in the north of Ghana in the traditional homelands of his people, the Frafra. He travelled south seeking work and found it with two missionary families, assisting them in their homes. During this time he learned to speak English.

I first met him when he was training as a pastor at the Kpandai Bible School. Despite having no formal education, he proved to be a gifted evangelist with an amazing ability to get alongside people and share the relevance of the power of God to their daily lives and struggles. After graduating as a pastor, he mentored many men in his various churches. Both his wife and daughter suffer from sickle cell anaemia, making them much more prone to serious attacks of malaria. Despite their own struggles as a family, they have a huge capacity to reach out to others with God's love. Their joy and enthusiasm are infectious and touch many lives.

When our family moves to Tamale, Pastor Samuel shares with us that he feels God is calling him to go too. He is the first ECG pastor to take up the challenge to move into a city.

He and his family endure many testing times, and although we support them where possible, they are careful not to be dependent on us but to rely on God for their needs. We know what it is like to trust God for His provision, but we have never got to the point they have of sitting down for breakfast one morning without anything to eat. Samuel leads the family in prayer and tells their Heavenly Father that they still trust Him and know He is faithful. Before long a Muslim neighbour, unaware of their situation, gives them some food left over from a gathering the night before.

It is not easy for Samuel's family initially. They live in rooms in a compound shared with people of another faith. Later we have the joy of seeing money come in for the building of a pastor's house close by. It is so encouraging to see Ghanaian pastors living in dependence on God as Marj and I chose to do so many years ago.

One day while we are still living in the missionary couple's home, three Dagomba men ride in on their bicycles to see us. 'We have heard you are missionaries. We are looking for someone to come and teach us God's word. Will you come?' they ask.

As our brief is to be full-time leaders, we consult the field committee first. They agree that we should at least explore this amazing opportunity.

We find the villagers enthusiastic and responsive, and our small team starts a regular outreach. What an open door! We recognise God's higher plans and rejoice in the wonderful way He has prepared their hearts to receive the 'good news'. The Dagomba are a people group that most people put in the 'too hard basket'.

***

We carry our excitement with us as we return for home assignment. It is 1986, and we are well aware that when we go back to Ghana it will be for just three more years. The children will then need to return to Australia to complete their education.

Chapter 33
Finishing well

Tamale, Northern Ghana
1987–1989

We arrive back in Ghana for our final three years, wondering what they will hold for us. Having this limited period in view adds an extra sense of urgency to all we do. There are many opportunities; there is so much we could do. What are the priorities? What does God want us to concentrate on in these next three years?

***

Reaching the Dagomba people is our goal. Our leadership responsibilities continue, but we now have a small team to assist us in church planting, so we set out to survey additional towns and villages to ascertain where there may be openings. Past attempts to reach them have met with a lot of resistance.

To our surprise, we find the people very open. They are keen for us to promote Dagbane literacy classes and to teach the Bible. One Muslim chief tells us, 'I am the area chief over 72 villages and I give you freedom to teach in any one of them.' This is an incredible opportunity—God given!

But where are the workers? Our small team cannot take on much more. With a government quota restriction on each mission organisation, we cannot allocate many new missionaries to join in this outreach to Dagomba people, as the Field has goals to reach other people groups as well. Each team will need to have a small number of missionaries working together with ECG workers and local Christians.

Those of us involved in the Dagomba ministry begin monthly training days. New believers from our church plants who show leadership potential are invited to come and learn. We provide them with resources, which they can then use to teach others. Eventually

Pastor Peter Nseakyure joins Pastor Samuel and me. Then new workers from Korea, Shin Chul and Sung Sook Lee, begin learning Dagbane and eventually take over responsibility for the work.

***

Despite taking regular malarial prophylaxis, I continue to have frequent bouts of malaria. The parasites are developing immunity to the treatment, so we keep changing medicines in an effort to find a better solution. In the end I have to revert to using quinine to rid my body of the disease. This is quite drastic and leaves me debilitated and wrung out, the way a severe bout of the flu would. It seems at times as if the cure is worse than the sickness.

I am mindful that our time in Ghana is limited and am disturbed to notice my workaholic tendency coming to the fore. I place a greater emphasis on doing rather than being. Ultimately, this causes me to lose my sense of balance in life, something that not only affects me but also impacts negatively on those around me. God draws my attention to this fact during the malarial attacks when I am flat on my back and more ready to listen.

For me the first sign of malaria is during the daily afternoon cold shower. Although we now have running water, we don't have a hot water system. Most days a cold shower is refreshing, but when Marj can hear my chattering teeth and the groans and shivering noises from the next room, she does not have to be told another batch of malaria parasites is trying to squeeze the life out of me.

The fevers tend to increase late afternoon and evening, and the curative treatment takes time to have an effect. When the fever abates, my body feels like I have been battered and bruised in a boxing match. After two days, as the symptoms dissipate, I am left weakened and drained of energy. But on the third and fourth days, as I regain strength, my mind is alert and I am able to spend time thinking, praying and seeking God's direction for the coming months. Often I come out of these times with creative ideas and plans to pass on to our team.

These attacks are not enjoyable, but God often uses the down times free from activity to communicate with me. As Scripture says, 'God causes everything to work together for the good of those who love God and are called according to his purpose for them' (Romans 8:28 NLT).

***

The Ghana field has reached a new zenith. Our ministries are bathed in prayer; we have clear goals and a new focus on unreached people groups. God blesses the team with a new influx of workers. We now number 35 missionaries from thirteen different nations. There is a wonderful sense of unity and a clear sense of purpose. New workers spend their orientation with us, visit Dagomba outreaches and become increasingly excited at the prospect of beginning ministries among other unreached peoples.

It is definitely 'harvest time' in Ghana. The years the pioneers invested are bearing fruit. We are reaping what they have sown. The 1988 publication of the Northern Regional Church/Evangelism Survey confirms this. In the period 1977–1986, the Evangelical Church of Ghana grew by 159%—a cause for much praise.[1]

One of the keys has been the strong sense of unity and cooperation between church and mission. Pastor John Kipo Mahama, the general secretary during our last term, is now the ECG president. A wise and godly man, John has a lovely way of being firm when highlighting inconsistencies in mission practice. He is bold when challenging us to consider alternatives and yet humble enough to listen to the opinions of others and open to correction. He is a wonderful servant of God and a great model for the younger pastors.

Even with the exciting growth taking place, the full National Church Survey released in 1989 reveals that there are still 15,000 unchurched towns and villages in the country.[2] This highlights the fact that two million unreached northern people are living in southern Ghana and three million in the northern regions. This provides even greater motivation for ECG and WEC to work in partnership. Their greatest desire is to see churches multiplying and for these people to have the opportunity of hearing of God's love for them.

***

It is 1989 and we will soon be returning to Australia. Towards the end of our time, we hand over leadership to the first non-Western field leaders in WEC worldwide, P.M. John and his wife, Wabangla. A committed and gifted couple from India, they come to us via the UK sending base.

Our daughter Julie has a head start on the rest of the family. She is living for a year with my parents in Adelaide while doing her final year of high school. Paul and Merilyn will complete their education in Adelaide and, together with Julie, seek God's pathway for their lives.

After almost 18 years in Ghana, we leave with mixed feelings. We are amazed and humbled by the ways in which God has empowered us and equipped us for each task and role we have been given. He has stretched us in leadership roles beyond what we thought possible. In the natural, I would have run from these, preferring to follow rather than lead.

As we reflect on the journey, we are blown away by all that God has done in and through us. Our faith has grown stronger and more resilient. We are more convinced than ever that living in total dependence on God is the way to experience God's greatness first hand. We are sorry to be leaving behind so many friends, both Ghanaian and missionary, but we are sure that the work is in good hands.

***

Years after we leave the field, we hear that an ECG training and conference centre has been established close to Tamale in the north and a national headquarters built in Accra. The church has continued to grow and has expanded into other regions of the country, planting churches in many of the main cities. It has taken over management of the Kpandai Health Centre, established local schools and a computer training school.

ECG has embraced the vision of becoming a truly national church. By 2013, according to figures supplied by the General Overseer, Pastor Daniel Gbande, the church had grown to 10 districts with 300 churches and preaching points attended by 18,676 people, who were cared for by 69 pastors and church planters. God is building His church!

***

As our time in Ghana draws to a close, we write to inform the WEC Australia leaders that we plan to be based in Adelaide on our return. We feel right about locating where the children can once again attend Southern Vales Christian Community School. The staff and students there have been such a blessing to our family on each home assignment; to finish their schooling there, would provide our children with the least re-entry stress possible.

Having lived outside Australia for so long, the prospect of a more permanent re-entry is daunting. Added to that is the uncertainty as to what we will do. We are still keen to be involved with WEC but don't know if there are any options open to us in Adelaide. We ask if they have any advice or suggestions for us.

SOUTH AUSTRALIA
(1990–1995)

Graham and Marj, Merilyn, Paul and Julie

Graham, 2 helpers, Kevin and Rodney

Chapter 34
New property

Adelaide, South Australia
1990

The 1990s stretch out before us like a huge blank canvas. At times I wish we could see around the next corner, but it's not to be. The chorus of an old hymn throws light on the next step: 'Trust and obey, for there's no other way, to be happy in Jesus, but to trust and obey.' Trusting our future into God's hands takes the worry out of the question 'What will we do next?'

We know it is right for us to return to South Australia. I would love to continue in mission, but I am aware that there are limited positions available at home. If that door is closed to me, I will need to go back into secular work and try to find a job. Prospects for doing that are not great with Australia facing a dramatic rise in unemployment and on the brink of 'the recession we had to have'.

***

A letter arrives inviting us to become the South Australian WEC directors. We had no inkling the present directors were thinking of leaving.

We share our thoughts and feelings in a letter back to the leaders in Sydney. 'We are open to discussing this possibility, but we have some concerns. We feel that the present HQ is too far out of the city, and local involvement with WEC has declined in recent years. Really we need to find a new location more accessible to the majority of the Christian public. Such a move could form part of a new thrust to rebuild interest in WEC. Another concern is more personal. If we live in the present HQ location it will not be possible for our children to attend their normal school, and that is one of the essential elements in deciding what we will do.'

We are given three months for readjustment, medical examinations, relating to family and reconnecting with our church and friends. During this time we talk with our GP about a dark patch which has been growing on my left cheek. It had concerned Marj in Ghana, but typically I had delayed doing anything about it until I got home. The GP, with a sense of urgency, pushed to get me booked in with a plastic surgeon as soon as possible.

"Would you mind if I take some photos?" The surgeon asked. "I haven't seen a skin cancer as developed as this for some time so I would like to show my students". As he snaps away, I start to wonder if I should have listened to my wife's concerns and made it a priority. "We will need to get this cut out immediately".

"I had to go deep to make sure I got it all, and put a skin graft to cover the hole. Thankfully it wasn't as developed as I first thought". The surgeon reassures me. "However, it was a Stage-4 melanoma so we will need to check regularly to ensure there is no reoccurrance".

***

The HQ at Stirling in the Adelaide Hills has been a wonderful provision of God for many years and has served its purpose well. Now the leaders agree with us that it is time for change and a fresh start, but they warn us there are no extra funds available at present. So even before our official three-month rest period ends, we begin contacting real estate agents to explore alternative possibilities.

In view of the unusual design of the HQ, an auction is advised and arranged. But it attracts very little interest. Now what do we do?

Once again we are cast upon the Lord. We are so thankful for the help and encouragement of the local WEC council. These men and women, all volunteers, are mature in their walk with Christ, active in their churches and experienced in many different aspects of work and ministry. They all have a desire to contribute to God's kingdom purposes. They are very supportive of us and willing to help where they can. With no extra funds available, we agree that we need to sell the present property for enough to cover the purchase of a new property and all the agent's fees and government taxes involved in both buying and selling. Our experience years before of seeing God provide a house for us reassures us that this challenge is not too big for God.

We agree with the real estate agents on what we feel is a fair price for the property. We encourage friends in South Australia to pray with us both for its sale and for another suitable property to become available. We are looking within a particular area south of the Adelaide city area, large enough for a HQ and within our price range. Fitting all the pieces together at just the right time is yet another opportunity for God to show His goodness and greatness.

***

After three months of rest, Marj and I assume responsibility for the WEC work, and I begin commuting from our own home to the office in Stirling each day. There are a few enquiries about the property, but none of them progress further than that. Likewise our attempts to locate a suitable alternative HQ are not promising. It looks like we might have to purchase two adjoining properties to meet our needs.

Then comes the breakthrough. One weekend, looking through the real estate section of the daily newspaper, I notice a property with 16 rooms, five toilets and three bathrooms. Just reading the advertisement I sense this is the property God has for us. On inspection we are even more excited, as down stairs as well as room for an office, there is an area that is suitable for our regular public meetings. Upstairs there is room to accommodate our family and visiting missionaries as well! We try not to let our enthusiasm show.

Council members agree on its suitability, and we are able to negotiate a good price as well as a 90-day settlement, which will allow time for the sale of the existing property. Not only are the price and size right, but the property is located just inside the southern boundary of the area we were interested in. From here our children will be able to travel to their school easily. Encouraged by this very specific answer to prayer, our friends continue praying with us for the sale of the original HQ at a suitable price.

***

Pressure mounts as time flies by and we start to get a bit anxious. We are beginning to wonder what is happening when the phone rings.

The agent has received a cash offer. It is for $5000 less than we were asking but with settlement in just 14 days. Interest rates are currently high and we realise that after the sale we can invest the total amount received and, by the time we need to pay for our new property, earn $5000 interest. A sold sticker goes up on the For Sale sign out the front of the house.

Elated and with no time to waste, we work hard to pack up the office and equipment. The owners of the property we are buying are very happy to hear the news, and allow us to store equipment and furniture in a shed on the new property.

On settlement day, there are sufficient funds to cover all costs, with a small amount left over. This small amount is enough for us to make an alteration. It provides a better entry for public meetings and eliminates the need to walk through the whole house to get to the meeting area. MMM (Mobile Mission Maintenance), a service mission that coordinates volunteer tradespeople, does the work for a donation. Once again our hearts are filled with praise as God does more than we could ask or think.

***

One hundred people cram into the new property for the Saturday dedication and official opening. The chatter and excitement among those gathered fills us with anticipation and hope for this new phase of ministry.

On Monday, after everyone has left and we knuckle down to the day-to-day challenges, we feel very much alone. After years of working with a team in Ghana, we find ourselves the only couple, so we really value Peggy Kingham's part-time help with finance and secretarial tasks. There are a million people and many churches in this city. Once again, we are in a place of having to depend on the Lord for His direction and enabling.

Chapter 35
The Bees are back!

Adelaide, South Australia
1990–1995

'We are not here to "hold the fort". We want to see an increasing number of South Australians reaching the world for Jesus Christ.' So we declare in a magazine article announcing our appointment as state directors for South Australia.[1]

***

'Marj, isn't it great to see God work in amazing ways?' My excitement bubbles over.

'For sure!' she replies. 'But now there's an even bigger challenge ahead of us. Seeing the property issues come together is one thing, but seeing God move in people's hearts is another.'

'I agree. So what do you think our goals should be?' I have been thinking and praying about this myself and have a few ideas. Together we need to nail down some specific targets that will help us to remain focused and to pray specifically.

Marj replies thoughtfully, 'Well, obviously our main work is to promote the challenge of the unfinished task.' She is talking about the fact that 2000 years ago Jesus gave us the 'great commission'—to go into all the world and make disciples. 'That's why WEC exists, and it's the primary reason why God has placed us here.'

'OK, so how's your faith? I suggest we trust God for two people from South Australia to move into missions each year. What do you think?'

'I think it may take a year or two to see it happen, but yes, let's pray and work towards that.'

Bouncing ideas off each other is part of the process of discerning

God's will, and agreement gives us greater confidence as we work toward those goals.

We are well aware that not everyone is called to go, and that not everyone who is called will actually go. As we begin to reintegrate into society and church in Australia, we are burdened by the fact that many, including Christians, seem to drift through life without any clear purpose. It seems they are only concerned about themselves and life here on earth.

Marj and I want to encourage people to view life differently— to gain a vision of God's kingdom purposes and His desire that we should be His representatives wherever we are, whatever we are doing. We believe that we can all be intentional in discovering what God is doing in the world and how we link into that. There is no sacred/secular line dividing the things we are involved in, so saying 'I haven't been called' is never an excuse for doing nothing.

***

As we have been overseas for most of the past 18 years, we rely on the WEC Council and friends for guidance in many areas. Their encouragement is a blessing to us personally as well as a strong point in the redevelopment of the work. They are a wonderful example of being God's people in the place He has positioned them.

'Well, here we are again, Marj, standing in the need of prayer.'

'Yes. We didn't realise how long it would take to adjust back into this culture, did we? So much has changed, and we've changed too'. Having a job to come back to and a continuing sense of purpose helps to minimise the stress and the adjustments involved in re-entry. Our children are benefitting by already having connections with friends at school. It still takes time but we are thankful that we are not unduly stressed. We'll have to break new ground and see what opportunities open up to us.'

'I know that prayer will be a priority if we are to see God work in new ways,' I continue. 'But I've also been thinking about God's question to Moses: "What is that in your hand?" '

A good number of retired missionaries and friends who have had strong connections with WEC over many years rally around us.

Now the HQ has shifted, they are within easy travelling distance. We invite them to join us one morning each week for concentrated prayer followed by lunch. With the produce from my new garden, we can easily provide a chunky vegetable soup.

These dear friends really know how to pray and are keen to learn all they can about the various missionaries and where they work. They form the foundation of the new season of WEC in South Australia. Over the years, we have remarked that, while missionaries are the ones in the spotlight, we will only know the true extent of the commitment and faithfulness of their many supporters when the full stories are revealed in heaven. We are so grateful for the many hundreds of people who have stood with us personally in various ways over the years, and who have so often been the channel of God's provision and blessing.

People like Don and Grace Jamieson, who printed and distributed our prayer letters for 18 years mostly in the days of manual typewriters, duplicators and hand addressed envelopes. The welcome mat was always out at their home for our family of five whenever we were in Sydney.

After concerted prayer, we set goals and use them as prayer targets for growth. We are also believing for an increase in the number of regular 'Prayer Forces' (prayer groups) and prayer chains that we would like to see established.

***

During the time we were in Ghana we experienced great support and encouragement from home staff. Now it is our opportunity to provide that care for those serving around the world.

We commit to writing each month to all the workers who joined WEC through the South Australian HQ. In addition to circulating their prayer needs and relating to their sending churches, we also hold occasional meetings for their families. This helps to establish a rapport so they feel free to approach us with their questions or fears in times of stress or political uncertainty. Many of their loved ones live and work in areas where they experience danger, loneliness and discouragement, and where communication is not always easy.

***

In the first few years we see significant growth in interest and in attendance at meetings, as well as in the various avenues for prayer. But we have to hang in for several years before we see the first new workers heading off for missionary training and service overseas.

Marj and I are active in promotional tours in various parts of the state. I travel widely, but Marj also takes a turn travelling to some areas while I stay at home with the children. There are also opportunities to speak and promote missions within the city of Adelaide.

We discover once again, as we did during our home assignments, that openness to missions has changed considerably since we first went to the field. No longer do churches seek to have missionary speakers in their pulpits. It is much more difficult for us to find opportunities for visiting missionaries to share in churches. Congregations expect their pastors to do most of the speaking. In terms of mission interest, many churches are concerned almost entirely with their own backyard rather than seeing the 'uttermost parts of the earth' as their responsibility too.

I am appointed chairperson of the South Australian 'Missions Interlink', and, together with other mission representatives, we do our best to promote missions around the state. Many people have the perception that mission organisations compete with one other, and to a certain extent we do 'fish in the same pool'. But we recognise that our primary aim is the extension of God's kingdom and are always glad to see people going out, no matter what mission they are connected with.

There are a large number and variety of mission organisations operating in Australia, and we are convinced there is a need for them all. But we are disappointed that some missions, while trying to promote their own organisation, denigrate the efforts of others. This can be particularly so when it comes to training and supporting national workers. Some promote the idea that this is the only way to go and that the day of missions is past—just send your money.

However, in many of the hard-to-reach places, there are not yet any local Christians to be trained, and others need someone to come alongside to encourage and equip them for the task. Many people will never hear unless someone leaves home and crosses cultures to tell them the good news. They need people to live among them and demonstrate in practical ways the love and power of God.

***

Much to my surprise, I am elected on to the newly formed WEC Australian Strategy and Personnel committee whose role is to assist the leaders in the oversight of all Australian workers. This has a side benefit of keeping me up to date with exciting things happening across Australia and around the WEC world. There is in turn a flow-on effect: the excitement and passion it arouses in our team enhances the local ministry too. This responsibility also expands my understanding of mission leadership and the sensitivity and care needed in handling personnel and the matters associated with them.

***

The world is changing and the way young people approach missionary service is changing accordingly. Many of today's young people prefer to have a short-term experience before committing to the longer term.

There can be many benefits in doing that. Moving out of one's comfort zone and into unfamiliar circumstances can help create a deeper dependence on God that enriches one's own life. Among other things, it can help those who go to better understand the long-term workers' needs and how to pray for them. The experience can also open their eyes to the needs and give them a vision to train and serve long term in missions themselves.

Feeling frustrated that our mission is not providing enough opportunities for short-term opportunities, I volunteer to lead a 'WEC Trek' to the Middle East as part of my mobilisation efforts. This will also widen my experience so that my promotional activities will have a broader background in addition to my years in Africa. Little do I realise what an emotional time this will be for me as well.

Chapter 36
Middle East bomb shelter

Jordan and the West Bank
1993

'Sorry, guys, but we only have two bedrooms vacant at present,' Kevin says with a smile. 'Rodney and Christine, you can have one, and Willy, you can have the other one in the nurse's quarters.'

'Hey! What about us? You're not leaving us out in the cold, are you?' I ask with mock indignation.

'You two come with me. Look over there across the field; you can sleep there.' Kevin is a bit of a joker, so I am not quite sure if he is being serious or not.

'Are you sure there's enough room for two?' I enquire a little facetiously. 'It doesn't look like it to me.'

'Oh, what you can see from here is just a covering to protect the entrance. You'll be sleeping underground!'

***

Planning the trek to the Middle East is made easier by the fact that we are initially heading to Jordan where my sister and brother-in-law, Val and Kevin McCallum, are working. Kevin is manager of a farm connected with a hospital for chest diseases.

The five of us on the team (not exactly young people) have two main aims: to get an insight into the life and culture of one area of the Middle East and to give some assistance to those working sacrificially and tirelessly to assist the local people. Despite our inexperience and lack of language, we hope that by giving some practical support, and even by our presence here, we will be an encouragement to the hospital staff.

Well, I never anticipated sleeping underground—in a bomb shelter! That is a shock to the system. There is just enough room for two beds and a simple bathroom. At least there is an electric bulb so we can see clearly and not fall down the stairs.

Kevin explains, 'This was built at the time of the Six-Day War in 1967. Fear, tension and uncertainty were high at the time. Who could predict how it would end and the areas that might be affected? It was wise to be as well prepared as they possibly could be.'

I share the shelter with the fifth member of our group, Mark. We feel safe though slightly claustrophobic—and a bit envious of the others in their 'five-star' accommodation (relatively speaking, that is!).

As a team we are very well looked after. The culture and the foods are vastly different from what I experienced in Africa. However, I thoroughly enjoy them and determine to make the most of this experience.

Enjoyment isn't really our aim, though. We are not in Jordan as tourists; we are here to serve. What we observe happening at this hospital impresses us. We appreciate the staff and form good friendships with them. They often go the proverbial 'second mile' as they provide assistance to the mainly Bedouin people.

Rodney, a good friend and the dentist on our trek team, has an eye for detail. He remarks one day, 'I've seen people being treated here from Syria, Saudi Arabia, Lebanon and Jordan.'

Obviously we are not the only ones impressed by what we see—word has spread to the surrounding countries. People are prepared to travel from near and far to get the help they so desperately need. TB and other diseases can ravage families and populations unless appropriate medications and support are given.

***

Our team's normal daily program commences with breakfast and prayer at 7.30 am before working from 8.30 am to 4 pm. We enjoy morning tea with local staff in gender groups. We observe closely the cultural differences and try to fit in as best we can. This interaction with locals is a highlight. We spend as much time as possible listening to stories of their backgrounds and experiences, and they in turn enjoy hearing us share something of our lives.

As evening approaches, we spend time visiting patients in the wards before they are served their evening meal. Our interaction is limited as we rely on interpreters, but people are generally welcoming and happy to see us. It is amazing how a smile can transcend cultural barriers.

Christine and Willy enjoy working in the dispensary making bandages from sheets and bottling and labelling tablets. Their efforts in the children's and babies wards are also greatly appreciated. We men get on with the real work—from our perspective, that is!

Our job is to convert a storeroom into a much-needed hospital ward. The large room previously stored bags of food aid, but hearing positive reports about the hospital, patient numbers are swelling. The room will have a more illustrious future once we have finished work on it. The main challenge for us is installing a drop ceiling and drilling into the concrete roof to support it. The drill bits are not good quality and blunt easily. That completed, we paint the room with the help of the two women.

Happy with the result, we men move back outdoors to dig trenches. Soon local workers will begin installing new pipes and irrigation pumps for the orchard.

***

We are amazed to hear accounts of how the hospital has developed. Two amazing single women had the vision, bravery and commitment to see it established in an area where that is normally a man's responsibility. The hospital plays a crucial role in the health care of thousands. They could use many more workers, so we keep beseeching the 'Lord of the harvest' to send more workers to this corner of the world.

All five of us thoroughly enjoy the whole experience. We learn much about Middle Eastern culture and develop a real appreciation for the workers here. At the same time, we learn lots personally as we face the challenge of working in a team; some of us had not met before we left Australia. As in any team, we have our unique and different personalities—some more different than others! It is a test of character and an opportunity in an unfamiliar location and unusual circumstances to prove God's enabling.

We have some good times of relaxing, too, roaming around the town, looking in the shops and observing the people and their lifestyle. We feel privileged to visit a local church and observe Christian worship, Arab-style. Christians anywhere in the Middle East face lots of opposition. Here they are a small minority in the face of the dominant religion. We admire their steadfastness and courage.

***

One night we stay out a bit late and return to the hospital grounds to find the gate locked. 'Watchman, are you there?' we call out repeatedly over the high fence. There is no sign of him at all. He is meant to be guarding the property.

There is only one thing to do—climb over. We feel like thieves on a night-time raid. I help the others over and then, as I am following up and over, a bright light flashes in my eyes. The honourable team leader is caught in the act.

I am the only one photographed and become the subject of some good-natured jokes. 'We'll show folks back home what you've been up to. We have irrefutable photographic evidence!'

***

A long drive south enables us to observe a permanent clinic outpost staffed by two nurses and an administrator. It does not have the same security as the hospital. Suspicion abounds. The local inhabitants wonder, 'Why are these medical people here?' False rumours fuel the community's suspicions, making it much more difficult for the clinic team to gain acceptance.

It is barren out here, and from the top of the escarpment where the clinic is located we can see the steep road winding its way down to the plains below. The Wadi Rum and the rail bridge filmed in the making of *Lawrence of Arabia* are a bit further on. We are amazed at how nomadic Bedouin people can survive out here, and we admire greatly the clinic workers who have chosen to live here in order to serve them.

***

Back at the hospital, work stops during the Easter period. We decide to take advantage of the break and cross over to the West Bank. We want to visit some of the biblical sites around Jerusalem.

Kevin, who has been there before, is our guide. His Arabic skills enable us to stay in the Arab quarter and to eat at their restaurants, which are much cheaper than those in the Jewish section. Travelling by bus and locally hired vehicles costs much less than organised tours.

We feel blessed to be in the Holy Land, particularly at Easter. However, the blatant idolatry saddens us. People have come from around the world to see, touch and kiss historical sites and icons. They almost worship the items that may or may not have been there at the time Jesus lived. We do not enjoy that aspect of our time here. For us, following Jesus is all about having a living personal relationship with Him—very different to being consumed by all the peripheral things associated with religion.

The most significant time for me is on Good Friday afternoon. Sitting across from what may have been the place of the skull, I reflect on Jesus' suffering and death on the cross. It is a deeply significant and emotional time, the impact of which will stay with me for years. On Resurrection morning, we gather near the Garden Tomb. It is 6.30, and although conditions are frosty, excitement and anticipation are evident on the faces of those gathered. With thousands of others, our voices crescendo in a wonderful time of worship in the place said to be the Garden of Gethsemane. From where we sit, we can see the Garden Tomb close by.

We appreciate the guides who tell us the unvarnished truth: 'This may have been where Jesus was buried. We can't be sure, but it would have been in a tomb like this.' Walking where Jesus walked and ministered is a humbling and meaningful experience. Knowing that He walks with us now and in the future gives us all fresh vision.

***

After completing our project in Jordan, three members of the trek team return to Australia. From the beginning, my dentist friend Rodney Ferry and I planned to stay on to help Kevin with an even more dangerous assignment.

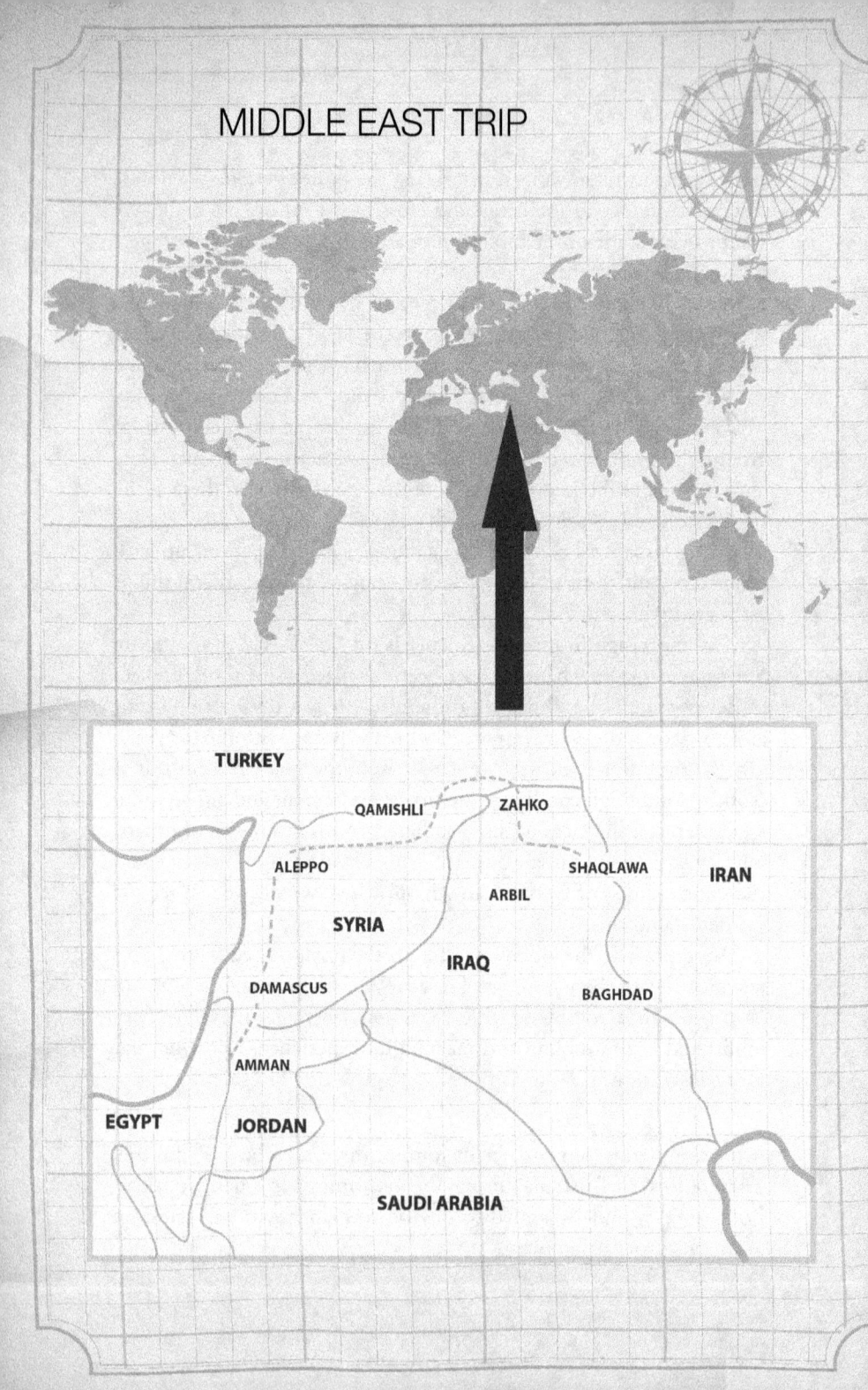

Chapter 37
Kalashnikovs, Kurds and land mines

Jordan, Syria, Kurdistan
1993

The men carry Kalashnikovs like women carry handbags. They pick them up every time they walk out the door. We want to see as much as possible in the short time available, but we have to be extra vigilant when taking public transport. Whenever the bus rounds a corner, everyone sways and sometimes, unintentionally, the guns end up pointing in our direction!

***

Graphic new details emerge about the Kurds as they often feature in world news. Saddam Hussein's shocking mistreatment of them has finally caught the attention of some US senators. For years these people without a homeland have pleaded for the world to take notice of Iraq's malevolent oppression. Their pleas have been largely ignored by the outside world.

Now, suddenly, the world is listening; they are aware of Kurdish suffering and appalled by this blatant persecution. International opposition to Saddam's activities is growing. In response, he prohibits people from travelling through southern Iraq into the Kurdish area in the north. Consequently, the degree of difficulty for our next assignment increases dramatically.

***

Our mission is to help Kevin transport his family's belongings to northern Iraq. Kevin, Val and their children are moving to work among the Kurds, but there is no easy way to get there. It is not possible to pass through Baghdad, nor is it feasible to have one vehicle take us all the way by a circuitous route. We will have to journey the hard way.

The McCallums pack all their belongings into suitcases and sacks that can be loaded and unloaded by hand. Schooling materials, bedding, cooking utensils, clothing and more needs to go, so we end up with 45 pieces of luggage to transport. Once we deliver their goods, the family can travel by a similar route, but without the hassles of luggage. Even then, it is a huge challenge for a young family to face in light of all that is happening in the region. Only those following God's clear call and direction would even contemplate this.

Kevin hires a good-sized truck for the first leg to Damascus. Early the next morning we load everything and set off. There are frustrating delays at the Syrian border. We have difficulty convincing customs officials that we are just taking this luggage through Syria. They suspect we might be importing it all to make a profit.

Unaware Kevin understands and speaks Arabic, the men say to each other, 'That's a likely story! They don't look like a normal family. What would three guys be doing with stuff like this? They'll probably sell it as soon as they get out of here.'

Initially, they request we pay a huge sum in US dollars as security, but we have legitimate concerns that the money will not be returned when we leave the other side of the country. We keep talking and in the end the three of us pool our resources and Kevin negotiates a reduced amount of US$974. In my experience, border crossings are very good places to increase the intensity of your praying—even when you know you are not doing anything wrong. This one is no exception.

Finally, we get through and make it safely to the Damascus railway station. In this ancient city we unload everything for the first time. We have to wait several hours, so we take the opportunity to stroll down Straight Street where the Apostle Paul walked long ago. We return to the station in time to load everything onto the train for the long overnight trip that will take us right through Syria.

From the rear looking forwards, the train looks like a huge snake as we wind our way alongside the Orontes River and pass through Aleppo. It is interesting to reflect on geography classes from years before when I studied this region of the world. On one side of the tracks there is barren desert while the lower side has lush green crops irrigated from the river and Lake Homs Dam, the oldest dam in the world.

To me this paints a vivid picture of the difference the Living Water of Christ makes in our lives. My heart cries out, *Lord, keep me from such dryness and barrenness. I long to be refreshed, productive and fruitful. Keep me drinking from the waters that never run dry.*

***

Early next morning, we arrive at the Qamishli railway station in northern Syria; that was the easy part. We unload everything again and negotiate for two small rickshaws (motorised three-wheeled vehicles). The bargaining over, we pile them up with all the luggage. With the three of us on board, the rickshaws career through the town to customs at the border with Turkey. The unusual sight of foreigners and so much luggage arouses much curiosity and draws quite a few stares.

Once again, we unload and carry all the luggage into the shed for inspection. Oh, what we would give for a drive-through customs shed! As the inspection begins, we earnestly pray we will not have to open every single piece. After selecting six pieces at random, the search convinces the officers that these are indeed used household items and personal belongings. We obtain clearance to go.

However, there is still a major issue that has us calling urgently on the Lord. The customs officials think of all the excuses why they cannot repay the security money that day: 'An official has already done the bank run today. The bank will be closing early afternoon.'

We are not prepared to take no for an answer. We keep talking and reasoning with them and explain the urgency of our plight.

Finally, Kevin overhears them say, 'These people won't pay us anything; we may as well give it to them.'

They send someone racing off on a motorbike to the bank in town. I am sure he has never had so much prayer covering in all his life! We hope and pray he makes it in time before the bank closes for the day. We certainly do not want to spend the night here; we've already been negotiating and waiting for eight hours as it is. We are greatly relieved when the officer returns with the money. He just made it to the bank in time.

We hurriedly carry the luggage out of the shed and load it again. Rejoicing in the Lord's goodness, we head for the border. There, we have to carry the cases and sacks across the no-man's-land bridge piece by piece. Just as well there are three of us. We take it in turns: one remains to guard the pile, one carries some across, and the other guards what we have already taken across.

From there, we arrange with two more small vehicles to take us to the Turkish customs just up the road. They have to clear us for entry. What a process this is! We unload, check, gain clearance and then reload for a short trip to the lorry parking area. Kevin negotiates with the driver of a large minibus to take us across Turkey to the border with northern Iraq.

We load everything yet again and set off. Our vehicle travels only a short distance before corrupt police officers looking for bribes order us to stop. They do their best to find something against the driver and vehicle. Noticing the foreign cargo, they think this is too good an opportunity to miss. We manage to talk our way out of handing over money to them. This delay at the end of the day means we will now have to race to arrive at the Iraqi border by 6 pm.

We make it by 6.15. 'Sorry, we are closed,' the border official tells us. 'We have already packed up for the night. Please come back tomorrow.'

Our best attempts at reasoning and our sense of urgency do nothing to change his mind. Dejectedly, we make our way back to the nearest town. It has been a long, tiring day and we didn't sleep all that well on the train. Now we need to find a hotel that will accommodate us together with our 45 pieces of luggage!

On the third try, we find one with accommodation upstairs and a lockable room downstairs. Once again, but at a much slower pace, we unload and carry everything inside. Walking through the bar to get to our rooms, we encounter a cloud of smoke—thick smoke. We try to stoop lower to avoid the worst of it, which is trapped by the ceiling. Anti-smoking advertising obviously hasn't reached here yet.

***

After a reasonable sleep, we decide that I will stay by the stuff while Kevin and Rodney cross over the border to locate friends with a vehicle in Zahko. After some hours and just as I am starting to get anxious, they return. It is time to load up again. This time we are able to drive across the border into Kurdistan in northern Iraq with the luggage and without unloading and reloading.

Thank you, Lord!

The rest of that day is spent looking around and arranging for the trip the following day. We hire two utility vehicles with armed guards. That evening we dine at a local restaurant where the danger in this part of the world is dramatically brought home to us. As we leave, our host checks under the vehicle for any bombs or dangerous devices before we get in and head home for the night.

The following morning we load everything again. We travel mainly on back roads and pass a huge, dark brick prison at Dohuk. Many Kurds have perished here at the hands of Saddam's men. Signs along the roadside warn of land mines, so we decide not to go mushrooming!

Travelling down through Kurdistan, we encounter many security checks. We have been advised that the easiest way through is to mention that we are journalists. There is some truth in this: we are coming to observe Kurdish suffering and plan to write several articles on our return as well as speak at many meetings highlighting their inhumane situation. So we feel justified in making that declaration. It seems to work. There is a warm acceptance of us and we pass through without undue delays.

Chatting at the checkpoints, we listen, observe and gain further insights into the suffering endured by the Kurds. The people are happy to receive anyone who can advertise their plight to the rest of the world. We hear first-hand reports of bombings and chemical attacks on Kurdish villages in mountain areas. In Halabja, 5000 civilians were killed. The Kurds hope international pressure will be brought to bear in order to relieve their oppression.

What a relief, after a long day's drive, to finally arrive at Shaqlawa. We are met by friendly faces. We unload everything at the English Language Centre, where it will be kept safe until the family's arrival. On final count, we have loaded and unloaded these 45 pieces of luggage 16 times!

Kevin warned us that the weather would be hot, so we did not bother bringing warm clothing. On the way, we notice in the distance that there is still snow on the mountains. The next morning we are freezing, but Kevin seems to be coping pretty well. We tease him mercilessly when we discover he has been able to get into his luggage and find his thermals!

***

We hear some terrible firsthand stories of suffering. A teenager turns up looking for medical help. He has one eye hanging out of its socket. We witness misery, destruction and injury all around, seeing man's inhumanity to man on a scale we did not believe possible. Many houses have been not just knocked down but pulverised into gravel by Saddam's bulldozers. We witness a public street auction of used furniture and clothing. Some desperate families are selling anything they can do without in order to buy food.

***

The United Nations has established a no-fly zone in the northern part of the country. We meet many Kurds and hear stories of their suffering while fighting in the mountains as part of the Peshmerga (freedom fighters). They live in constant fear of their men being captured and imprisoned by Saddam's forces.

We are also warned that Saddam has placed a bounty of US$10,000 on the heads of foreigners, so we are careful where we go, particularly when visiting towns close to the southern areas of the country. Saddam controls these areas and sometimes his men infiltrate the Kurdish area. It is encouraging to drive past one of the newly established premises of the Kurdistan Regional Government and realise some progress is being made.

It is a delight to observe significant differences between here and other parts of the Middle East. We drive past groups of Kurds celebrating picnics and special occasions with mixed gender dancing. The women always dress in spectacular brightly coloured dresses and the men wear their distinctively Kurdish outfits.

We develop a real appreciation for the Kurds and their struggle for recognition and freedom from persecution. As Christians, we are concerned that the 30 million Kurds should have normal human rights and freedoms, and the opportunity to hear of a God who loves them. He longs for them too to be present on that day when people from every nation, tongue and tribe worship before the throne in heaven.

***

Despite their struggles, the Kurds are a friendly, generous people and we are the recipients of warm hospitality. At one meal, Rodney and I struggle to swallow the thick goat's milk yoghurt. I slowly sip at it without making much headway. Rodney takes a different approach: hoping to please our hosts and not offend them in any way, he downs his in a few gulps. As the meal progresses, they take away my unfinished glass and refill Rodney's!

After commencing negotiations for a house for the family to rent, we leave others to finalise an agreement. We make the return journey to Jordan with much less effort and stress than the trip in. The way is now clear for Kevin, Val, Cara, Sam and Jenn to move across to Northern Iraq. The children can face the tiresome journey without all the hassles of handling luggage that we encountered.

***

Rodney and I return home to Adelaide with full hearts, our lives touched by all we have seen and experienced. After clearing customs, Rodney puts on a Kurdish cap he purchased and I don a wrap-around Kurdish headdress. Rodney, being taller and having a fairer complexion, easily stands out as an Australian. With a much darker complexion, swarthy from not shaving and wearing a black windproof jacket, I could pass for a Kurd.

Although I am right beside Rodney, Marj starts to worry. 'Where's Graham?' Her eyes keep searching for someone more familiar. She is so relieved when she finally realises it is me under the turban.

Once before, when speaking at a Greek Evangelical Church, people remarked, 'We thought you were Greek until you opened your mouth.' I seem to blend in with the locals pretty well in many places I go.

After our return, I have over twenty opportunities to share about the Kurds and the ministry that is seeking to demonstrate God's love to them. I usually end up quite emotional each time I share about the Kurdish suffering. This trip, along with another one I make later to Hong Kong and China with my daughter Julie, gives my presentation of the challenges and needs in world missions more credibility.

It is important in my current role, but even more so in helping to equip me for the bigger challenges ahead.

SYDNEY
(1995-2002)

Australian Leaders - 1996
Left: Marj, Graham, Helga Meinel, Pauline Pembridge

Korea - Byung Kook Yoo and Graham

Chapter 38
Bigger challenges ahead

Strathfield, Sydney
1995

The cloud is moving! As with the children of Israel, we feel God is moving us on. Our children have flown the nest, the work in South Australia is functioning well and there will be other workers who can take over from us. We are fit and well; the needs are great; why shouldn't we go?

***

Our plan has always been to return to Ghana after five years in South Australia. We anticipated that during that period our children would complete their education and be making their own way in life. They are well aware of this, and in the last eighteen months of our time in Adelaide, they move to Queensland one by one.

Julie works as a travel consultant in Adelaide but the office there closes and the company offers a transfer to the Gold Coast. Paul finds employment in a plastics manufacturing factory, and three weeks after he enquires about the possibility of a transfer to the Gold Coast, a position close by in South Brisbane opens up for him. Merilyn, meanwhile, tries to gain experience in customer service with a view to becoming a flight attendant, but can only find infrequent opportunities. Eventually, with the encouragement of her siblings, she moves to the Gold Coast and finds greater opportunities there.

Now they are independent of us and there is nothing to prevent us from returning to Ghana.

***

We remind the WEC Australian leadership of our original intentions and that we are beginning to think about a return to Africa. They will need to find replacements for us here in South Australia.

At a strategy and personnel meeting in Sydney, Australian director Trevor Kallmier takes me aside and says, 'Jen and I are not standing for re-election as Australian directors at the end of this term. We think you guys are the "first cab off the rank".'

I am blown away by the fact that they would even consider us, let alone ask us to follow on from them. I assure Trevor our heart's desire is to return to Ghana.

Wisely, he suggests, 'Why don't you pray and ask God about it?'

On my return to Adelaide, I share this proposition with Marj. Within a week she gains a sense that this is right and is God's plan for us. I am still struggling with the old feelings of inferiority and inadequacy. Besides, this will mean a definite closure to ministry in Africa where life was fulfilling and enriching.

After learning the language and adjusting to the culture and living conditions, it now seems such a waste not to return to ministry there. What about the rich friendships we formed there? And the spiritual lessons we learnt through the tough years of struggle? Our experience would be valuable in encouraging and helping new workers become established. On a human level, it just doesn't make sense. It seems so often that when a person does well in a role, they are placed in a position of leadership and can no longer do the things they have done so well!

***

Usually, when I look to God for guidance, I keep moving forward confidently with the assurance that in His time He will direct my path. His direction generally comes through a quiet witness in my heart that 'this is the way; walk in it'. Just now, however, it doesn't seem so easy to know which path to follow, especially as the challenges we face are way beyond my own abilities. No, this time I will need to hear God's voice even more clearly before I am prepared to take this new role on.

In my times with the Lord each day, I am reading through the book of Isaiah. Although God has spoken to me through Isaiah in the past, nothing I read now seems to speak to me at all. I begin to feel that perhaps I am right—that Sydney is not for us and we should go back to Ghana. Then one morning I turn the page and read in chapter 40 verses 21 and 22: 'Don't you know? Haven't you heard? God created the world ... He rules the earth ... He spreads out the heavens ... He brings down rulers' (paraphrased).

Slowly I see the bigger picture. Even though I doubt my ability, this should not be my primary concern. God is far greater than I am, and He is more than able to help me in the challenges ahead. I went through this same kind of struggle years ago. I confess that I am slow to learn, just as the Israelites were. The question is, will I trust Him now?

The next morning the Father's patient and loving encouragement comes as I read in Isaiah 41:9–10: 'I took you from the ends of the earth ... You are my servant; I have chosen you ... So do not fear, for I am with you; do not be dismayed, for I am your God. I will strengthen you and help you; I will uphold you with my righteous right hand' (NIV).

I'm sorry, Lord, that I've made this decision more about me and whether or not I'm able or capable rather than resting in your power and promises. I'm willing to live in dependence on you, trusting that you know best. Thank you that as I step out of my comfort zone you will prove you are indeed a great and awesome God.

We write and confirm our willingness, if elected, to take on the new task, confident that 'for this we have Jesus.'

***

The Australian WEC Conference unanimously elects us as incoming directors and appoints replacements for us in South Australia. We spend three full but happy weeks in the Australian Office with Trevor and Jen Kallmier, Helga Meinel and Pauline Pembridge. They do their best to cover everything we will need to know. My brain is struggling to retain all the details and I am so thankful that Helga and Pauline will be staying on in their current roles. They will be an immense help as we settle in to the job.

In March 1995, we pack up all our possessions and move across the continent to Sydney. We were prepared to serve the Lord far from our grown children, but now that we are moving to Sydney, we will be just 800 kilometres from where they are living in Queensland. We are overjoyed. We have missed not having them close by. Sometimes, in the course of our regular ministry, we will be able to visit them, and at other times they will be able to come to us in Sydney. Just another one of the Father's loving gifts that He delights to give His children.

***

Our time in South Australia has worked out better than we could ever have imagined, and we leave Adelaide grateful for all those who joined with us and contributed to rebuilding the work. Now we feel like 'the new kids on the block', but knowing clearly that this is where God wants us encourages us as we join the team in Sydney.

Chapter 39
Here to make a difference

Sydney
1995–2002

It is never easy to swim against the flow. As a child I never had much opportunity to develop swimming skills, so I struggle to make headway if there is a strong current. In life though, once I know what God's will is, I have always been ready for a challenge. My desire has always been to live above the level of mediocrity and to resist the temptation to drift and go with the flow. Thankfully, it is not a case of struggling, as with my swimming, but of using the gifts and resources I have been given and persevering.

***

Marj and I share very openly with Australian WECers that we are not in Sydney to fill a position but, with God's help, to make a difference. We do not see ourselves speaking at conventions as leaders who challenge and motivate people for missions in a large public speaking capacity. Prayer and building relationships are the keys for us.

With a little research we discover that the number of Australians serving with WEC Australia, both in Australia and internationally, has remained almost the same over the last ten years at around 245.[1] In the six years between 1989 and 1995, our numbers increased by just four workers. In the same period, WEC worldwide grew by 23%. In a climate where many local churches are placing less emphasis on the overseas missionary task, to see any growth is a challenge.

We feel that the only way growth can happen is if we mobilise people to pray. After all, Jesus told us to 'pray the Lord of the harvest that *He* will send out workers'.

Some of the challenges we face are summarised in the handbook for WEC Prayer Forces in 1996:

Australia has become one of the most multicultural nations on earth. Cultural diversity has brought with it changes in values, beliefs and behaviours. Most of us welcome the variety we now have in foods, restaurants etc.; however, there are less popular effects on our Australian identity and way of life. Pressure is constantly being placed on Australian authorities from special interest groups, both secular and religious, to have a voice in Australian society. This affects the uniqueness of the Christian message in the eyes of the general populace, devaluing it significantly. Christianity is now seen as just one of the major world religions. To talk of Jesus being the only way to the Father, and the Way, the Truth and the Life, is perceived by many as being intolerant.

On the positive side, multiculturalism has brought with it the growth of many ethnic churches. We still need to take the Gospel to the unreached in the furthest places of the earth, but God is bringing these unreached people to our own doorstep.

Although the major interdenominational Bible colleges are full, many mission societies are struggling to recruit new workers. Young people are passionate and ready to take an active part in global evangelism, but most of this is for short-term experience.[2]

***

We begin our new role with 241 Australians serving with WEC internationally. After much prayer, we propose to the Australian staff that we adopt the slogan/prayer target '301 by 2001'. This is a simple but challenging faith target that our workers and supporters can easily remember.

After discussion and prayer at our annual conference, this is agreed to and together we begin to pray, trust and work towards achieving the goal. We commit to pray for 15 new Australian missionary candidates each year to be accepted as career workers with WEC. We set faith targets for growth in the number of Prayer Forces and prayer chains as well. As a mission, we have a very strong constituency in the various states of Australia. Our desire is to build on this so that we encourage and facilitate their active involvement with us.

We embrace WEC's core value that prayer is a priority. We become more intentional in our mobilisation efforts and our workers see unprecedented interest as we go into churches, university groups and Bible colleges. We recognise that our nation has been blessed with much. By sending out workers, we can be a blessing to others.

Through the faithful work of earlier Australian WECers and the generosity of God's people, a strong network of state headquarters was established across the country. Many graduates of Worldview in Tasmania are joining WEC. We sense a strong bond of unity in our team, and in answer to our prayers our numbers begin to grow—slowly at first, but then with greater momentum. We are on track to reach our goal. Other mission leaders involved in Missions Interlink begin to ring up asking how we are managing to grow when they are finding it difficult to recruit new workers.

One factor in our favour is highlighted by Dr Kath Donovan and Ruth Myors in a survey of 1,398 Australian missionaries from 34 different societies.[3] In a private summary of responses from WEC missionaries, they inform us that WEC has the lowest attrition rate. They attribute this to the strong bond new workers develop with our organisation through the longer than average orientation period (four months). Retaining long-term workers is as important as attracting and recruiting new workers. Making them feel cared for, appreciated and supported is strongly embraced by the staff in each state base—very much a team effort. We feel God's blessing and favour resting on us.

***

In nearly every location we have served, we have seen God at work wonderfully providing new buildings, and Sydney is no exception.

WEC owns a smaller property adjacent to the main HQ in Strathfield. The dilapidated old house is now barely habitable. It is in such poor condition, we joke that in the next big storm the wind might relocate the family living in it to the next suburb.

There is a pressing need for new accommodation. But we have only $76,000 that we can put towards it.

Remembering Hudson Taylor's statement that 'God's work done in God's way will never lack God's supply', we arrange with a Christian builder to take on the project. He estimates it will cost $245,000 for a main house with a smaller self-contained unit attached. This plan will provide not only replacement accommodation for the family but also badly needed accommodation for an additional couple.

The builder understands WEC's faith policy and accepts that we will pay as God provides. However, as it is a business agreement, we agree on a date for final settlement and handover.

No pressure! Well, there shouldn't be. But as work progresses, we are anxious at times as bills become due and we have no idea how they will be met.

Our faith feels like it is stretched to the limit; we can do nothing but rest in the Father's promise that He will provide. And wonderfully, God does provide through some generous donations. During this period, the mission receives three very timely estate gifts from long-time supporters of WEC. I do not know of any other time when this has happened.

The task of mobilisation and member care of our workers continues. As the building nears completion, Marj and I need to make a visit to Western Australia. Having a great staff team to handle mission affairs and oversight of the building while we are away is a blessing. It enables us to give ourselves fully to those we are visiting.

On our return, we enquire how finances are going. We are aware the final deadline is approaching. All along, we have invited people to pray with us for God's provision, but never mentioned the amount involved or appealed to people to give towards the project. Yet our treasurer, Rhonda Sallaway, informs us of another large gift—enough to cover the remaining $23,450.

Once again, Jehovah-Jireh, our provider, confirms that when we are prepared to step out in faith in dependence on Him and His promises, He will provide. There is great rejoicing when the final amount is paid with a week to spare. Seeing God at work, Australian WECers, together with friends and supporters, are encouraged to keep trusting God—in the little things and the big things.

During these years, the Lord wonderfully provides a property in Launceston to be used as a Tasmanian HQ (separate from the Worldview training centre) and funds for the building of a large education block at Worldview. The current principals, Ron and Margery Perschky, are instrumental in seeing this dream accomplished.

***

As leaders of the second largest sending base within the WEC structure, we also have the privilege of being members of WEC's International Coordinating Council and Leaders Council. We have regular correspondence with other leaders and attend meetings in various parts of the world. Because of distance and expense, we usually combine these trips with visits either before or after the meetings to encourage Aussie WECers in their places of ministry.

On one trip we are able to make a return visit to Ghana and speak at the opening of a permanent building for Tamale Central Church, which Samuel and I commenced years before. Three hundred people are present!

In the periods between meetings, we are required to give input into decisions that affect the progress of the work internationally, including decisions regarding the opening of new fields. On behalf of WEC Australia, I accept responsibility for supporting a new initiative in Korea.

I am constantly amazed at the way God continues to use me, a quiet farmer from the Adelaide Hills. Years ago, all of this would have been way beyond me, but now, with God's enabling, I am even enjoying the privilege.

Chapter 40
Amazing Korea

Seoul, South Korea
1997

'Byung Kook, there must be a mistake,' I call through the doorway. It is Sunday morning and we are getting ready for church. 'These are not my trousers. Maybe mine got mixed up with yours.'

'Let me see,' he says, examining them closely. 'It is true they are not yours, but they are not mine either!'

Bemused by the confusion, we both chuckle and wonder.

***

I am in Korea as part of my responsibility as Australian director. Byung Kook Yoo and his wife, BoIn, are the newly appointed leaders of WEC Korea. My role is to assist them and the new WEC Korean board in whatever way I can—to advise and empower the new sending base to function like our other sending bases.

During the week, I travel by train to visit several cities and renew fellowship with Shin Chul and Sung Sook Lee, friends and colleagues from Ghana days. Knowing I am to preach on Sunday morning, I leave my suit trousers in the wardrobe so that they will not be creased by the train journey. Now, reaching for my trousers, I discover the ones hanging there are different from the ones I left!

Byung Kook says with a smile, 'I can't understand this. They are Korean trousers but they are too small for me as well.'

'Well, if they won't fit you, they certainly won't fit me,' I reply, patting my stomach.

We ponder the strange predicament with great amusement.

'How is this possible? What could have happened?'

'More to the point, where are my trousers now? I have to get ready.'

Just then the phone rings. Dr Ok InYoung, chairman of the WEC board in Korea, wants to confirm the time he will pick me up. Byung Kook chuckles as he shares our dilemma.

'Don't worry; I will look after him,' Dr Ok responds reassuringly.

But curiosity won't let us rest and we are still laughing and speculating when Dr Ok arrives. The only possible explanation we can think of is that an older relative, doing the housework and wanting to be helpful, took my trousers to the dry cleaners. Mistakenly, she may have brought the wrong ones back.

'It is time to go,' Dr Ok says, looking at his watch.

Aware that Koreans dress impeccably for church, I am very conscious of my mismatched trousers and coat. On the way we converse comfortably and he tells me not to worry.

After the service, we chat briefly with some church members, and then Dr Ok indicates that we need to be on our way. He parks outside a department store and hurries me inside.

Looking at the racks of suits, he asks, 'Which colour do you prefer and what size do you wear?' Once I decide on the colour and size, we sit and wait patiently while staff cut the trousers to the right length and sew up the cuffs. By the time they finish, other shop assistants are standing by the door anxiously looking at us—it is closing time. We apologise and hurry out the door, but suddenly they call us back. 'We have a special deal going at present,' they explain, 'and because you have spent over the required amount, you can choose a small suitcase for free!'

It has been quite a morning. Thanks to Dr Ok's kindness and generosity, I now have a new suit, a new case and a good story to tell friends back home.

Each time our paths cross, Byung Kook and I have another good laugh. But the answer to the question, 'Whatever happened to my trousers?' remains a mystery. I secretly wonder if there is a man somewhere in Seoul eating a lot of fast food so he can fit into them!

***

This is my first time in Korea and there is so much for me to experience and learn. Some of the things that strike me are:

- Flying in at night to the amazing sight of red neon crosses on top of every building where there is a church.
- Huge blocks of accommodation units, which all look the same in size and height but are identified by their numbers—up to 150 or more in one area alone.
- The density of the population and the fact that it is 98% ethnic Korean. I am from Australia, the second most multicultural nation in the world. No wonder Koreans find adjusting to an international mission a challenge. Their preparedness to learn English and make the effort to equip themselves for future ministry causes me to admire and respect them even more.
- Discovering the mind-blowing fact that there are more than 100 different Presbyterian denominations in Korea.
- Taking a short drive to one of the Prayer Mountains, where we view the hundreds of small cubicles where people go to pray and be alone with the Lord. It is humbling for me to witness their ardent dedication to God.
- Hearing about their 4.30 am prayer meetings, as well as long work hours. This reflects the commitment of Christian men, but I wonder how they fit in time for their families.
- Their generosity and warm-hearted hospitality, which we can definitely learn from.

One outstanding experience is attending Sarang Community Church in Seoul. Just getting into the church grounds is like trying to go against the flow of traffic after a football match. The parking attendants are essential in helping us find a place to park. By the time we enter, five minutes before starting time, the sanctuary is already full and we are ushered into an overflow room where we watch proceedings on the big screen. They have seven services every Sunday attended by a total of 10,000 people. I have never seen anything like it.

How will I describe the experience when I am back in Australia? It feels like a foretaste of heaven. It is a privilege to preach in my new suit at the English afternoon service, where I am encouraged by people's responsiveness.

***

For quite some time, it has been the desire of our mission to set up a sending base in Korea. A few people thought we had 'missed the boat' since some organisations are already established and recruiting workers. But God's timing is always right, so we trust for His guidance and wait patiently for the right people to head up a Korean base.

In 1996, the WEC leadership feel the timing is right and approach an experienced couple: Byung Kook and BoIn Yoo. They agree to finalise their ministry in the Gambia and return to Korea to lead this new ministry. WEC Australia is asked to be the sponsoring sending base to help them become established—hence my involvement.

The Yoos return to Korea in early 1997 and my first visit is in March. I am met by Byung Kook and Chul Hee Choi, a company CEO and leader of the founding committee, which has been meeting regularly to prepare for launching WEC in Korea. I meet with the committee and explain more about how WEC functions and guide them in various aspects of operating a sending base. Apart from the Yoos, I am their first contact with WEC.

I am amazed to hear that even before the Yoos arrived back in Korea, the committee had been meeting monthly and making regular donations from their own resources. On their return, Byung Kook and BoIn were presented with a large sum of money to use as a bond in renting accommodation. In Korea, a bond is given to the landlord to invest while the tenant has the use of the residence. When the agreement ends, the tenant is refunded the money, which can then be used to invest in the next property.

It is amazing for me to witness firsthand the excitement and commitment of these people to see WEC up and running in Korea. Having a committed group of people like this is a wonderful blessing for this fledgling work.

***

The new sending base is officially launched on June 5, 1997, just as the Asian financial crisis hits. Replacing the founding committee, a board is appointed with Dr Ok InYoung as chairperson.

The Yoos are well-respected and many doors open for them.

Not many Koreans have been able to integrate into an international mission and remain on the field for ten years or more, as they have. As we would say in cricketing terms, they have the 'runs on the board'. Returning to Korea was a sacrifice for them. They loved their time in Africa and developed good relationships with the Gambians. The emotional effect of leaving is still weighing heavily on BoIn.

Despite the cost to themselves and the loss they feel, they willingly throw themselves into the work with a conviction that this is God's will for the next phase of their lives. In a sensitive environment, they tread carefully to ensure that WEC Korea is not linked to any particular denomination and that the mission is accepted as being truly interdenominational.

***

It doesn't take long before committed, well-trained Koreans are lining up to join WEC. I visit again in 1998 and guide the board regarding the requirements for new applicants, as well as interviewing and processing procedures.

The Yoos visit Australia and the USA to observe functioning sending bases. They make the most of these opportunities abroad to minister to Koreans resident in those countries. Now Koreans from other countries are keen to join as well.

God honours the Yoos' commitment and hard work. The rate of growth of this sending base is unbelievable—within 15 years Korea becomes the largest sending base and there are more Korean workers on WEC fields than any other nationality. Typical of their commitment to Jesus and the missionary mandate, Chul Hee Choi (aged 57) and his wife Hye Sook, along with Dr Ok InYoung (aged 66) and his wife Myung Ae, later resign their jobs and join WEC.

***

With my interest in Korea truly aroused, I discover back in Sydney that more than 100 Korean churches exist in the city. We develop links with some of them. A Korean Olympic gold medallist comes for candidate training with us, and as she walks from the WEC base to the train station at Strathfield, many of the residents and shop owners acknowledge her presence and fame by bowing.

A large number of Koreans have moved to Australia. There is now a substantial Korean community on our own back doorstep!

Not only the eyes of Koreans but the eyes of the whole world are focused on Sydney as the year 2000 approaches. As a team, we discuss the ramifications for us and how we might benefit from the strategic location of our centre.

Chapter 41
The winner is Sydney!

2000

'And the winner is … Sydney!'

Sydney has been abuzz with excitement ever since it was named host city for the 2000 Olympics in 1993. However, as the event approaches, many locals decide they will leave town during the event to escape the traffic congestion and noise.

WEC, on the other hand, seeks to capitalise on the fact that we are strategically located close to the railway line and barely ten minutes from the Olympic Stadium at Homebush.

***

At the WEC base in Sydney, there is quite a lot of extra accommodation normally used for Candidate Orientation and visitors. With the upcoming Olympics on our doorstep, the Sydney team decides to liaise with the Olympic organising committee on how we might use our facilities to take advantage of this opportunity. One thought is that we could host overseas support staff, with the possibility of building bridges of friendship with them.

In the end, we are allocated a group of Australian trainee chefs who will assist in the catering department at the athletes' village. One of them turns out to be the son of a family I met while on my first deputation tour in Port Lincoln.

We enjoy the contacts and they appreciate getting to know us too. The income we make from the agreement is sufficient to purchase new beds and mattresses for each room and to repaint the whole heritage-listed building before they arrive. With paint peeling in places it has badly needed a makeover for some time. Building maintenance was neglected for a while as we investigated a possible relocation. We made the decision to stay, and we are grateful for that decision now.

God's creative way of providing for us this time is to have the world's biggest sporting event in our neighbourhood! I am sure many others in Sydney also benefit from what the IOC President called 'the best Olympic Games ever'.

***

At the same time, we have a number of situations for which solutions are not immediately evident. Some of these concern personnel needs.

Helga Meinel has been assistant director for years and stayed on when we became directors. One day she shares with us that she feels God is calling her to the Middle East. A traditional response would have been, 'We'll pray in a replacement, and when they are here you will be free to move.' In this situation, however, we realise that if Helga doesn't go soon, there will not be much point in her tackling Arabic language study. We release her to go when she feels the time is right while we make approaches to fill her position.

The next couple of years are challenging as we cope as best we can with various staff shortages. Several people are approached but after prayer decide this is not the right time or place for them. Other team members, including Pauline Pembridge and Warren Griffin, are gracious in shouldering extra responsibilities to help us through this period. Finally Terry and Diana Freeman, who are working in Asia, agree to assist us, but it will be some time before they are free to come. Just knowing help is on the way is a relief in itself.

Being understaffed certainly keeps us in a position of dependence on God. We need His strength and wisdom daily as we cope with the regular program of overseeing staff and assisting with the training of candidates and pastoral care of workers, as well as our international responsibilities. The number of Aussies in WEC continues to grow so that by the end of 2000 there are 293—well within sight of our '301 by 2001' goal.

***

In April 2000, Marj and I fly to the USA to attend the International Coordinating Council meetings. We arrange to travel to a number of countries afterwards to visit Aussie WECers in their fields of service.

During the meetings, Marj has a sudden, unusual and unexplainable physical feeling in her body. But it only happens once and seems to pass. Her strength returns to normal after a few days.

The particular type of round-the-world air ticket we have enables us to travel to the various countries we want to visit while returning to a hub several times. By the time we reach India, our last stopover, we are both very tired. In addition to visiting members of our organisation, we are delighted to spend time with our daughter Julie, who is in Delhi for a period of two years with a like-minded group. We spend the first few days visiting projects and seeing some of the tourist attractions.

Then, very quickly, Marj becomes seriously ill. She is weak and needs to rest, but she encourages me to continue sightseeing with Julie. We are very concerned for her and pray, trusting God to strengthen her for the long flight back to Australia in a few days' time. Thankfully, she regains some strength and we are able to make the journey home.

On our return to Sydney, we have only a few days before we are due to fly to Tasmania to lead the annual Australian staff conference. Our doctor agrees with us that it appears Marj has a very serious case of dysentery or some similar condition. He arranges for further tests and to our dismay informs us Marj is not well enough to travel. The tests will take some time, so Marj encourages me to stick to our original plan to go to Tasmania. She assures me there are others who can help look after her during my absence.

In my heart, I am very concerned for her. I have never seen my dear wife so sick and weak. Reluctantly, I head for Tasmania.

Chapter 42
The dreaded C word

Mention 'the C word' and most people know you are talking about cancer. Marj and I discussed years ago what we would do if either of us contracted it. We have a surety of heaven and look forward to being in Jesus' presence for all eternity. We both desire that over chemotherapy with its harsh side effects.

***

The conference in Tasmania is going well and I am feeling 'carried'—in the arms of the Father and by the prayers of so many. Marj is in my thoughts and prayers continually. Each phone call we share, she reminds me of the Lord's great faithfulness and encourages me to press on with my responsibilities.

Towards the end of the conference she phones to say the test results have come back. She has secondary cancer. This comes like a 'bolt out of the blue'. However, she assures me that our doctor still thinks the symptoms are consistent with amoebic dysentery and has asked pathology to redo the tests.

As planned, I stay on for a couple of days after the conference for some interviews and debriefing sessions with workers. The day before I am to travel back to Sydney, Marj phones to say the results of the second tests are in and they confirm she definitely has cancer.

I am stunned by this diagnosis. Thankfully, I am able to change to an earlier flight home, and a few hours later we embrace emotionally.

After a biopsy, the oncologist shares the diagnosis with us. 'We are not sure where the primary is, but Marj has an aggressive secondary sarcoma of the liver.' We are both devastated.

Having discussed such a possibility long before this, we share with the doctor our response. 'We are Christians, and we've agreed that neither of us will undergo chemotherapy if it is ever recommended.

We're sure of going to heaven, so we see no reason to prolong our time here, especially if it means diminished quality of life.'

He listens attentively, then replies, 'I understand that. But I'd like to suggest an alternative option. There's only a 30–40% chance that chemo will help, so I recommend that Marj has three doses three weeks apart. After that, scans will show if it is having any positive effect. If there is no improvement, the chemo will be stopped and we'll accept there is nothing further we can do.'

We feel right about proceeding on this basis.

The chemotherapy causes Marj to be very sick, with constant nausea and weakness. Her hair comes out in clumps, adding emotional stress to the physical symptoms. Despite enduring all of this, the chemo has no positive effect, so it is stopped.

We look forward to Marj's recovery from its effects and trust she will enjoy improved health in the immediate future. However, it soon becomes obvious that her heart, which was deemed to be strong before the chemo, has suffered damage. Now she is unable to go anywhere or do anything without being connected by a long plastic tube to an oxygen bottle.

Julie comes back from India to help care for Marj at home. It is an enormous blessing to have her with us and to have an extra pair of hands. My office is just next door from our unit, so I am able to keep working each day. The many cards, letters and emails Marj receives lift her spirits and remind her she is loved and appreciated.

***

Marj's heart problems necessitate a couple of emergency trips to hospital by ambulance, and she has several blood transfusions to help rebuild her strength. Her well-being fluctuates from day to day and sometimes even from hour to hour. Medical personnel assure us that we are doing a good job of caring for her at home, with assistance from a palliative care nurse who visits regularly. Marj would not receive such personalised care if she were admitted to hospital.

One day in the midst of all of this, she asks, 'Graham, it is clear where I'm going. I want you to answer me: would you think of getting remarried?'

I am stunned by her question—such a notion has not entered my head. 'Darling, I'm here to love and care for you,' I assure her. 'I'm not thinking about what lies ahead. I know my future is in God's hands.'

She persists and presses me for an answer, so I respond hesitantly, 'Well, at 54, I guess guys my age would probably consider it. But I wouldn't want to get remarried just because I was lonely. I know some men whose marriage the second time around didn't work out so well. I would only consider it if I had a clear sense that it was God's will for me.'

Marj then astounds me by saying, 'I think Becky would be a nice wife for you!'

Meryl Beckman—'Becky' to us all—is part of WEC's strategy and personnel committee and we have worked closely with her, meeting for three days every three or four months. She lives in Tasmania and is on the faculty of the now renamed Worldview Centre for Intercultural Studies. Over the years, Marj and Becky have become good friends and prayer partners.

Marj and I do not discuss this again, but her suggestion is filed away in my mind to ponder at another time. It was obviously not an idle comment and I need to consider it prayerfully. Right now, however, handling work responsibilities, caring for Marj and keeping friends and family informed of developments is all I can cope with.

***

Although the Sydney 2000 Olympics are in full swing, I decide not to attend any events as I do not want to enjoy the excitement alone, knowing Marj is so sick and cannot attend. However, one day when Julie has already gone to the stadium with friends, Marj answers the phone. It is my brother Greg, offering me a ticket to go the track and field events that evening.

She tells him she knows that I would love to go and phones me in the office to inform me. I have to rush to get ready and meet Greg, but we are comfortably seated among a record 112,000 people in time to see Australia's Cathy Freeman burst through the finish line to win the 400-metres gold medal. It is a highlight for the whole of Australia, and for me in the midst of a very heartbreaking and tiring time.

***

WEC colleagues and friends from Narwee Baptist Church surround us with their love and care; through visits and gifts these dear ones do all they possibly can to support us. As Marj's strength diminishes, she asks me to limit the number of people who come. Although she greatly appreciates their concern, even short visits become exhausting for her.

We receive a host of suggestions from people about diets, programs and even a machine that others have found helpful. Many assure us they are praying, and some indicate they believe she is going to be healed. I pray that she will be, and this is certainly what I desire. *Lord Jesus, I firmly believe that you can heal Marj, if it is your will to do so. Help me to understand what your will is.*

One morning in my daily Bible reading, I am reading Luke 14 in The Message, a contemporary paraphrase of the New Testament. The following words about the cost of discipleship speak to me: 'Simply put, if you're not willing to take what is dearest to you, whether plans or people, and kiss it goodbye, you can't be my disciple … Are you really listening to this?'

The words register in my heart as though they were written personally for me. I know that this unusual turn of phrase, 'take what is dearest to you … and kiss it goodbye', is Jesus' word to me. It helps me accept the imminent prospect of losing Marj. I am well aware that, in Hebrews 11, some people of faith received miraculous deliverances while others were given faith and grace to endure.

With my heart breaking and the tears running down my cheeks, I pray: *Lord, thank you for your constant presence with us both. I trust you for all the grace I'll need in the days ahead.*

***

While many complain about the inadequacies of the Australian health system, we find people very helpful and are thankful for such thorough care. They guide us in managing Marj's pain with appropriate medication. It is a fine balance giving enough morphine to keep her comfortable without leaving her drugged and unable to respond.

As Marj's health deteriorates, we have visits from various family members from interstate. We are grateful for accommodation provided on site. Watching our dear wife and mum, daughter and sister go through all this is not easy and is the beginning of our grieving process.

Aware that her ability to communicate is diminishing and becoming an effort, I suggest to Marj that we can still communicate by squeezing each other's hand. Three squeezes in quick succession convey 'I ... love ... you'. A flicker of a smile conveys that the message is received. We cherish these moments of intimacy in the midst of struggle and suffering.

Early one morning, just five months after her diagnosis and with all of the family around her, Marj passes into the glorious presence of her Lord.

We have a precious and memorable thanksgiving service. As well, we receive over 600 emails, cards and letters from friends and colleagues around the world expressing their sympathy and giving thanks for Marj's life. Many share tributes of the ways Marj was a blessing to them during her life. The service is truly honouring of a lovely lady who gave herself in sacrificial service to her Lord and other people.

How do you sum up the life of the woman you have loved for more than 30 years? During the thanksgiving service, I share a poetical tribute entitled 'My Precious One', and in my next prayer letter I share some of what was said during the service. 'I have lost a wife, mother of my children, constant companion, best friend and lover, co-worker, encourager, navigator, barber, housekeeper, cook, prayer partner and a true example of a Christ-like person.'

An article in the Christian newspaper *New Life* highlights Marj's commitment and contribution in Ghana.[1] 'Working alongside

Graham in vision-setting and strategy formulation, Marj's caring ministry also came to the fore, especially to wives in isolated locations.' Then, in South Australia, 'the Bees saw new vigour and fruit for missions.' In national leadership, 'Marj's life focus was to know God and please Him. And she did. She pleased Him by her faith. Marj simply believed God—that He would pull down strongholds, that He would save the difficult individual, that He would provide for His children; she prayed accordingly. Her strength as a leader was that she led by example.'

Typical of the words of appreciation that flowed in from around the world were these: 'Many have prayed for us, but Marj's ministry was outstanding … without your strategic contribution we would never have made it this far.'

***

As the moving tributes, the celebration of Marj's life and the many encouraging words from friends recede, I am alone. Alone with my loss, my memories, my thoughts and questions, I now have to face the future.

Chapter 43
On my own again

On our wedding day we promised to love each other 'till death do us part'; now the reality of that graphic moment confronts me. Marj has been sick for just five months, but in one painful moment, she is gone.

Paul wrote in Philippians 1:21, 'For to me, to live is Christ and to die is gain' (NIV). Marj lived for Christ and now the 'gain' is hers—no more pain, no more tears, no more suffering. She has been released from her earthly body into the light and love of Jesus, who met and welcomed her with open arms and a heartfelt 'Well done, good and faithful servant.'

I am relieved and happy for her. Yet in this same poignant moment, I have gone from being a husband caring intensively for his wife to being a widower. There is a feeling of finality about this. Life will never be the same.

It is difficult for my children, too, coming to grips with why Mum and Dad should have to endure this after 30 years of faithful service. One comments, 'Surely God rewards His servants better than this.' They feel the loss of their mum deeply and experience a natural disappointment that she will not be there to attend their weddings and hold their babies. I strive to cope with my own loss and grief and try to help them through theirs. However, I understand they are facing their own journey, which is different from mine. I feel for them; my own mother is still alive, and hopefully I will have her for years to come.

Losing Marj hits me hard. As the reality sets in, I realise that for the first time in my 55 years I have a bedroom to myself! I am on my own as never before.

Marj and I enjoyed almost 30 years of togetherness. Many men go off to work at 7 am and return home to their wives around 6 pm, but we worked together closely and shared every aspect of our life and ministry with each other. I miss her terribly. I am not angry with God. I accept that Marj is rejoicing in the presence of Jesus. But I feel numb.

For months the tears flow freely at unexpected moments, and for much of the time God seems distant. Sometimes it feels as though my prayers are getting no further than the ceiling. Yet I know He is with me, and I hang on to the promise that 'He will never leave me nor forsake me'. Although I feel at rock bottom, I find the Rock, Jesus, is beneath me—I am on solid ground, shaken but not shaky. Gradually I experience small but encouraging evidences of the Father's loving presence with me.

God, you are Emmanuel, and although it doesn't always feel like you are with me right now, I know you are, just as surely as you were with Shadrach, Meshach and Abednego in the fiery furnace. More than at any other time in my life, I need your help. Thank you for loving me and ministering to me at this time when I feel so alone.

***

Julie stays on and we grieve together, just as together we cared for Marj night and day. After attending to formalities, thank yous and other arrangements, we travel to the Sunshine Coast for some holidays. The early morning beach walks and daily swims are beneficial in easing the shock and tension I have been feeling.

Over the Christmas/New Year period, we travel together to South Australia and Victoria to spend time with both my family and Marj's. Her mother Bobby and father Steve live in country Victoria. One night, as we are still sitting at the table after the evening meal, Steve suddenly says, 'Well, Graham, you've been a loving husband to Marj, and you're still young, so we hope you find another lovely wife.' There is a stunned silence at this unexpected statement. Julie is the first to respond: 'Thank you, Grandpa. It's nice to know that if it does happen, Dad has your blessing.'

We return to Sydney and I resume leadership responsibilities. I am still grieving and often feel emotional and teary, but life moves on. I wish the world would stand still while I process all of this, but it moves on relentlessly.

After a couple of months, Julie feels it is time for her to return to her work in India. I have some health issues myself and the doctors discover that once again I have developed Type 2 Diabetes. It will require daily medication and a careful diet. They tell me it has most likely been triggered by the stress of Marj's illness and passing.

Folk at Narwee Baptist and WEC colleagues continue to walk with me through this time of transition. For many bereaved people, the care and concern of others ceases soon after the funeral and the person is left to cope in their loneliness. Australian WECers, especially those in Sydney, have lost a dearly loved colleague and friend. We are all grieving Marj's death. We benefit individually and corporately from having a professional counsellor come in to debrief us.

Things that were never issues before suddenly confront me. Where will I sit in church? Whom will I sit with? I become aware that relating to women and to couples is different now. Where do I fit? I feel this difference acutely, and I am aware that, consciously or unconsciously, people relate differently to me now. It is a lonely period in my life.

Over the months, in my alone times, I begin to think and pray about Marj's recommendation of Becky. I need to be sure myself that this is God's plan for us. In the meantime, WEC New Zealand has 'borrowed' Becky for 12 months to be their candidate director. For the year following Marj's death, Becky lives and works in New Zealand. The distance between us could potentially make it more difficult to discover if we are meant for each other.

Chapter 44
A second treasure

2001/2002

One evening I make a phone call to Becky, both to ask how she is coping in New Zealand and to update her on the progress of the work in Australia as she is still a member of our strategy and personnel committee. After we finish talking, I try to sleep but am restless and struggling about when to share with her how I am beginning to feel. Finally, about 1.30 am, I send an email asking, 'Would you be willing to explore a relationship with an old man like me?'

***

Meryl Beckman is her given name, and she is still called Meryl by her family and older friends—but most people call her Becky. She is 47, has never married and originally trained as a high school English and German teacher.

Like me, Becky studied at Worldview in Tasmania (1979–80), afterwards joining WEC for service in French-speaking Africa. Knowing she would need a high level of French for teaching in the Bible school in Isiro, Becky spent two years studying French in Switzerland. Thankfully she loves learning foreign languages, for on arriving in Zaire (now the Democratic Republic of Congo), she discovered she would need to learn Lingala as well. She loved the Zairean people and spent five very fruitful and satisfying years there before evacuating in 1991.

Becky comes with good credentials and experience to take on leadership with me. She was candidate director in Australia for 18 months and in New Zealand for a year. At Worldview she was part of the leadership team and spent time as academic dean and dean of women. And for ten years she was greatly appreciated as a creative lecturer.

To me it is amazing that such a lovely, warm, outgoing, gifted person, who is well respected and a friend to many, is still single. As another female colleague joked years earlier when asked why she was still single, 'My singleness stands as a monument to man's stupidity!' I can't help but agree in Becky's case!

***

Two long days pass, then on the third day an answer to my email finally comes. It is a 'yes'—a 'yes' on Becky's part to exploring a relationship, but I take it as a definite indication that God is in this.

We begin to phone and email regularly. By the time Becky returns for the Australian WEC conference in June, we both have a clear assurance that the Lord is leading us together.

When I share the news publicly at the first night's meeting, there is both surprise and excitement. After the meeting, many people go walking outside in the chilly Mt Tamborine air to use their mobile phones. Talk about the WEC grapevine! Word spreads quickly. The next morning there is even a congratulatory email from Gambia.

Meanwhile, WEC New Zealand, unaware of our developing relationship, has decided it would be good to have an outside person come to guide leadership discussions at their September conference. Becky is in the field committee meeting when they mention my name as a possibility. She is calm on the outside but laughing with secret delight inside. They offer to fly me over and of course I agree to go. I am hardly able to control my eagerness.

Now that news of our relationship is in the public domain, I decide to make the most of the opportunity and go a few days early to have some time with Becky. Thanks to this unexpected but God-given chance to be together, I propose with a poem I have written, 'Becky BEE mine!'

She responds with tears. Surprised and at a loss to understand her reaction, I say, 'You're supposed to be happy!' Through her tears, she manages to smile and say, 'I ... a-am ... h-happy!'

This expenses paid trip is a real bonus and another indication that our loving heavenly Father is smiling on our relationship.

***

At the conclusion of Becky's time in New Zealand, she comes to the Sydney base to live and prepare for our wedding. Soon afterwards, I have a major bout of diarrhoea, which I am hoping will just go away, but Becky encourages me to go to my doctor.

My GP is very thorough; he sends me for several tests and then refers me to a surgeon. Amazingly, the X-ray centre has just had a new machine installed—the radiologists confirm that had I had the test a week earlier, the mass would not have shown up on their old, less accurate equipment. More evidence of the Father's loving care!

A year after losing Marj it is confirmed that I have a tumour in my small bowel.

The doctors want to operate immediately, but I ask for a three-week delay so that I can attend my daughter Merilyn's marriage to James in December. Having lost her Mum so recently, it is important that Dad be present on this special occasion. It is a lovely wedding and a huge morale booster to celebrate as a family after all we have been through.

I feel strongly I need to chat with Becky and give her the option of calling off our engagement. When she agreed to marry me, I was well; now the circumstances have changed dramatically. We are not even sure if I will survive this insidious form of cancer. I tell her I am releasing her from our engagement if she would like to opt out. With a smile, my dear fiancée looks me directly in the eyes and says, 'What would you do?' The matter is settled and we do not discuss it again.

Immediately afterwards I am admitted to hospital to have a tumour the size of my fist removed. It is a Stage 4 melanoma—a secondary growth from a melanoma that was removed from my left cheek twelve years earlier. Medical staff are amazed that it was found before it spread.

They also intended to take out my gall bladder at the same time to remove some stones that are causing severe pain. However, because of the risk of cross-infection, that is not possible. They place a plastic tube into the gall bladder and tape the tubing to the outside of my stomach. This will form a channel through which doctors can deal with the stones later, once I have had a chance to recover from the major surgery.

The first attempt to break up the stones and remove them is unsuccessful, so we are married and go on our honeymoon with the tubing still in place. Patrick Johnstone quips, 'You are the only person I know who has taken a piped organ on his honeymoon!'

Our wedding is an amazing event with over 200 people present at Fairfield Christian Family, Becky's sending church in Brisbane. Her friends there are overjoyed that she is finally getting married. There is a loud cheer as we are presented as Mr and Mrs Bee to a beautiful rendition of the 'Hallelujah Chorus'! Becky's friends have taken charge of all the catering arrangements, the wedding cake, the flowers, the photographer and video, and all the decorating of the church and hall. They provide a sumptuous afternoon tea, and there is a real buzz as everyone interacts. Friends and family have travelled from interstate and from Canada and New Zealand. We feel blessed, loved and supported as we begin married life.

We honeymoon on Norfolk Island in the Pacific Ocean, staying in a small privately owned house in Dead Rat Lane. Despite the name and my condition, we have a precious time together. The history of the island is intriguing, going right back to the Mutiny on the Bounty and convict days. While we are there, the first murder in 150 years occurs. Along with everyone else on the island, we are fingerprinted and asked to give an account of what we were doing every 15 minutes of that day.

Murder aside, the island is peaceful and quiet, a great place to rest, to be alone and to get to know each other more intimately. Many people struggle to find one suitable life partner; I am overwhelmed to be blessed with a loving partner a second time—truly a treasure saved up for me.

***

After our return home, the gall stones are successfully dealt with and I have no further problems with either the cancer or the stones. I have regular oncology check-ups and we are advised not to live overseas for prolonged periods. Doctors say that if the cancer does reappear, the only medical hope for me is to find it early and remove it surgically. We pray against any recurrence.

I feel like I have been through a dramatic couple of years health-wise. After watching and caring for my beloved wife dying with cancer, I had to cope with it myself just twelve months later. Now I understand and agree with the Psalmist's declaration that 'though I walk through the valley of the shadow of death, I will fear no evil, for you are with me'. God has been my 'very present help in trouble'.

In the years following, many friends, colleagues and acquaintances walk similar paths. My experience, and a genuine testimony to God's faithfulness in it all, enables me to come alongside and offer support and prayer. Twelve years on, I am well but do not cope with emotional stress as easily—a small price to pay for the physical wellbeing I enjoy.

Chapter 45
How much more, Lord?

Sydney

What a two years I have been through! With my wife's cancer and death, then my own loss, cancer and facing the prospect of death, the story of Job's struggles suddenly takes on new meaning. The wonderful way the Lord has brought Becky and me together, and her loving companionship, seems to indicate the dark clouds have lifted and now at last there is sunshine ahead.

I am unaware of another dark cloud hovering close by.

***

Despite being a follower of Jesus for many years, I still find there are lessons to learn on the journey. Throughout our lives, God uses experiences of all kinds to mould us and prepare us for what is ahead. In every situation, I try to look beyond the current circumstances to understand what God may be saying to me. Knowing He is with me and is always planning good for me gives peace in the midst of the storms that invariably come.

Even when my prayers seem to go unanswered and I don't know what the future holds, He is still guiding, still transforming.

I have always found the illustration of a tapestry a great help.[1] We see the underside—the tangled threads, the knots and the loose ends in our lives. But as God looks from above, He sees the top side—the intricate weaving of lovely colours to form a beautiful picture. The darker threads as well as the vibrant ones are all used to create a masterpiece.

Only in hindsight do we realise the full significance of what God was doing in our lives. We begin to see circumstances from His perspective and can praise Him for His loving dealings on our journey. I find that, even when I am unable to discern His purpose in the midst of pain and hurt, I can trust His loving heart.

I know the theory well, but acting on it in the rough and tumble of daily life is a process. There are further challenges ahead of us as a team. Terry Freeman, who with his wife, Di, joined us as deputy directors just before Marj passed away, is diagnosed first with multiple sclerosis and then with multiple myeloma. This makes three Australian WEC leaders who battle cancer in three years. It is a difficult time not only for us personally but for the whole of WEC Australia.

The number of Australians in WEC reaches 293, and remains constant during the following two years. We don't quite make '301 by 2001'. But God has certainly blessed and honoured the faith of our Australian workers. There are now more Aussies involved in reaching the unreached with WEC than ever before. We pray, and God in His unique ways calls and sends out labourers into His harvest field.

***

The WEC Australia team has already extended my time as leader beyond two three-year terms, and I continue in this role after Marj's death. I have a sense that my time is coming to a close, but I do not have a clear idea of who should take over. I indicate that I am willing to stay on for a further two years, even though I am still working through the impact of the last couple of years and do not have the same capacity to cope with stress as before.

In consultation with the International Office, it is agreed that after our marriage Becky and I will have six months leave for rest and recovery before continuing in leadership. This will also allow time for adjustment to each other without the pressures that leadership brings.

Already on the calendar, organised before we were married, is a trip to Germany for a month. We are there for Coordinating Council meetings followed by Intercon, our large international leadership conference. This is a strategic conference when we wonderfully see the Lord confirm Trevor and Jen Kallmier as incoming international directors. During the session when they are elected, the sense of unity in the Spirit is almost palpable as together we wait on God for His leading.

The irony is that we are there as Australian leaders, representing

WEC Australia, but are no longer Australian leaders. How can this be?

Earlier, during our six-month time out, the Australian committee meets and decides that it is time for us to move on. They will take responsibility for finding new leaders. When this is communicated to us, my initial response is, 'I have no desire to hold on to a position. If this is God's direction I will accept it.'

However, as I process the news and the abruptness of the decision, I feel disillusioned and extremely hurt by the way the decision was reached and communicated. Normally, a decision of this magnitude would proceed to the Australian conference to be voted on by all Australian workers. This conference is only six months away.

My heart is heavy. *How much more, Lord, are you asking me to endure?*

In my missionary training days, visiting speakers warned us to ensure our trust was in God and not in people or organisations. During my 35 years of involvement with WEC, I have loved, appreciated and fully supported the organisation and its people. I have many special friends all over the world and cherish the WEC family. We belong. We feel privileged to serve with such a passionate and committed group of people; they inspire me to seek after all God has for me and to give myself wholeheartedly to it.

Right now, however, and even more so over the next few years, I struggle to understand how I can feel so disheartened in WEC. After all the fulfilling years, how has it come to this? Then I remember what I was told in Bible school days and realise I am not the first, and won't be the last, to feel let down, and that our organisation is not alone in this.

I feel blessed to have Becky by my side during this traumatic time. It is not easy for her either to deal with this as well as the early days of marriage, living in the home I shared with Marj, and shattered expectations. We do our best to support each other and spend a lot of time praying.

***

In the absence of a new leader, a leadership team is put in place. With good intentions, radical changes are made and the work is restructured with different priorities. Within the new structure older experienced workers do not have the same opportunity to give input as before. Methods of recruitment are suddenly changed, the traditional state representatives are replaced and the processing and care of workers is handled nationally. Properties are sold without the consultation and agreement that we are used to.

It is difficult watching all of this—not the concept of change in itself, but the fact that years of invested time and prayer seem not to be appreciated and the benefits largely discarded. We try to voice our concerns, but it is never easy for former leaders to have input and I am too emotional to do a very good job of it anyway. We are not the only people affected by all of this; others inside and outside of WEC are hurt. Many WEC supporters and friends share that they are confused and disappointed.

Becky and I get to the point of discussing resignation. As we chat and pray for wisdom and guidance, we agree that our concerns are with WEC Australia, not WEC internationally. By this time we have new areas of ministry to concentrate on that come under the International Office. We feel we should 'draw a line in the sand' and move on positively with what God has given us to do.

As painful as it is to see numbers dramatically declining in Australia, we know it is no longer our responsibility and that we can hand our concerns over to God.

***

In more recent years, it has been recognised that while some of these changes were good, others were not successful. There has been a return to more mainstream WEC practices and apologies have been made to those of us who were hurt and disappointed over those years.

I know from experience that it is not what happens to us but the way we respond that determines how problems affect us. Psalm 13 impacts me during this period of deep distress. The psalmist asks four questions, three of which begin with the agonising phrase 'How long?' But although I resonate with David's pleas and fears in the first half of the psalm, I rest in the final two verses: 'But I trust in your unfailing love; my heart rejoices in your salvation. I will sing to the Lord, for he has been good to me' (NIV).

The Lord *has* been good to us and we have learnt from this difficult experience. Letting go makes it possible for us to embrace what God has for us around the next corner.

GOLD COAST YEARS
(2003–THE PRESENT)

Graham and Becky

East Timor Team, 2001

Chapter 46
A home on the Gold Coast

Gold Coast, Queensland
2003

'When we married, I joined you in your house, your work, your church, your friends and even your car,' Becky says to me. 'In thinking about another place to live, it would be good to look for somewhere neutral. Brisbane is home for me, so that wouldn't be neutral, but I don't want to be too far from Mum. She's getting older and frailer, and I'd like to shoulder some of the responsibility for her that my sister Jude has carried for so long.'

'I understand and I'm happy for that,' I reply. 'Our new ministry will be itinerant, so we can basically choose where we like as our base. Since my children and their families all live on the Gold Coast, why don't we think about basing ourselves there? That's only an hour's drive from Brisbane.'

As we pray about this option, we feel right about heading for the Gold Coast.

***

Our move from the familiar in Sydney to the unknown in Queensland is not as daunting as Abraham's challenge, but it does stretch our faith. In Sydney we have been living in WEC accommodation, enjoying the benefits of community living. Now we need to see God provide not only a house, but the furniture and all the equipment needed to operate our own office and maintain the property. The sale of my house in South Australia and bank approval for a small loan mean we are able to start looking within a specific but limited price range.

In December 2002 we head north from Sydney. On our journey, God gives me an assurance about the house He is going to give us. In that day's reading in *The Message* I am amazed to read, 'My choice is you, God, first and only. And now I find I'm your choice! You set me up with *a house and yard*. And then you made me your heir!' (Psalm 16:5–6).

We house-sit for a few days on the Gold Coast but resist the temptation to start looking for a property before our holiday is finished. We don't want anything to disrupt this much-needed break. I say to Becky, 'The house that God has for us may not even be on the market yet.' We continue the drive north and spend two weeks on the Sunshine Coast.

On our return to the Gold Coast we start looking in earnest. On the first day, a Monday, we visit ten real estate agents situated between the northern and central areas of the Gold Coast. We explain to them that we are looking for a three-bedroom house with a large backyard for under $200,000. One by one, they smile and say that with recent rises in house prices, we should look at duplexes, which will be more in our price range.

We do look at one duplex, which has been fully renovated and is for sale for $212,000. Becky loves it, but I believe we will do better to buy something cheaper that needs renovation. I can work on it between ministry commitments. We are trusting for a place with a reasonably sized backyard—I am hanging on to the promise I believe God gave me from Psalm 16. I have always had a garden and want to grow fruit and vegetables.

On the first evening, after leaving our contact numbers with the agents in case something comes up, we head back to my son Paul's place, tired and very aware of how difficult and frustrating this house hunting might be.

The next day, Paul and I go to look up an agent friend of his. We find he has moved to work with an agent we visited the day before. As we enter, a salesperson remembers me and says, 'Oh! I was about to contact you regarding a property that came on the market last night. It's a three-bedroom house for sale at $199,000 and it has a large backyard.'

Paul and I go to look at it, like what we see and arrange an inspection the next day for Becky.

One of our 'wants' is a flat block. Though the house is on a flat pad, the drive is steep. I am afraid that Becky might find it difficult to walk up and down, so I warn her about it. My description must have embellished reality, for when she sees it she wonders what I was worried about. We really like the house, including the fact that it has a large room in addition to the three bedrooms. This has been used as an extra living area; however, with some improvements it will suit us for a home office and storage space. I ask a question about whether the carport meets regulations and am assured that there have been no problems with the local council.

We go home very encouraged and pray overnight about what we should offer. On Thursday, we make a formal offer of $192,000, and the real estate agent assures us he will meet with the owners that evening and get back to us the following day. On Friday, the fifth day of our search, the agent calls to say the owners have agreed provided we are willing to sign a clause saying the carport may or may not meet council specifications. We feel that at that price, even if we have to pull the carport down, we have a good deal.

We discover that the house has not yet been advertised and does not even have a 'For Sale' sign out the front. God has wonderfully led us to it, despite real estate agents themselves telling us there were no houses with yards available at that price. Our unbelievable God strikes again!

We are later told that when the agent put up a 'For Sale' sign with SOLD sticker already across it, a man walking past asked how it could be sold when there hadn't even been a sign up. He had been waiting years for the property to come on the market. Amazingly, the vendors agreed to sell to the first offer, for less than the advertised price. They are good Catholic folk who built the house and lived there for 22 years; we have the impression that knowing we are missionaries, they are happy for us to have it and care for it.

***

One month later we move in, and gradually we discover what a wonderful location it is—backing onto bushland, close to the motorway, on the central part of the Gold Coast and between the ocean and the hinterland mountains. It is on a large sloping block with plenty of space to make an attractive garden at the front and lots of room for fruit trees and vegetables at the back.

Little by little, our house becomes a home. In time we add on a large pergola, which is ideal for entertaining and provides an undercover area where grandchildren can play and ride bikes. It is a delight to be creative with my hands once more. I build retaining walls (one from rocks on the property), make a water feature and establish the gardens. We install subsidised water tanks at a time of severe water restrictions and take advantage of the free ceiling insulation offered by the government. The fruit and vegetable garden gives me a workout each day and provides us with lots of healthy produce.

Despite the circumstances that led to us moving to Queensland, there is a song of joy in our hearts. We want to say along with the Psalmist:

> He has given me a new song to sing,
>   a hymn of praise to our God.
> Many will see what he has done and be astounded.
>   They will put their trust in the Lord.
> O Lord my God, you have done many miracles for us …
> If I tried to recite all your wonderful deeds,
>   I would never come to the end of them.' (Psalm 40:3, 5 NLT)

Chapter 47
The recent years

Who wouldn't want to be based on the Gold Coast? It is Australia's theme park capital and a preferred holiday destination for world travellers. Our slogan is: 'Beautiful one day, perfect the next!'

***

Though we are not living here for the climate, beaches or tourist buzz, we grow to love our little corner of the world. It has an international airport and is a suitable base from which to continue ministry; at the same time, we are able to relate to our families and the growing number of grandchildren. We are blessed to belong to a healthy, life-giving church and enjoy being part of its pastoral care team.

In reviewing my medical history, doctors reiterate their advice against prolonged stays in other countries, though short periods overseas are fine. Over the next 10 years we receive a number of invitations to live and minister in various countries on a one-year basis, but each time we sense we are where God wants us for now.

On our leaving Sydney, the Australian leaders agree that we will have three main areas of ministry:
- We will have responsibility for handling the supporting sending base responsibilities for WEC's work in East Timor.
- I will continue as chairperson of the international committee revising WECs Principles and Practice, and assisting with some rewriting of the International Guidelines.
- We will be involved in WEC's Rainbows of Hope (ROH) ministry, facilitating training and continuing (in my case) as a member of the ROH international committee (and chairperson for a time).

Rainbows of Hope is a department of WEC that focuses on children, youth and families in crisis and/or at risk. Our role with

ROH involves helping formulate policies and guidelines for the development of the ministry, visiting some of the projects, speaking at its first international conference, encouraging workers who are directly involved in these projects, and advising others preparing to go.

When I step down from committee membership after about six years, both Becky and I train as facilitators for ROH under the founder, Phyllis Kilbourn, and Becky is appointed Australasian trainer. This enables us to conduct training courses for prospective workers, those wanting to advocate or intercede on behalf of children, and those who are simply interested in what is happening in our world. One church in New Zealand has all the folk going on a short-term missions trip to South Africa and Senegal do the course on street children.

Over the next eight years, courses are held in New Zealand, Tasmania, Queensland, Hong Kong and Zambia. One young man, Nate, working on the streets of Cairo, flies all the way to New Zealand for the training!

The courses run as interactive workshops with thought-provoking discussions, case study groups, creative activities and DVD clips. Though Becky is the main trainer, I assist with sharing devotions and some teaching times, helping to carry resources and looking after the practical arrangements and set-up. Twenty-five hours over five days is a heavy load, especially when we are facilitating courses on sexually exploited and trafficked children.

Becky visits projects in various countries to keep up with the needs and opportunities there, which ensures the training is relevant. As well as having up-to-date stories and photos from the ministries she visits, she is able to encourage the workers and give pastoral care when needed.

Participants learn how to minister to children in crisis; however, during the seminars many become aware of issues in their own upbringing which they need to deal with. Around 90% of students at Eastwest College of Intercultural Studies in New Zealand have participated in one or more of the courses. Not all will pursue ministry with children or youth, but they are all better equipped to serve.

As we say during the courses, 'Every adult has been a child, and many struggle right into adulthood because they never received the help and support they needed earlier in life.'

***

We appreciate the fact that when we are not travelling, we do not have to adhere to a fixed daily program. This gives us greater flexibility to help our young families when they need it. The children are thankful to have us living close by. In the years they were at boarding school, then during our busy years in Sydney, opportunities to relate to them were limited. Now it is good to have time with them and to share the privilege of having input into the lives of our grandchildren.

Reflecting on their years at boarding school and the sicknesses they have endured, including Paul's two bouts of cerebral malaria, we are thankful to God. They have grown into healthy, mature adults, passionate about Jesus and with friends all over the world.

For part of the last few years, we were able to help care for Becky's mum and give some assistance to my family in caring for my mother until they both passed away. My mother lived to 89 years and continued to be a godly and loving influence in our family until she was 'called home'. Dad has just turned 92.

***

As we plan for each year, Becky and I try to spend time listening, to discern what opportunities God wants us to participate in. I feel I am in a time of transition, seeking to reduce my involvement in view of decreased energy and physical well-being. I find it a challenge to know what is right to take on.

In 2013 Becky and I, along with four others, co-facilitated a Member Care workshop in Chiang Mai, Thailand, for WEC member carers and leaders from around the world. These workshops will continue on a regular basis, perhaps in different parts of the world. Becky is sure of her involvement; I still need to listen, to hear and to obey what I hear the Father saying to me.

I want to keep a healthy balance between accepting my limitations and trusting God to empower me when I am weak.

***

We are blessed to be able to serve God together. Often Becky and I look at each other, smile and say, 'We are team!' We are so different, yet our strengths are complementary and we work well together. Becky is creative, a starter; I am a finisher/completer. Like Marj, Becky's personality (ENFP) is directly opposite to mine (ISTJ). We each have our strengths, but there is also the potential for misunderstanding and frustration.

I assure Becky a number of times that I don't compare her with Marj but appreciate both with their differences. I do admit, though, that God was gracious in helping me to adjust to Marj first so that when I married Becky, I was able to cope with being stretched a bit further! Becky's bubbly and godly personality is appreciated by people all over the world. She is a loving, generous and fun grandma, loved and respected by all our families.

Becky is a trainer par excellence. In addition to her work with ROH, from time to time she co-facilitates Sharpening Your Interpersonal Skills (SYIS) workshops, lectures at Worldview and teaches in leadership development courses in the Asian region. Nine years younger than me, she revels in new opportunities that open up. At 68, I am seeking to support Becky in what she does but gradually taper off the amount of international travel I do. I can still assist with the arrangements, do the correspondence and support her in various ways.

Travelling less has provided more time to concentrate on the writing of this book, which I trust will be an ongoing blessing. It may open up more local opportunities for ministry.

***

Our role in helping with the development of the work in East Timor has continued longer than first anticipated. The immense privilege of identifying with our team in the challenges they face, as well as the joys and victories they celebrate, allows us to see Jesus at work in the lives of others in an exciting way.

Chapter 48
East Timor miracles

So close and yet so different! Just a one-hour flight from Darwin, this tiny mountainous island nation of just over a million people has broken free. The East Timorese are fighters and survivors. They have struggled for an independent future and now that day has dawned.

As the plane banks and turns before landing in Dili, the capital, I catch a glimpse of the 'Cristo Rei'—a 27-metre high statue of Jesus standing on a globe of the world. It highlights the fact that this is only the second nation in Asia, after the Philippines, where 'Christianity' is regarded as the major religion.

This prominent landmark is a reminder to visitors like me of the traumatic history of these people. They endured more than 450 years of colonisation by Portugal. In 1975, nine days after declaring independence, and just when they thought they were free, Indonesia invaded. The Indonesian government gave the statue to the East Timorese as a gift, but it was only a token—for over a quarter of a century, the brutal occupation by Indonesia squashed their resistance and struggle for freedom. More than 200,000 people (one-third of the population) died through slaughter, starvation or disease, and many more were forced into exile.

While much of the world turned a blind eye to Indonesia's invasion, gradually the atrocities being inflicted on the East Timorese were publicised, and in 1999 Indonesia reluctantly agreed to a UN-sponsored referendum. Nearly 80% voted for independence. As the Indonesians left, militia supported by the Indonesian military—and the Indonesian forces themselves—ransacked the country, destroying 70% of all buildings and infrastructure.

Finally, in 2002, the Democratic Republic of Timor-Leste, known in the English-speaking world as East Timor, was inaugurated.

***

WEC leaders have been concerned for East Timor for years, and have had one worker there seconded to another organisation. Finally in 2000 they agree to open a new field there. Australia is appointed as the supporting sending base. Luise Laufer and Hildegard Berg, along with David and Else Meader, form the new team. All have experience working in Indonesia so are able to transition culturally to this new context.

My first visit, as part of the supportive role we have been assigned, is in 2001. The destruction I see, and the stories of suffering I hear, touch me deeply.

The country will take years to recover. With infrastructure destroyed and shops, homes, churches, schools and government buildings nearly all burnt-out, accommodation is hard to find. Very few food items are available. Power and water supplies are spasmodic and limited to a few hours each day. UN vehicles and a few minibuses and taxis drive on badly neglected roads. Virtually every person in the country has been traumatised; they have all lost members of their families and many their homes. The situation is still unstable and they are still not sure who to trust.

The children's eyes haunt me. A deep sadness and fear is reflected in them. The children in particular seem to be without hope and without any appropriate support in their desperate need. Their drawings are usually of people fighting, wounded and bleeding.

On subsequent visits, and as more workers join the team, project Esperanca (Hope) is established in a poor part of Dili. Children flock to the kids' clubs and students attend the various classes in English, Portuguese, dance, drama and computer. They begin to laugh, trust and hope again. Church planting work and medical, media and training ministries are commenced.

It is crucial to the well-being of each worker that they have an opportunity to debrief—to talk about what they have seen and experienced, how they are helping the children and youth through their grieving process, how they are doing as a team and what they need in terms of support. Our brief when we visit East Timor is to spend time with each worker, mostly listening, sometimes asking pertinent questions—always praying. We share devotional times and do team building activities. Each day we go with them to clubs and classes. Together we enjoy meals, swims and other social activities.

It is a delight to have so many nationalities represented in the team at different times—German, English, Brazilian, Korean, Indonesian, Australian, New Zealand and Swiss. As in all international teams, there is potential for hurt and misunderstanding. So times spent with the team also involve looking at cultural and personality differences and how we can better understand one another. We are constantly impressed by the calibre of the workers in East Timor, but we need lots more like them.

***

On my first visit, six of us embark on the long, arduous drive to Los Palos where Luise Laufer runs a medical clinic. Lu, seconded from WEC to another organisation, has worked on her own for years. We want some footage of the clinic to include in a promotional video being made for WEC.

As we drive along the coast, it is quite unnerving to look over the edge of the road and see the steep drop to the sea below. There are no safety rails, and the edges of the bitumen are badly broken up. The sealed strip is just wide enough for one vehicle. At times we are suddenly confronted by oncoming vehicles heading right for us.

David Meader does a good job of getting us through this dangerous section of the trip. After some hours of driving, and with the worst hills behind us, he feels tired and hands over the driving to me.

With the road flatter and straighter I am able to increase our speed. Suddenly, rounding a corner, we are confronted with a tree lying right across the road directly in front of us. Travelling at 80 kilometres per hour there is not enough time to stop. Deep culverts on either side add to the danger.

We are going to crash. Instinctively I jam on the brakes and swerve towards the leafy end of the tree, trying to avoid smashing into the solid trunk. In the split second this takes, I notice a narrow gap. Someone has been here before and cut branches so they could squeeze through. We skid to a stop just the other side of the tree.

With hearts pounding, we breathe deep sighs of relief. 'Wow! How did you manage that?' someone asks. David adds, 'It's just as well you were driving, Graham, because I'm not sure I would have reacted quickly enough to get through.'

'I'm sure it was God guiding me,' I assure them. 'I know people at home are praying for protection as we travel. Let's thank Him for looking after us.'

I don't think I've ever been in a prayer meeting where more heartfelt thanks has been given to God!

David calls out to people from a nearby village and they help us roll the tree off the edge of the road so that other vehicles and lives won't be endangered in the same way.

***

It is a privilege to support our small team through challenging times. One of the most dramatic is in the midst of another violent crisis in 2006.

As tension mounts in Dili, I am asked to act as crisis manager. While monitoring the situation from Australia, I am notified that the hostility has escalated dramatically. There is an opportunity to evacuate all our workers to Australia on the last UN flights out of the country.

In the pandemonium and fear of that day, our workers are not able to phone each other, but, strangely, I can reach them all. I relay messages and news about what the others are doing. They all get out safely to Darwin, then on to Brisbane. WECers in Brisbane help with arrangements to accommodate and care for them for the next six weeks and we have some in our home as well.

Having them close by gives us the opportunity to debrief

appropriately, plan the future and decide when it will be safe to return. The time out from the heat and humidity, tension and uncertainty is good for each of them. They begin to relax and are more refreshed for their return to East Timor and the ministries ahead of them. We are grateful to God for His peace and protection, and for the wisdom given in the midst of fear and uncertainty.

During my thirteen years of involvement with the team, there have been four different team leaders and four different regional directors, so it has been good to provide some continuity and experience in a climate of great change, instability and uncertainty.

***

My visit in 2012 is a memorable one. The week before we are due to go, Becky is diagnosed with a triple whammy—whooping cough, influenza A and pneumonia—and is admitted to hospital. As the days go by, the doctor confirms that she is not well enough to travel.

We both sense, however, that it is right for me to go as planned. With just a one-hour margin before I need to leave for the airport, the hospital discharges Becky and I am able to bring her home. Friends assure me they will keep an eye on her, so with very mixed feelings I leave.

The visit is positive and an encouragement for the team. I stay healthy until the last day, when I develop a slight temperature and the beginning of a cold.

As scheduled, I fly to Darwin and stay overnight before another flight back to Brisbane. By evening, I am feeling a bit better. However, at 2 am I wake up in a lather. I am perspiring so much my pyjamas are totally drenched. I have a bad case of diarrhoea and spend a couple of hours feeling very uncomfortable before I am able to get back to sleep.

I wake feeling extremely weak so stay on my bed until it is time to go to the airport. A long queue is waiting to go through security, and by the time I make it to the departure lounge, it is almost time to board my flight. All the seats in the lounge are taken so I stand there waiting, only to be told the plane is delayed. By the time we eventually board, my strength is sapped.

I slump in my aisle seat. Immediately I begin shivering uncontrollably, just as I used to do when I had malaria. The flight attendants give me one, then two blankets, but I continue to shiver. Not knowing what dreaded disease I might have, they ask me if I should be flying. I assure them I will be fine. All I want is to get home.

After the flight takes off, one attendant tells me to let them know if I need oxygen. Half an hour into the four-hour flight, I rush to the toilet and vomit. I feel much better and start to warm up again. I pray for a tail wind to get us there sooner.

I arrive in Brisbane feeling much better than when I started the trip. Friends bring my car to the airport, but I do not let on what I have been through. There is still a one-hour drive ahead of me. I just want to get home without further delay or incident. After the most unpleasant flight in 45 years of flying, I am ready to collapse.

Becky is alarmed to see me so sick. Instead of caring for her, all I can manage is to fall straight into bed. Despite feeling weak and still quite sick herself, Becky now has to care for me.

Doctors confirm that I have dengue fever. This mosquito-borne disease is not common in our area, so they have me running from one test to the next. It has to be reported to government health authorities. I begin to feel I am some kind of rare breed! It is a full two months before I return to anything like normal health and strength. In Africa I experienced hepatitis and had dozens of malarial attacks, but this is my first experience of dengue fever. Now I can fully empathise with our friends in various parts of the world who have had it.

Even in this difficult time, I am aware my heart is at peace. I am secure in the knowledge that God is with me, working out His good purposes in my life.

***

In an effort to involve more Australians and New Zealanders in our work, I arrange for a short-term 'WEC Trek' team to travel to East

Timor in 2013. Becky and I assist with all the arrangements and team orientation, but we are not going ourselves this time. On the team is Rachel Moot, a student from Eastwest College of Intercultural Studies in New Zealand.[1]

On February 8 while ministering in East Timor, Rachel suddenly gets sick and is admitted to hospital. Over the next four days, she grows worse instead of better. Dayan and Mirna, the team leaders, decide to evacuate her to Darwin and inform me in Queensland.

We are in crisis mode again!

Despite communication difficulties, I am able to finalise arrangements for Rachel's flight even as she leaves for the airport. In Darwin she is taken from the airport in an ambulance and admitted to the intensive care unit in Darwin hospital, where she stays for two days. She then spends almost a week in a ward. I am thankful for good phone contact that enables me to coordinate her care, with the help of a family on the trek team who travelled with her to Darwin.

The doctors are baffled. They eventually diagnose her as having 'mononeuritis multiplex' causing drop foot. Once her condition is stabilised, but still walking with the help of crutches, she flies back home to Christchurch, New Zealand.

Rachel is given a brace to support her foot. Numerous medical specialists and multiple tests rule out the original diagnosis. She has an undiagnosed disorder and a paralysed foot. As the weeks go by, the prognosis becomes more pessimistic. She is unable to use her foot and has no central balance. She cannot stand without holding onto a fixed structure.

She is given three options:
- have an operation to permanently fuse her ankle joint at a 90° angle
- accept that it could be a lifelong paralysis
- pray for God to do a miracle.

People all over the world are already praying, so she informs her GP she is trusting for a miracle.

On Sunday April 14, 2013, a few friends gather in a park for lunch. They pray for each other and Rachel feels strength coming back into her foot. She removes the brace and shoe and for the first time is able to move her toes a little. Her friends help her to a standing position and she is able to stand without crutches and without falling over. The excitement mounts. As they pray, her foot continues to get better. She throws the crutches away, discards the brace and starts to walk around the park.

During the afternoon her leg grows stronger and stronger. She is able to walk freely. Calf muscles, which had atrophied, regrow, together with new nerves, enabling her to use her leg normally. She is completely healed with no swelling, numbness, pain or foot drop.

All praise to God!

***

The reaction of Rachel's GP is total disbelief, followed by excitement. He tells people in the waiting area that she hadn't been able to walk but now she can. He calls the nurses and receptionists to have a look. He says excitedly, 'This is the most amazing thing I've ever seen! There's no way I can charge a fee for this consultation, but please don't let anyone think you have any kind of super powers. I can't give you any answers, but we definitely can't rule out the spiritual aspect.'

The orthopaedic surgeon who organised her leg brace is a Christian. He finds her miraculous healing harder to believe than anyone else. There is such a tension in his thinking between medical impossibilities and the true power of God.

A member of the neurology team involved in her treatment rings Rachel and says that the GP has informed them of her healing. He asks if it is true. The team did not know what her problem was or what had caused it. They had done electric nerve conduction tests on her leg and found complete degeneration of nerves—they were non-existent. Rachel confirms she is walking around while talking to him, but he replies that he doesn't believe it and says they want to see her again.

They do the same electrical test on her leg even though she can now move her foot normally. They are amazed as the results are completely different to those obtained a month earlier. The team calls the head of neurology out of a meeting to see them. They say, 'Whatever you're doing must be working, so keep doing it!'

Rachel tells them confidently that she prayed and God has answered in an unbelievable way.

***

The battle for the minds and hearts of people in East Timor continues. Animistic beliefs and spirit worship lie beneath much of what is done; rigid Catholicism adds another layer, and now the Chinese influence is also increasing.

We pray for many more workers to share the liberating message that Jesus saves and sets free those who are bound by tradition and oppression.

Chapter 49
Green fingers: nurturing plants as well as people

Just before I started secondary school, our family moved from the city to the country. I had no idea this move would contribute to a change in my direction in life. Originally I wanted to be a teacher, but I quickly developed a love for all things 'country'.

On our small farm, I had the opportunity to help Dad grow our own vegetables. I discovered it was not easy to cultivate things; I had lots to learn to overcome the challenges of living in the driest state of the driest continent on earth. Early results were mixed. I learnt that getting a good outcome required lots of soil preparation and compost—there is much more to do than plant seeds if you want a harvest! But the challenges involved and the joy of picking and eating your own produce introduced me to a lifelong hobby.

Gardening has always been a stress release for me and a place to meet with God, especially in the quiet morning hours before the world wakes up. While others may consider it work, for me it is relaxing and enjoyable, and I love blessing others with the produce when there is plenty.

And beyond that, my garden has taught me many things about life and ministry.

***

One time, while living in Ghana, I needed to travel away for a time. I gave instructions to my helper to make sure he watered the vegetables. On my return, everything was dead and dry. His explanation was, 'I thought I only needed to water once a week.' The next time before leaving, I reiterated, 'This time please make sure you water the plants well.' On my return, all the cabbages had rotted because too much water had been splashed on top of them. He did not know that cabbages needed to be watered beneath the head.

At frustrating times like this, I really needed God's grace and patience. It was also a reminder that I need to give careful instructions and not assume people know what I mean.

In Tamale, we moved into a new house on a building site with very rocky soil. I took on the challenge of planting shrubs and trees to make the surroundings more aesthetically pleasing. I enjoyed the project even though I knew the benefits would mostly be left to someone else. Life can be like that: God blesses our faithful hard work even though it is often other people who benefit from the outcome.

***

In Adelaide, the produce from the small vegetable garden at the back of the WEC base enabled us to provide chunky vegetable soup to all who came to our weekly prayer morning. These times of prayer were for WEC workers around the world, especially those who had gone from South Australia. We did all we could to encourage Christians at home to pray for them and support them in practical ways.

***

In Sydney, I spent a lot of my spare time caring for the extensive gardens at the WEC centre. Previously a volunteer maintained the gardens, but, with a shortage of personnel, it largely fell to me. I found an hour or two of gardening helped release the pressures of leadership.

Some Asian candidates expressed concern to other staff members that I was working too hard in the garden and wondered why I felt the need to do that. For them, it is not cultural for a leader to do menial work like gardening; they found it difficult to understand that I enjoyed it. As well as the satisfaction I felt, it meant the grounds were attractive and the centre appealing to the many who attended our ministry functions.

***

When we moved to our own home on the Gold Coast, it was great to finally have a place where I could establish the gardens as I desired. Both the front and back yards were large and undeveloped, so there was a lot to do.

Initially, whenever we had tropical rainstorms, water rushed from the bushland behind straight over our land towards our back door. All the time and energy spent on drainage has turned out to be a great investment. When we are travelling and hear reports of tropical thunderstorms and flooding in our area, we do not have concerns.

Many of the hedges and plants that now adorn the property I grew from cuttings I propagated myself. It was all done on a minimal budget with lots of hard work. The gardens are now well-established and low maintenance.

Because of the tropical climate, I have had to think differently about what I grow. I now concentrate on plants with different coloured leaves rather than flowers, and spend most of the space available for growing vegetables. Our garden has produced much more than we can eat, so while we don't have much material wealth, we have plenty of fresh organic fruit and vegetables with enough to share with others.

***

Our grandchildren have always enjoyed coming to Grandpa's 'farm'. Although it is just a large suburban backyard it backs onto a farm and bushland. There are always interesting things for them to see or do, like watching cows, kangaroos and tractors through the back fence.

Sometimes they get their hands dirty and help with mulching or composting, but by far their favourite activity is helping to pick the ripe strawberries. One of them—needless to say a boy—is so eager he eats the strawberries without washing them or removing the green tops! Unlike the gardener's patient wait for plants to produce, the gratification for them must be immediate.

In Queensland we are blessed with much rain—nearly all the additional water we need comes from the water tanks we installed with the help of government and council rebates during drought years. There are various pests like fruit fly, grasshoppers and fruit bats. At times extremely hot, dry conditions require adapting the types of plants grown and the time of year to grow them.

The pleasure of picking and eating fresh, wholesome food is a lovely by-product of the stress release and sense of achievement that I derive from gardening. I believe that, along with drawing our resources from Jesus, it is important for all of us to have a hobby or some valid practical outlet that consistently helps us in coping with the pressures of life and ministry.

***

Gardening has not just provided me with delicious produce and many hours of quiet joy and deep contentment. It has also given me much time for reflection. I have derived spiritual lessons from various gardening practices such as transplanting, pruning, fruiting, weeding and maintaining soil fertility. Gardening illustrations have enriched my messages too.

After all, contrary to other suggestions, gardening is the oldest profession in the world. God gave Adam the job of caring for a garden in Eden. It was there in the garden that Adam and Eve sensed God's presence and communed with Him. As they walked and talked with Him they received guidance and directions for living; that is until bad choices resulted in them being expelled from the garden. Jesus used farming illustrations too. He spoke of hard soil, of sowing seeds, of waiting for the harvest, of vines and vineyards, of fig trees, of fruitfulness, or the lack of it. My experience in farming and gardening has not only helped in my understanding of spiritual truths, but has given a real connection with Ghanaians and a means of passing on truths to them too.

I have also learnt that gardening and leadership in missions have many similarities. Long-term mission teams are made up of widely differing personalities and are usually multicultural. In the mix there are some who are assertive, some impulsive and some who tend to dominate if given the chance, as well as the quiet achievers who have to be given space and encouragement to shine. There are some who have years of experience and some new workers who need guiding and nurturing in the early days. Leaders need to know their members well, to be understanding, discerning and compassionate, with an ability to handle each person according their particular needs—just the way we treat plants.

Likewise, many different kinds of plants make up a garden, and each has its unique requirements. Some need full sun; others prefer shade. Some have a tendency to grow too tall or to spread too wide and if allowed will take over. Consequently, pruning is needed. But it needs to be done carefully because if pruned too severely, some trees and shrubs will not survive the experience.

At times there is a need for more severe action. If a particular plant is not suitable at all, it may need to be removed for the good of the whole garden.

Maintaining healthy relationships within a missionary team is one of the greatest challenges leaders face. On several occasions, I have observed leaders helping others resolve their differences only for relationships to break down again later. Sometimes a physical change of location for one person proves to be a satisfactory solution. Both parties are then able to put all their energies into ministry and thrive with God's blessing. On other occasions, after doing everything possible to help workers, we finally conclude that it would be best for everyone if they returned home. Those decisions can be painful but necessary.

Thankfully, this has sometimes resulted in a person thriving in another location or organisation, and with a ministry more suited to his or her gifting and temperament. Some plants need to be transplanted because they haven't been thriving where they were. Queensland is not the most suitable climate for roses, so I have had to shift mine several times to find the right position, and they are now flourishing. A change of location can be beneficial for some people too.

I am anticipating less international travel in the coming years and perhaps a little more time in the garden. Psalm 92: 14 is my prayer— *Even in old age they will still produce fruit, they will remain vital and green* (NLT).

TRAINING LEADERS

Graham preaching in Ghana[1]

Training for ministry to Children in Crisis (NZ)

Chapter 50
Reflections

Gold Coast, Queensland
2014

As a boy growing up in the Adelaide Hills, one of the things I loved to do was to go up to Windy Point at night where I could look over the sparkling twinkling lights of the city of Adelaide. The air seemed so clear and the lights so bright. The city was so well planned it was relatively easy to pick out particular roads, landmarks and locations in various parts of the city.

Now, after more than 45 years of journeying with God in Christian service, it is a real blessing to look back and see the pattern of God's work in my life. It has been a wonderful adventure and I have no regrets. Along the way, the Lord has guided me, refined me, pruned me and moulded me—all so that I might be more like Him, reflecting His glory and being available to Him to use as He desires.

It has been an immense privilege to play even a small part in the extension of His kingdom here on earth. As I've picked out some of the highlights along the journey, my heart is overflowing with joy and thankfulness to God. What an unbelievable Saviour and Friend He has been!

Right at the beginning of this journey, I told Him I could not be a missionary. But God gave me the promise that if I would take the first small steps of faith, leave my comfort zone and give up my small ambitions, He would do the rest. Had I known at the beginning all the difficult situations and the losses I would face, the positions of responsibility and leadership I would hold, I doubt I would have had the courage to take those first tentative steps. Wonderfully, though, He has given grace and enabling every step of the way, just when I needed it. He has shed light on the path and guided my feet very clearly.

As you have read this book, I trust you have observed that this is not just my story, but also an illustration of what God can and will do when we give our lives unreservedly to Him. My story is such a tiny part of 'HisStory'. Recalling God's faithfulness fills me with gratitude, and gives me courage to face the future, whatever it holds.

In the Bible, we often read of memorials that were set up. Jacob set up a pillar in the place where he talked and wrestled with God (Genesis 28:18). Joshua set up twelve stones taken from the middle of the Jordan (Joshua 4:1–9). Samuel set up an 'Ebenezer' to remind him of how much God had helped him (1 Samuel 7:12). This book is my 'Ebenezer', declaring that God has helped and strengthened me right to this present day. He will do so until I meet Him face to face.

To explore more fully the key lessons I have learnt on the journey would take another book. Here are a few snippets:

- **Live in vital union with Jesus, God's Son:** My desire is to live in Jesus, drawing all I need from Him—love, strength, wisdom, faith, grace, power and direction. He saved me from the penalty of sin. He continues to save me from the power of sin. He frees me from those things that would bind and limit me.

- **Live in dependence on God:** My natural self longs to be autonomous and self-reliant—to be in control of my own life. Even as a Christian, I can be tempted to choose a lifestyle that allows God only partial control of my life. I have been tempted at times to do it my way—to save up, store up and do all I can to ensure I will be secure, satisfied and at ease for the rest of my life. Trusting God in the little things as well as the big has taken the worry out of life, and helped me see almighty God at work in my personal life and ministry. He is well able to deal with my fears, my feelings of inadequacy, my needs for today and my hopes for tomorrow.

- **Live in alignment with God's Word:** Daily I seek to feed on the Word, to walk in the light of what He shows me, guided and strengthened by the Holy Spirit. This results in a more authentic me, with nothing to prove, nothing to hide, nothing to defend.

- **Live with purpose**: My life verse has always been Matthew 6:33. My primary purpose in life is to seek first the Kingdom of God and His righteousness. As I do this, and as I share His love with others, the Father links me in with His plans for humankind: 'This gospel of the kingdom will be preached in the whole world ... and then the end will come' (Matthew 24:14 NIV). God doesn't call us to sit around waiting for His return—He is waiting for us to finish our work, the job He gave us to do.

- **Live with contentment**: I want to be thankful for what I have, rather than complain about what I do not have or desire what I cannot have. I desire to live simply; too many things complicate life. I am just a pilgrim passing through this world, and would far rather invest where the rewards are 'out of this world'!

- **Live in relationship**: God created us to live in relationship. In the times when I have struggled, and especially when I walked through the 'valley of the shadow of death', it was my relationships I treasured most. The children's chorus 'J-O-Y' has stuck with me: Jesus first, Yourself last and Others in between. It leads to joy deep down in my heart.

***

The Bible is full of stories of characters I admire and would love to emulate, but I do not have the courage of Paul, the boldness of Peter, the graciousness of Barnabas or the evangelistic gifts of Phillip. Yet I can do what one of my biblical heroes did.

He appears to be insignificant—the Bible doesn't even tell us his name. The miracle he was part of is mentioned in all four Gospels and twice in Mark, yet he gets a mention only once, in the Gospel of John. Even then we are not told his name.

It is the boy whose lunch consisted of five barley loaves and two fish.

Boys are not generally known for sharing their lunch and certainly not for giving it all away. Yet I believe that out of the thousands of people present on that day, this boy was the one who experienced the greatest joy. I can imagine him running down the hillside after it was all over, bursting with desire to tell his mother what Jesus had done with *his* lunch. Who could have imagined what Jesus would do with something so simple (certainly the disciples didn't)? He gave what he had, he gave all that he had, and Jesus blessed it and used it to bless thousands.

God has blessed me way beyond what I could ever have imagined. My prayer in writing this book is that you too will experience this same great joy as you give Jesus all you have and are.

NOTES

Chapter 1: Impossible? Not with God
1. This chapter is a development of my story 'All things are possible with God', previously published in Evan Davies (ed.), *Beyond the Edge: 100 Stories of Trusting God,* WEC International, 2012. Used by permission of CLC Publications. May not be further reproduced. All rights reserved.

Section: Australia
1. Dad and mum and 10 siblings R to L in descending age:
Dad, Mum, Graham, Heather, Marilyn, Greg, Brian, Rose, David, Val, Daphne and Peter.

Chapter 2: Born at Calvary—twice!
1. As usually described, 'Boosters' are those born up until the end of 1945, 'Baby Boomers' those born after the war from 1946 to 1964. I was born on December 29, 1945.
2. Adapted and used with permission from the Australian War Memorial, Canberra.

Chapter 3: Learning to appreciate differences
1. Aboriginal Protection Board report, 1951.
2. Australian Biography Series 3: Lois (Lowitja) O'Donoghue, Film Australia, 1994.
3. Doris Kartinyeri, *Kick the Tin*, Spinifex Press, 2000, quoted in 'Eden Hills Chronology', Mitcham Council SA website.
4. Excerpt from *Sydney Morning Herald*, Prime Minister's speech to Parliament 13/2/2008.

Chapter 14: Opposites attract—or attack?
1. Adapted from *Worldwide* magazine, WEC Australia, Nov./Dec. 1974.

Chapter 17: Tractors, tyres and tithes
1. Betty Theobald, *Battles, Bricks and Bees: Letters from Don*, unpublished, 1988.

Chapter 25: Coups and counter coups
1. 'Ghana: The 1979 Coup and the First Rawlings Government', <http://www.photius.com/countries/ghana/national_security/ghana_national_security_the_1979_coup_and_th-151.html>, accessed 24/1/14.

Chapter 26: Sssspitting cobras
1. 'Safe as Poison: An African Story' from *The Jungle Doctor's Fables* by Paul White.

Chapter 28: Twenty-two days
1. Part of this chapter was my story 'A table in the wilderness', previously published in Evan Davies (ed.), *Beyond the Edge: 100 Stories of Trusting God*, WEC International, 2012. Used by permission of CLC Publications. May not be further reproduced. All rights reserved.

Chapter 33: Finishing well
1. 'Northern Regional Church/Evangelism Survey', Ghana Evangelism Committee, 1988.
2. 'National Church Survey—Facing the unfinished task of the church in Ghana', Ghana Evangelism Committee, 1989.

Chapter 35: The Bees are back!
1. *Worldwide* magazine, WEC Australia, 1990.

Chapter 39: Here to make a difference
1. This figure includes a few people from other countries serving with WEC in Australia.

2. WEC *Prayer Force Handbook* 1996.
3. K. Donovan & R. Myors, 'Missionary propensity to resign: Summary of survey findings', paper presented at Missions Interlink Australia Forum, July 1997.

Chapter 42: The dreaded C word
1. *New Life*, Australia's Weekly Christian Newspaper, November 23, 2000.

Chapter 45: How much more, Lord?
1. Thoughts taken from the poem 'The Weaver', attributed to Grant Colfax Tuller, and later expanded by Benjamin Malachi Franklin.

Chapter 48: East Timor miracles
1. Much of the detail in the following story comes from Rachel's own account of her experience in personal correspondence with me.

Training Leaders
1. L to R John Kipo, Graham, Joseph Salifu and Samuel Apeligaba.

www.ingramcontent.com/pod-product-compliance
Lightning Source LLC
Chambersburg PA
CBHW051936290426
44110CB00015B/1994